IMAGES
of America

BOWLING GREEN

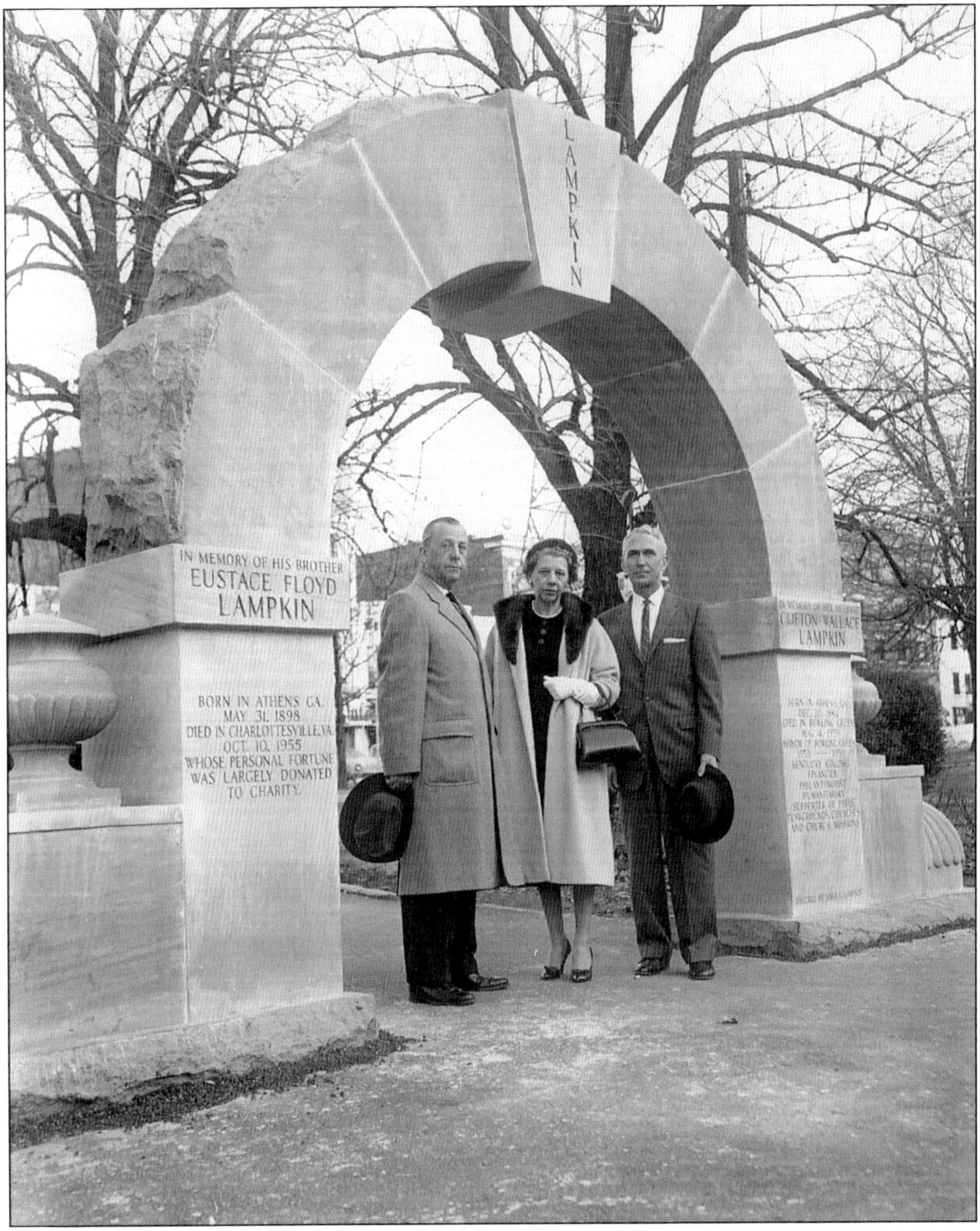

GATEWAY TO THE CITY. Mayor Bob Graham, Mrs. C.W. Lampkin, and county judge G.D. Milliken were in attendance on December 15, 1959, when the arch honoring Clifford Wallace Lampkin was dedicated. The arch was an entry to Fountain Square Park on the Park Row side and matched a similar arch constructed on the Main Street entrance almost 50 years earlier. Mr. Lampkin served as mayor of Bowling Green from 1953 to 1959 and died while he was in office.

IMAGES
of America

BOWLING GREEN

Jonathan Jeffrey and
the Kentucky Library

ARCADIA
PUBLISHING

ISBN 978-0-7385-1568-7

Published by Arcadia Publishing
Charleston, South Carolina

Printed in the United States of America

Library of Congress Catalog Card Number: 2003107852

For all general information contact Arcadia Publishing at:
Telephone 843-853-2070
Fax 843-853-0044
E-mail sales@arcadiapublishing.com
For customer service and orders:
Toll-Free 1-888-313-2665

Visit us on the Internet at www.arcadiapublishing.com

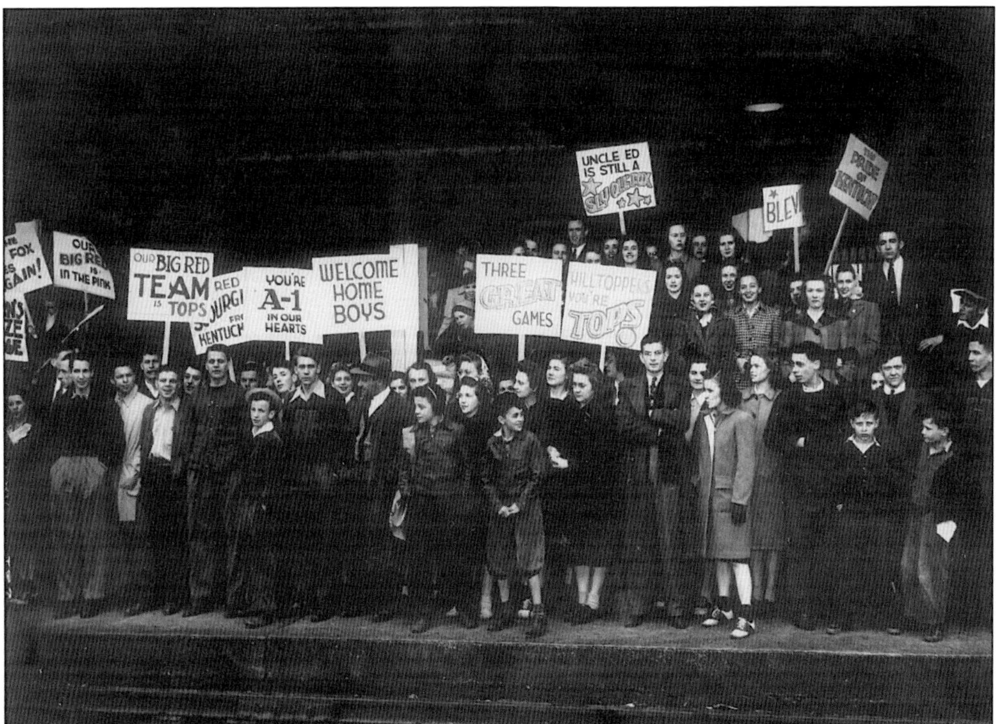

DIE-HARD FANS. These students and townspeople are awaiting the arrival of their beloved Western Kentucky University Hilltoppers via train after an appearance in Madison Square Gardens in March 1942.

Contents

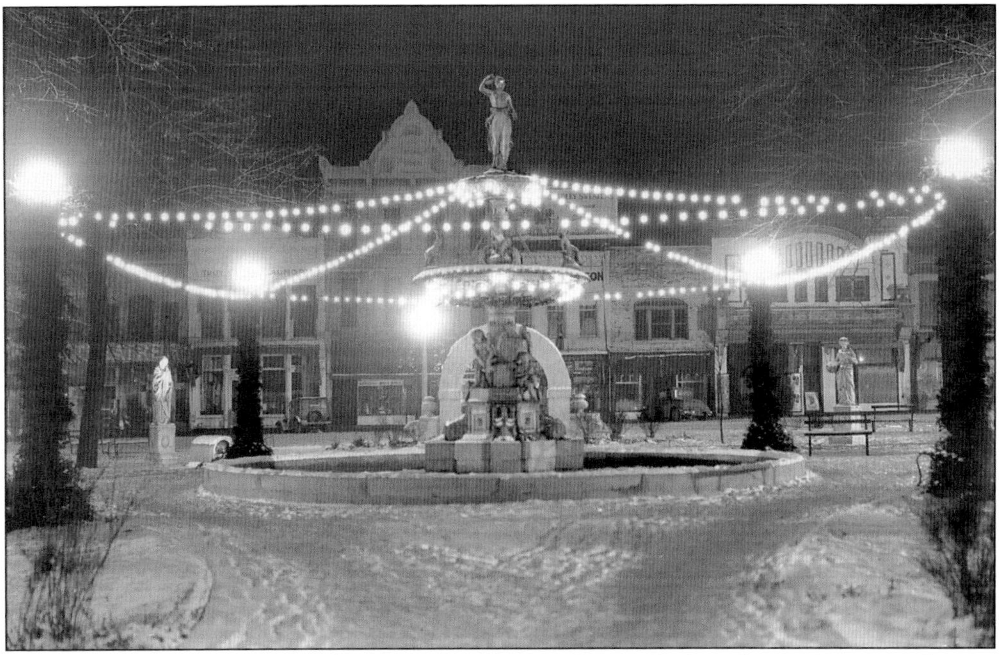

IT'S A WONDERFUL LIFE. Bowling Green's Fountain Square Park is the city's most endearing and enduring landmark. The city's second mayor, John Cox Underwood, designed the park in 1871. The first fountain was stone and was carved by James Ott, who also carved one of the Corinthian capitals on the Warren County Courthouse. This fountain lasted approximately ten years. The stone base from the original fountain is on the back lawn of Riverview at Hobson Grove. The city fathers then purchased a cast iron fountain with zinc decorative elements from the J.L. Mott Company of New York City. The cast iron fountain was dedicated by Henry Watterson in 1882. It remained until the late 1980s when the fountain was dismantled and taken to an Alabama foundry where it was completely re-cast. Some of the pieces from the 1882 fountain are now owned by the Kentucky Museum at Western Kentucky University.

ACKNOWLEDGMENTS

No project like this happens without assistance. I would like to thank my Kentucky Library colleagues, Nancy Disher Baird and Connie Mills, for their patience while this project was being completed. I would also like to single out Sarah Schmitt, one of our student assistants, who helped with a portion of the research on this work. A special thank you to William P. and Rosalyn Stamps for donating a number of photographs for this project. Lastly, I must thank all of the generous patrons who have donated photographs to the Kentucky Library over the last 65 years; without your generosity, this book never would have been possible.

INTRODUCTION

Since 1900 Bowling Green has been in almost constant momentum. During the first half of the 20th century Bowling Green evolved from a sleepy Victorian town into a thriving small city. This transformation was abetted by a committed cadre of creative and positive thinking leaders in all fields of endeavor: business, finance, religion, medicine, education, and law. This book concentrates on the period from 1900 to 1950 in which Bowling Green was just beginning to explore its potential.

One of the most significant factors in Bowling Green's emergence as a regional commercial center from 1900 to 1950 was the development and improvement of transportation routes and facilities. During these important years the city enjoyed access to good roads, river traffic via steamboats and barges, rail service on the Louisville & Nashville Railroad, and by the late 1930s a developing airport. These transportation routes made Bowling Green. Without them there would be no way to get goods in and out of the city, nor a means to bring people into the area.

Bowling Green needed ways for people to find this wonderful city as it emerged as a place of consequence. Some people came to the community's health facilities: the City-County Hospital (now the Medical Center), a tuberculosis sanatorium, the state board of health, and several private hospitals, nursing homes, and clinics. Thousands of students came to Bowling Green to continue their education at Ogden College, Potter College, Bowling Green Business University, and the growing Western Kentucky State Normal School (now Western Kentucky University). Customers visited regional banks, teeming department stores, legal offices, and numerous other types of service providers. Transportation helped the city and surrounding area get their products to the national market. Such commodities included agricultural products such as corn, grains, tobacco, hogs, horses, and strawberries. The area also boasted several important local natural resources—petroleum, limestone, lumber, and asphalt—that could be exported because of the transport availability. The city recruited new industry that depended on transportation, including Pet Milk, Honey Krust Bakery, Holley Carburetor, Ken-Rad, and Union Underwear. People also came to Bowling Green for entertainment, whether it was a week at Massey Springs, a bar-b-que at Beech Bend Park, a musical or sporting event at WKU, or an evening at Pauline's.

The first half of the 20th century also saw tremendous national events that affected our history: the invention of the automobile, World War I, Prohibition, Women's Suffrage, the Great Depression, the New Deal, World War II, and the Cold War. Warren Countians did not go unaffected by these events. Photographs help document local reaction to national events and thus are considered primary source material. They aid in interpreting significant happenings for future generations; they are evidence.

Fortunately, Bowling Green had several good photographers who helped document this significant era. One of the best known photographers was Edgar Cayce, the famed clairvoyant who spent six years in Bowling Green (1902–1908). Unfortunately, his studio burned twice while he was here. Most of his photographs that survive are portraits and some commercial photography for what was then the Southern Normal School (now WKU).

Perhaps the most prolific and accomplished photographer of the first part of the 20th century was Eugene Franklin (1886–1952). He was a native of Barren County and came to Bowling Green from Memphis in 1916. Franklin took some of the best surviving photographs of Bowling

Green businesses, events, and people. His skilled hand is seen throughout the pages of this book. After suffering a stroke, Franklin sold his photography business in 1946. Other notable local photographers who were just beginning their careers around the mid-century mark were Ches Johnson, Marshall Love, and soon afterwards, Tommy Hughes. All of these men have left an indelible mark on our local heritage, because photographs freeze history.

We are also fortunate that our city has a place such as the Kentucky Building at WKU, which houses the Kentucky Library and Museum. At this facility, professionals have faithfully cataloged and preserved photographs for the last 50 years. Photographs are selected for historic or documentary interest, visual or artistic merit, or interesting clothing or backgrounds. The library owns over 15,000 photographs ranging from daguerreotypes, to cyanotypes, to tintypes. Prints and negatives are cataloged and stored in acid-free folders and containers. The photographs create one of the most interesting and most used collections in the library.

In compiling this book I have tried to include a variety of photographs ranging from children playing to a church burning. With thousand of photos to choose from, I was looking for well-executed pictures. However, there were significant events, people, or places in our city that were only documented by amateurs, but thank goodness they were there to snap those shots for posterity's sake. I hope you enjoy watching Bowling Green's history through the camera lens of Bowling Green's past professional and amateur photographers.

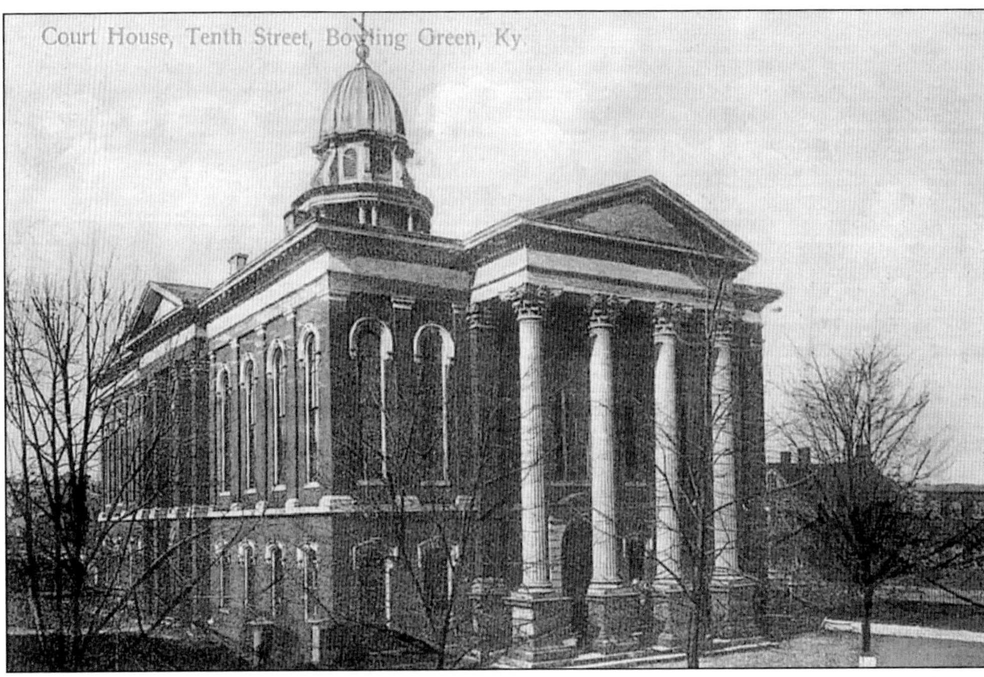

WARREN COUNTY COURTHOUSE. D.J. Williams designed the third Warren County Courthouse in 1867 and construction was completed in 1869. The Italianate structure boasts a Classical pedimented portico supported by magnificent fluted columns topped with massive Corinthian capitals, all carved from Bowling Green limestone. The architect masterfully crowned his creation with a lovely neo-baroque cupola, which has been rebuilt twice. The building's interior was completely remodeled in the mid-1950s, but little change has been made to the exterior.

One

Bowling Green in History

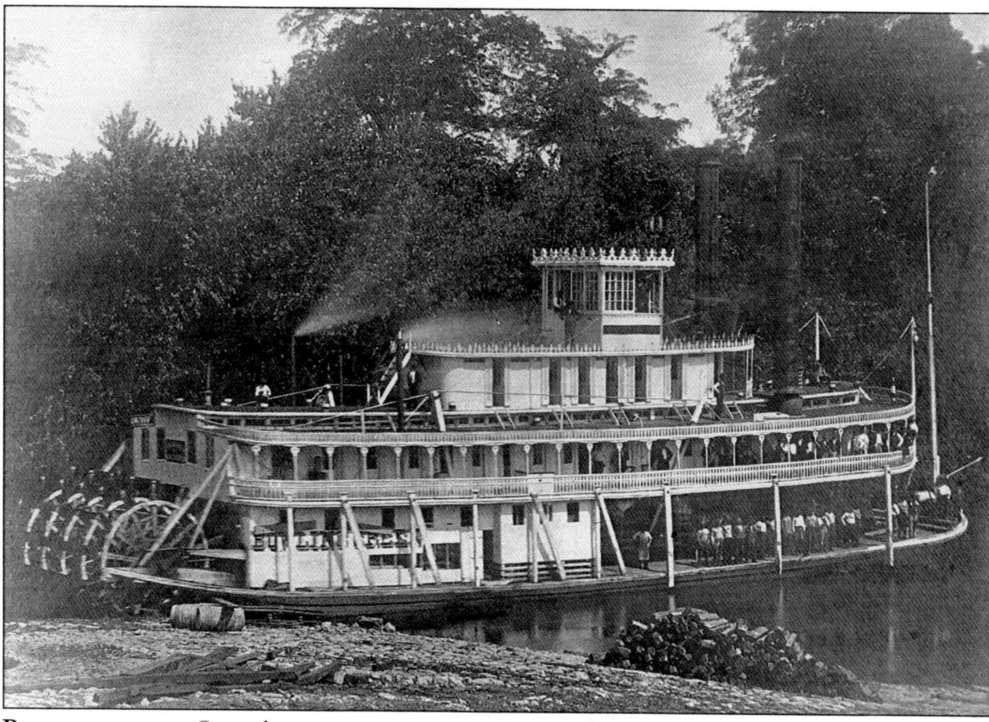

Paddlewheeler. Steamboats were a common means of transporting freight and passengers in and out of Bowling Green well into the 20th century. This proud boat was the third vessel to wear the name *Bowling Green*. The 132-foot-long steamboat was built in 1904 in Jeffersonville, Indiana. During a terrible 1920 storm, it sank near South Carrollton, Kentucky, and only the whistle was salvaged.

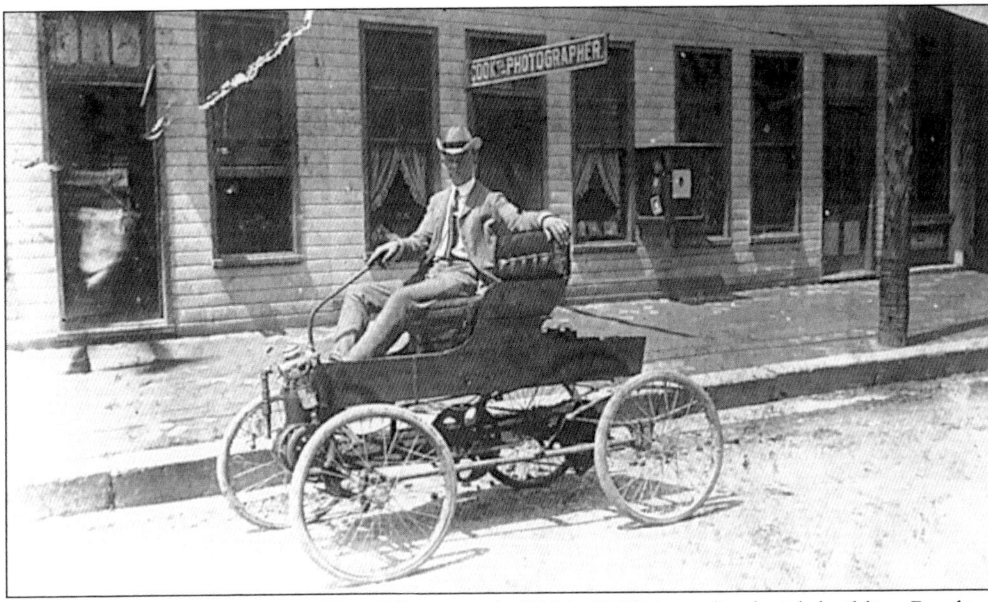

CITY'S FIRST AUTOMOBILE. J. Bland Farnsworth (1884–1962) is credited with building Bowling Green's first automobile in 1900 using castings from a local foundry and telephone batteries. He worked in a shop that adjoined his father's drugstore at Adams and Main Streets. The first factory-built automobile appeared in Bowling Green around 1903. This photo was taken in front of Cook Photography, which was located in the 900 block of College Street.

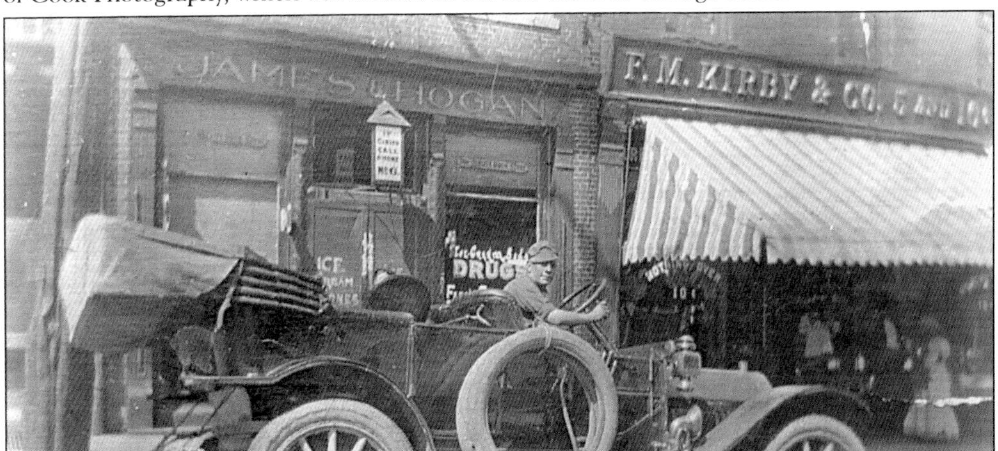

HOT WHEELS. W. Roy Hogan Sr. (1889–1947) opened a drugstore on Park Row around 1900. He soon tired of that business, decided to open a garage, and eventually became the local distributor for three different automobile manufacturers. When the oil boom took place in the early 1920s, he initiated a bus line between Bowling Green and Scottsville. He spent the rest of his life in the oil business.

McCormack Building Fire. Standing four-stories high at the corner of State and 10th Streets, the McCormack Building was Bowling Green's tallest structure, so when it burned on July 5, 1911, the damage was massive. In this photo, portions of the façade and a large chimney remain standing with the Presbyterian church's steeple in the background. To grasp the size of the ruins, observe the men at the bottom right margin.

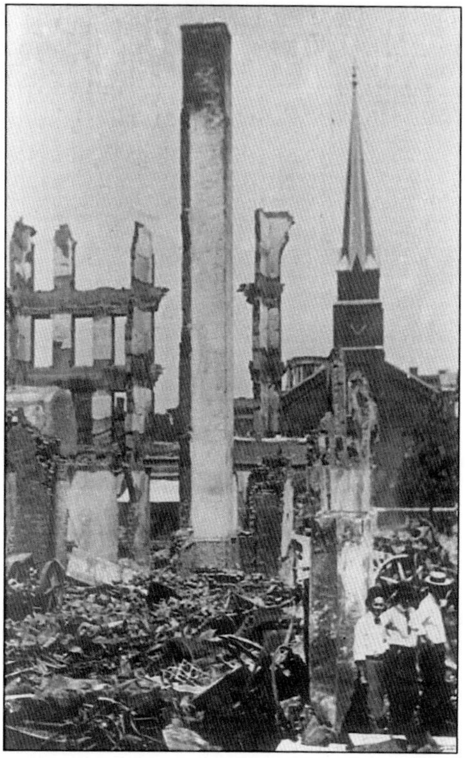

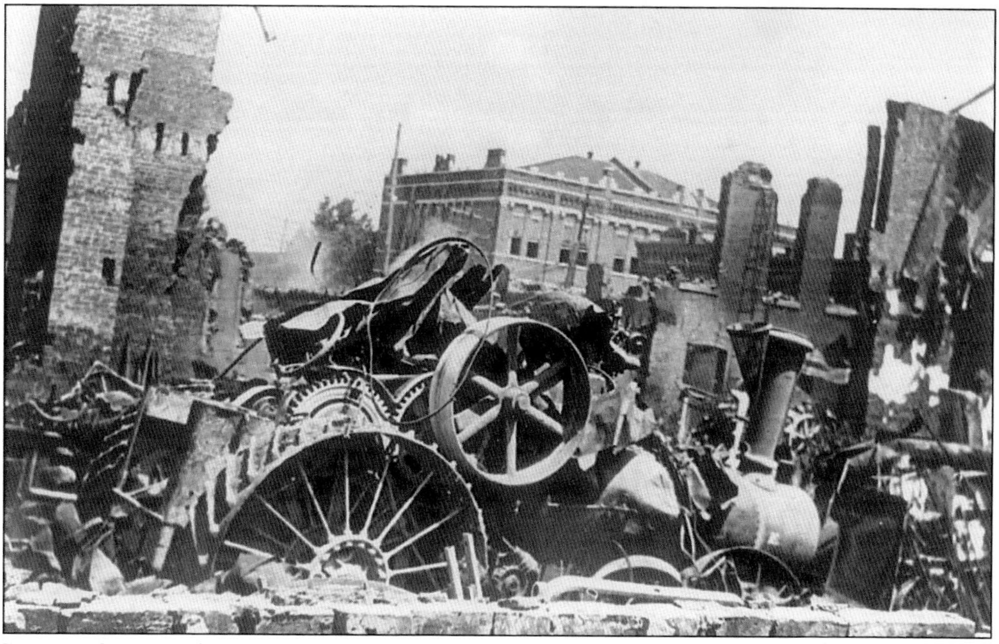

Ruined Goods. The McCormack Building housed a large portion of the Bowling Green Business University, a hardware store, a bowling alley, and professional offices. This photo documents a ruined steam tractor in one portion of the building. Material from the McCormack Building was salvaged and used in constructing the Price Building. The structure in the background is the Davenport Building, which was razed in the mid-1990s.

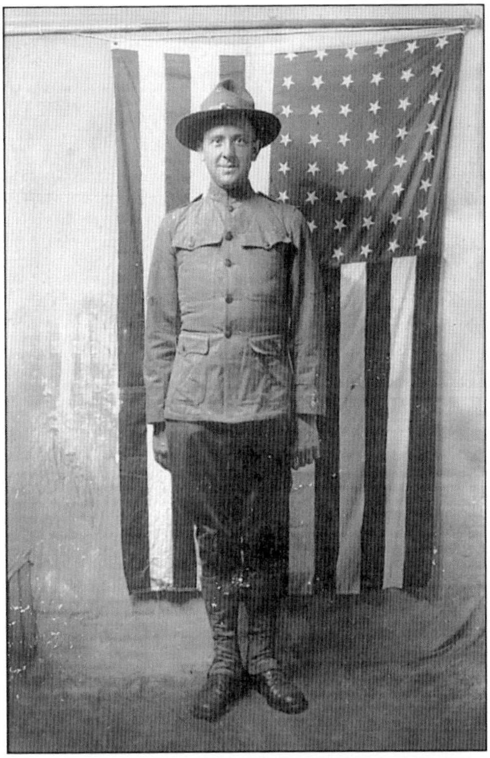

BOWLING GREEN IN WORLD WAR I. Almost 1,000 Warren county men and women served with 83,000 other Kentuckians during World War I. Sixty Warren County soldiers gave the supreme sacrifice and 129 more were injured during duty. Harry Gilpin, a native of Warren County, proudly poses for his patriotic portrait.

PATRIOTIC CONCERT. Western Kentucky University's Van Meter Auditorium has been a favorite venue for large concerts since it was completed in 1911. Here Franz Strahm (1867–1941), a German immigrant and head of WKU's music department, leads a grandiose musical spectacle during World War I. Franz's son Victor was a flying ace during the Great War and later had a distinguished military career. Notice the primitive lighting rigged for the event.

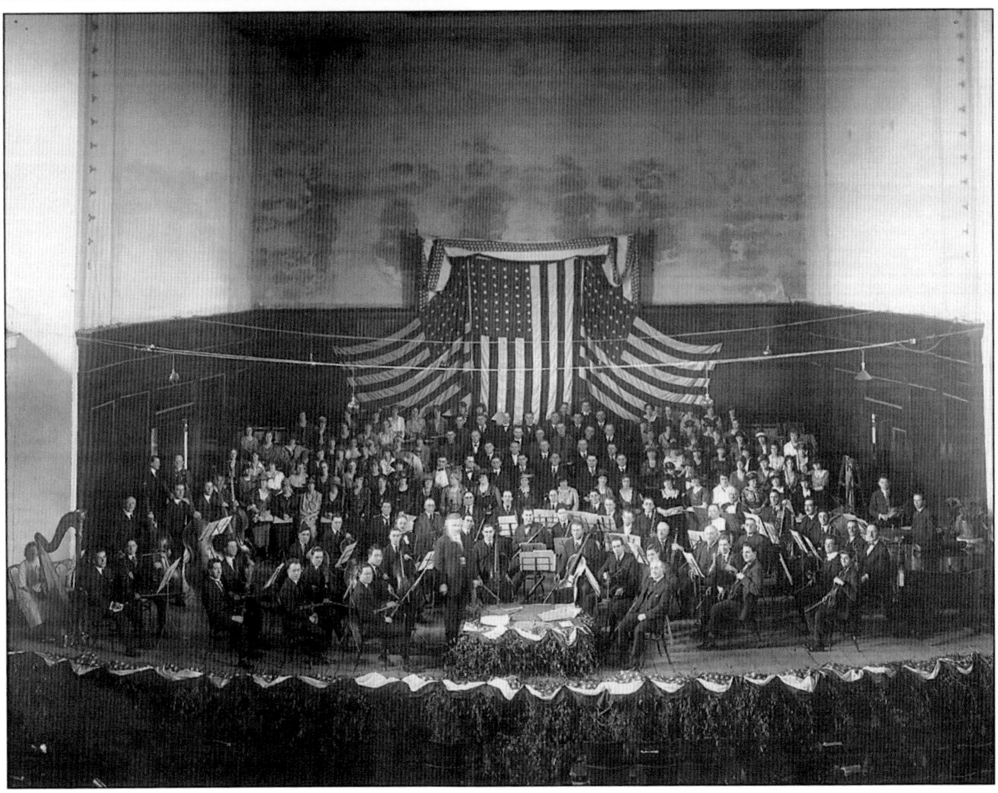

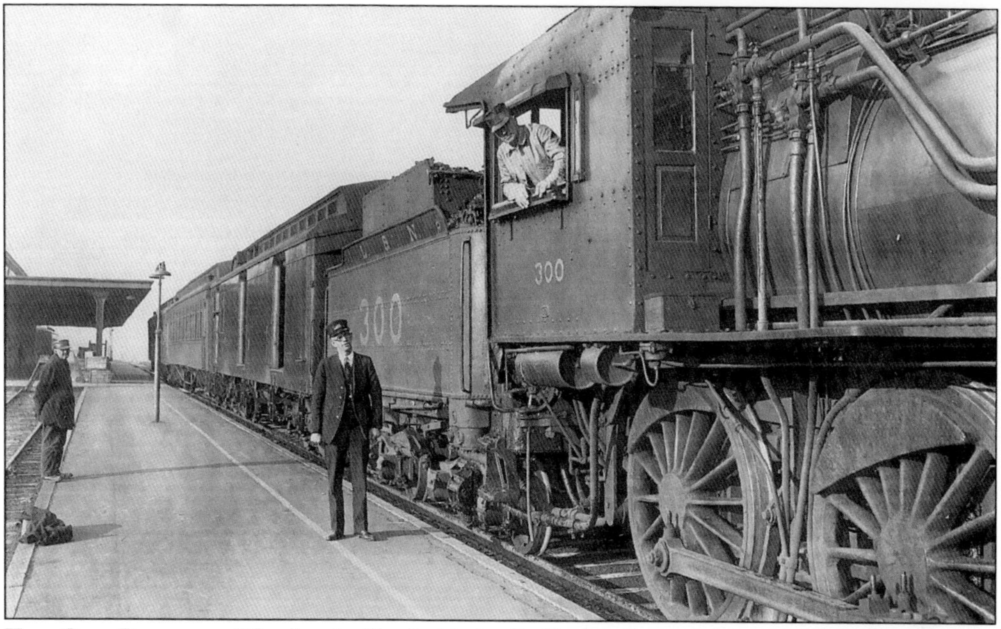

The Old Reliable. The Louisville & Nashville Railroad opened its mainline in 1859 and thrived despite Civil War setbacks. Bowling Green, on the mainline, was doubly blessed because a branch line to Memphis was constructed southwest of town. It assured Bowling Green's commercial success. This short train, pulled by coal-operated Engine 300, stopped at Bowling Green's depot in 1936 to pick up passengers.

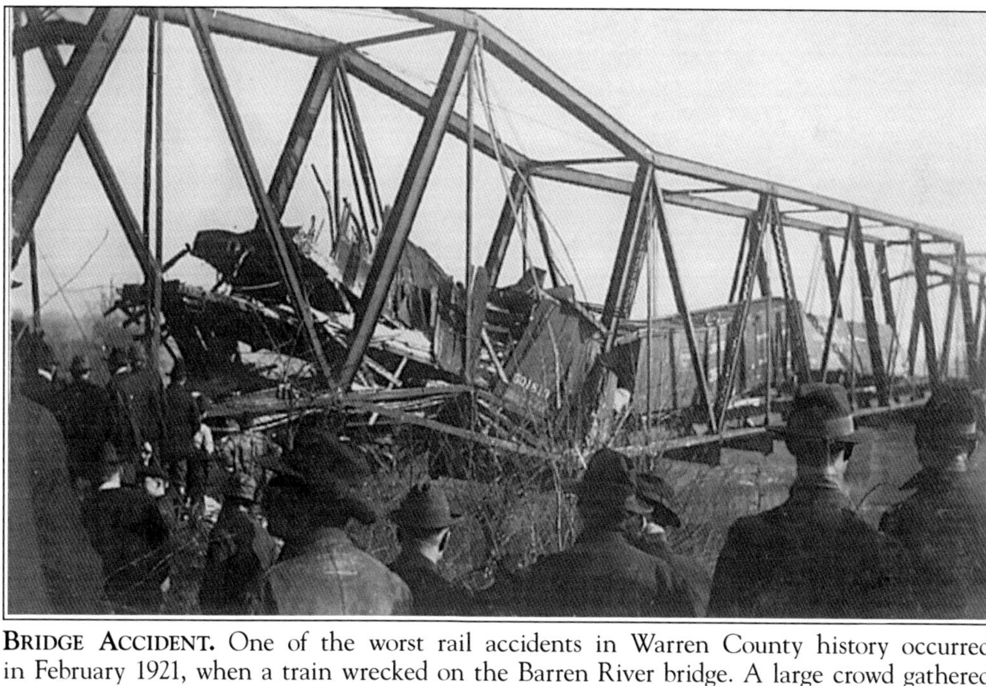

Bridge Accident. One of the worst rail accidents in Warren County history occurred in February 1921, when a train wrecked on the Barren River bridge. A large crowd gathered when the Louisville & Nashville Railroad decided to destroy the bridge on February 17th. Unfortunately Dan Cornwell, a spectator, was instantly killed when a piece of steel struck him, "lifting the top of his head completely off and strewing his brains on the ground."

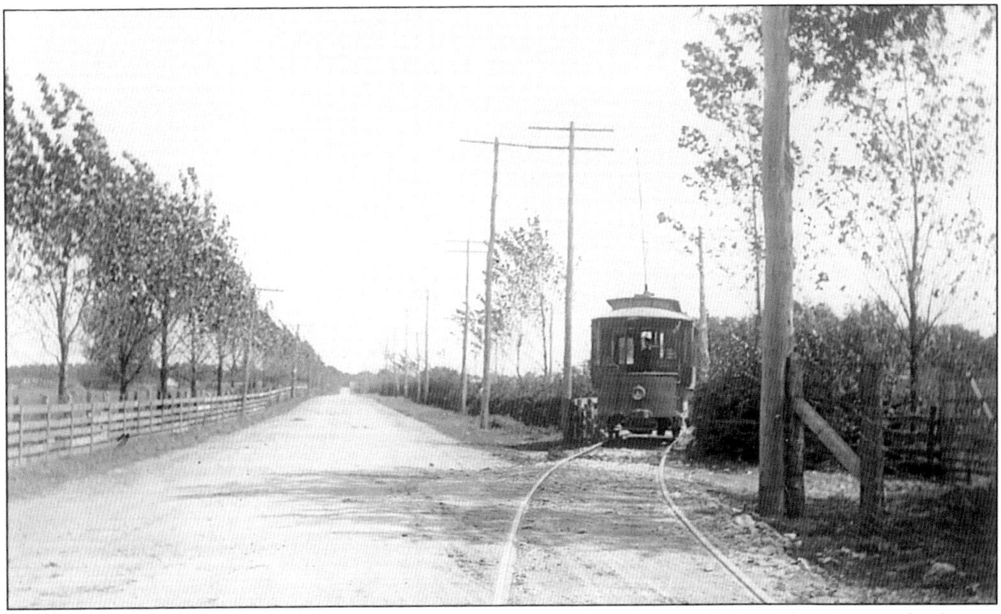

STREETCARS. Bowling Green enjoyed streetcar service as early as 1889. The first mule-drawn cars were abandoned in 1895 when the cars were switched to overhead electrical power, making it one of the first such systems in the Commonwealth. Eventually the local line had seven-and-one-half miles of track and passengers could ride for ten cents. The system was dissolved after a 1921 court case involving the victim of an accident.

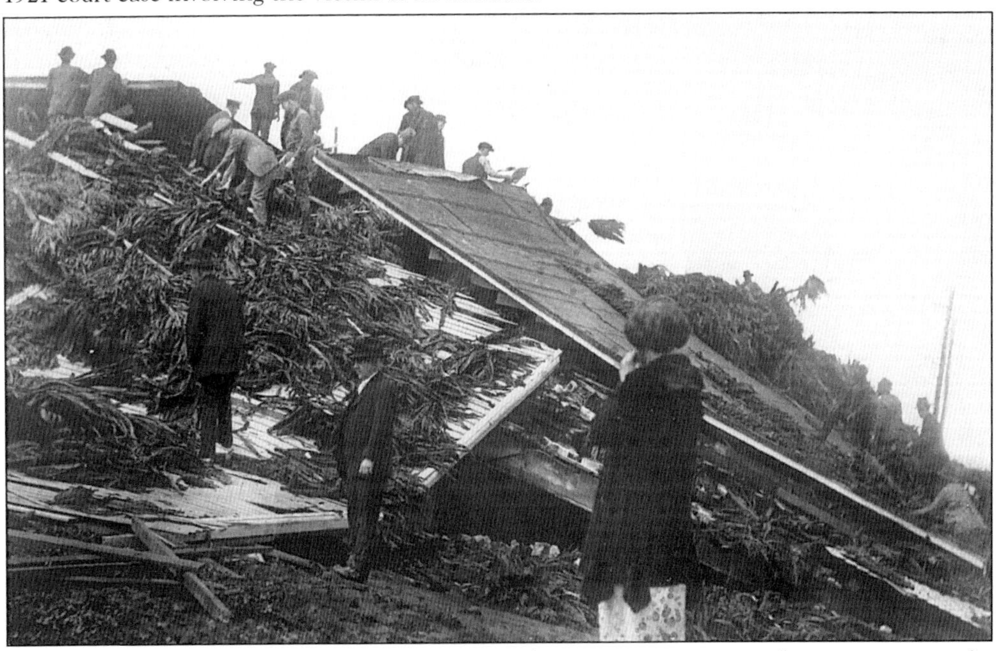

TOBACCO TRAGEDY. A woman looks on in apprehension as men scour the recent ruins of a huge, three-story tobacco processing plant owned by the American Tobacco Company. Located on the banks of the Barren River near the L&N railroad bridge, the structure fell shortly before noon on Mach 30, 1922. A ferocious wind leveled the building, killing three men and causing thousands of dollars in damages. Eleven men survived the tragedy.

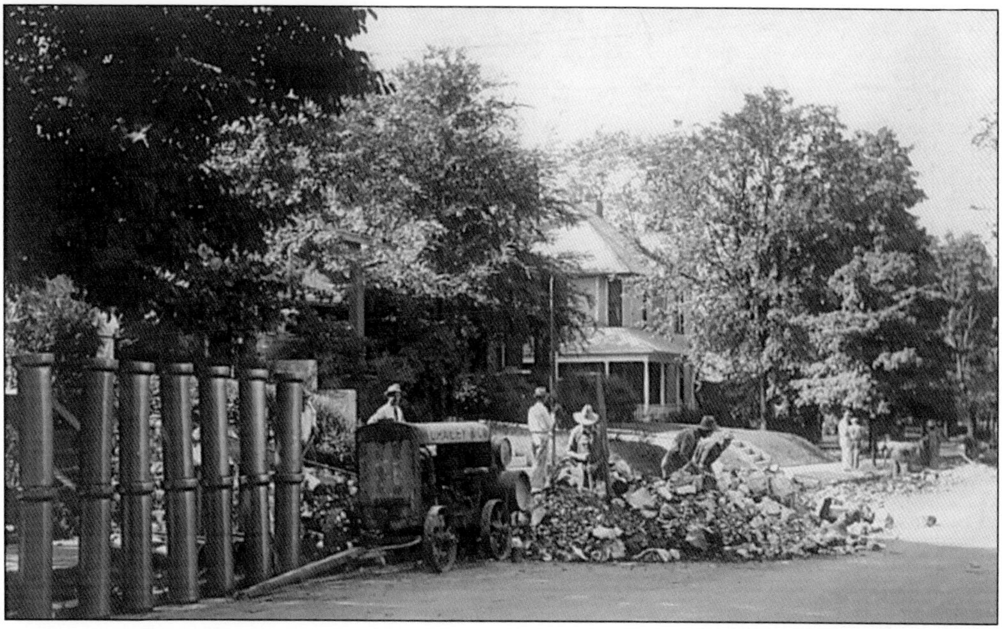

DEPRESSION-ERA WORK CREW. The Great Depression caused financial havoc for many Kentuckians and led some to accept temporary work with various New Deal programs. These men are taking part in an important local Works Progress Administration project: installing the city's first sewer system in 1933. The J.N. Chester Engineers of Pittsburgh supervised the surveying and installation of the sewer system.

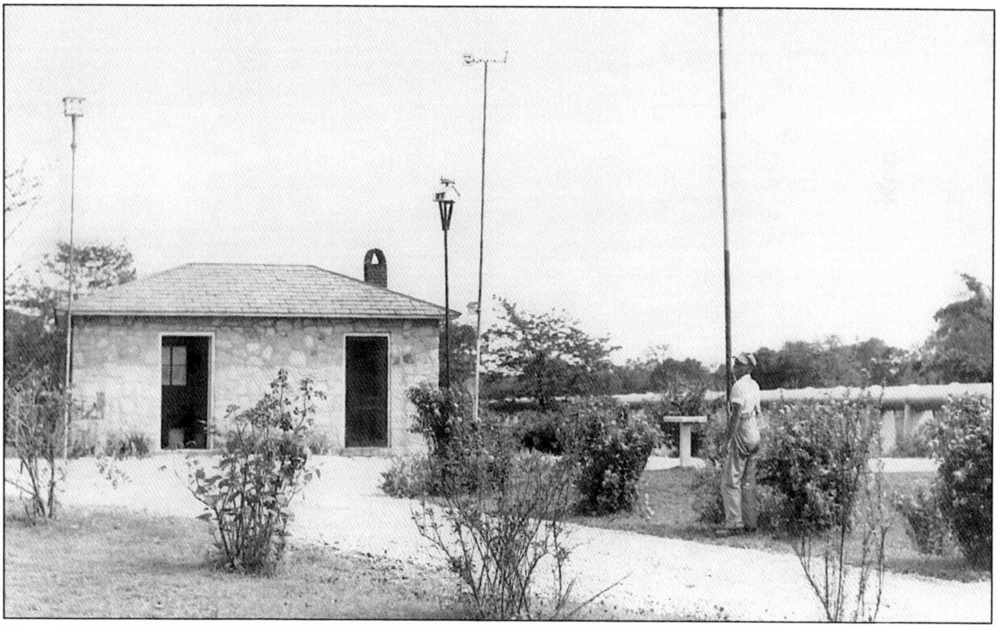

SMELLY BUSINESS. The sewer system installed in the 1930s included a disposal plant and sedimentation tanks located at the foot of Main Street near Hobson Grove. The grounds of the disposal plant belied the job performed there. Here a city worker views one of several birdhouses kept at the property. The grounds also boasted a number of bird baths and stone planters filled with colorful flowers. Notice the attractive path lined with rose bushes.

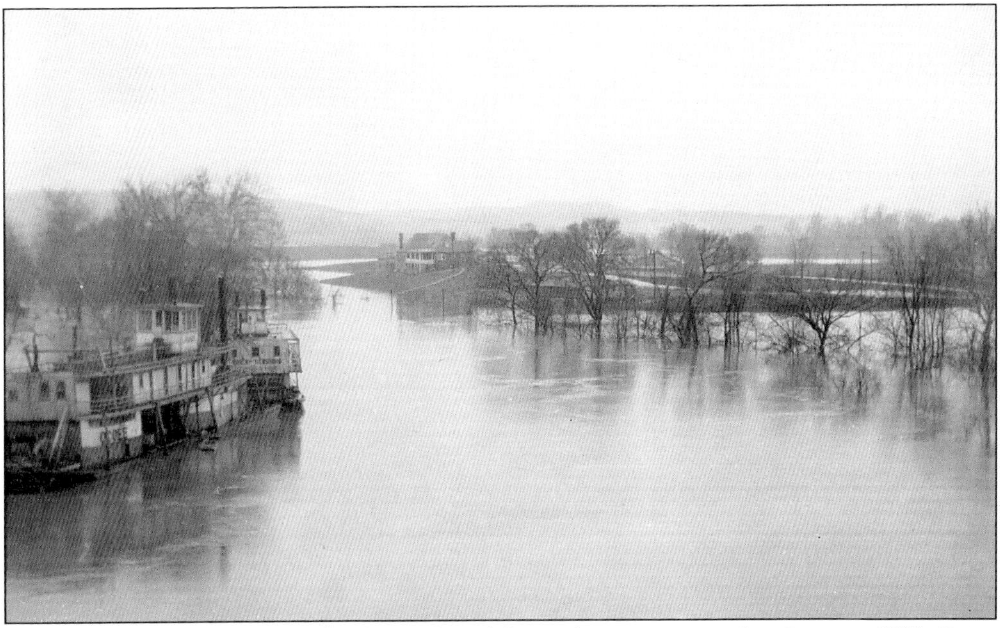

FLOODING. One of the worst floods in United States history occurred in January 1937. Cities and towns along the Ohio River were particularly affected, but Bowling Green did not escape damage. The Barren River swelled at the Boatlanding as seen in the top photograph. Because of the large quantity of water, many low places, such as the section of Nashville Road (below) just outside of the city, flooded. Refugees from the flood ravaged Louisville were brought to Bowling Green, staying in private homes and in the gymnasium at Western Kentucky University. Local citizens were generous in donating money, food, and housewares to those in need.

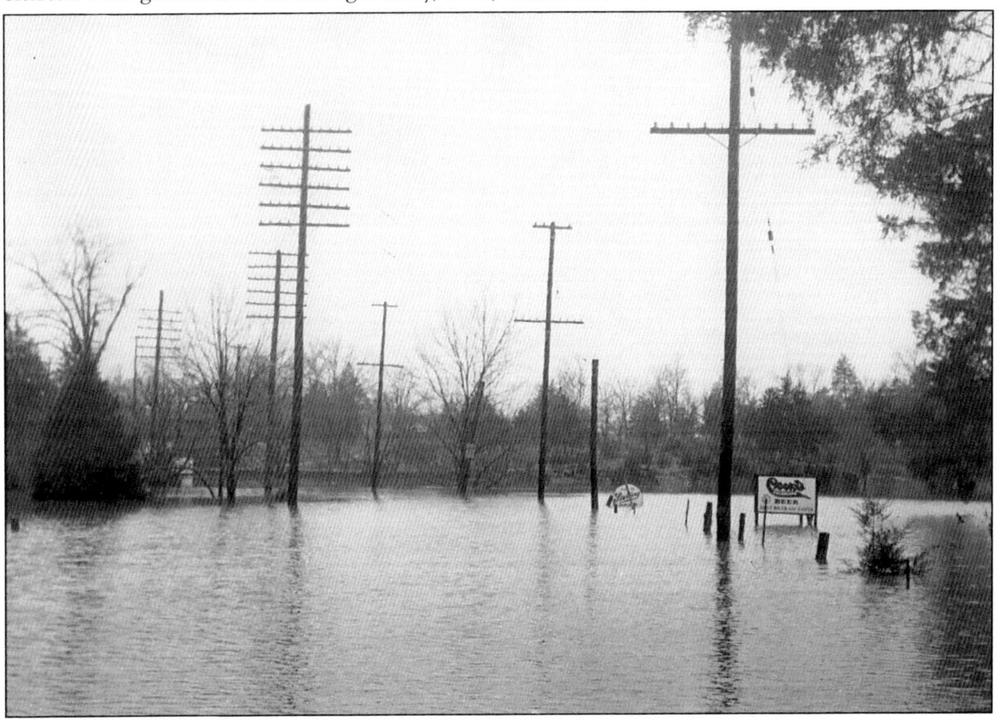

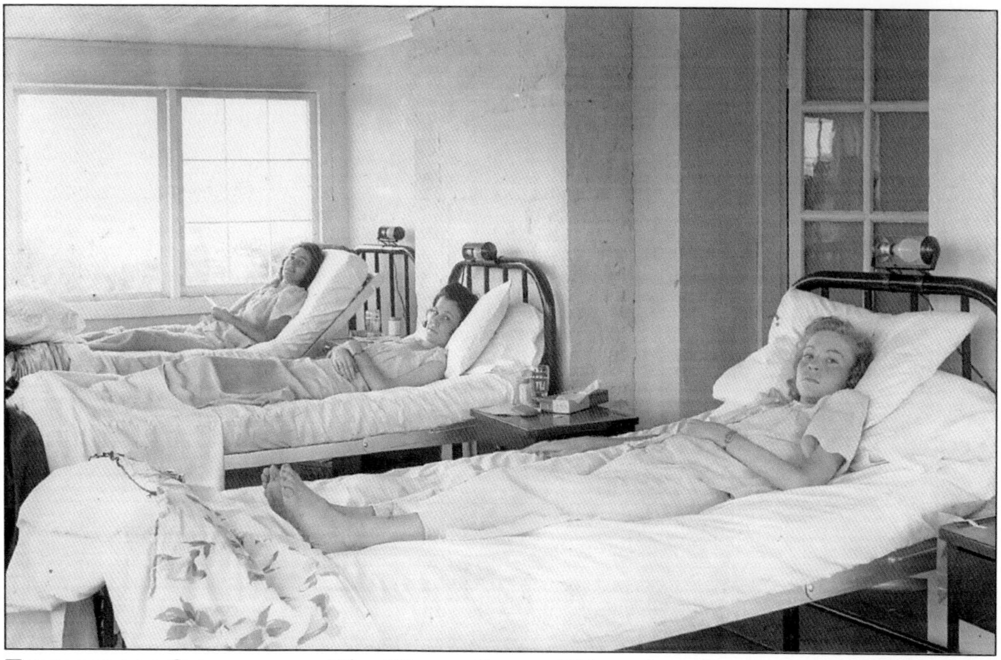

TUBERCULOSIS SANATORIUM. The Warren County Tuberculosis Sanatorium opened in 1940 near Riverside. The drive for the institution began in 1939 when a poor mother and several of her children were found by the Welfare Center to be suffering from the disease. Warren County citizens approved a special tax for maintenance of the facility, which was donated by C.W. Lampkin and J.L. Pushin. This facility operated until 1956.

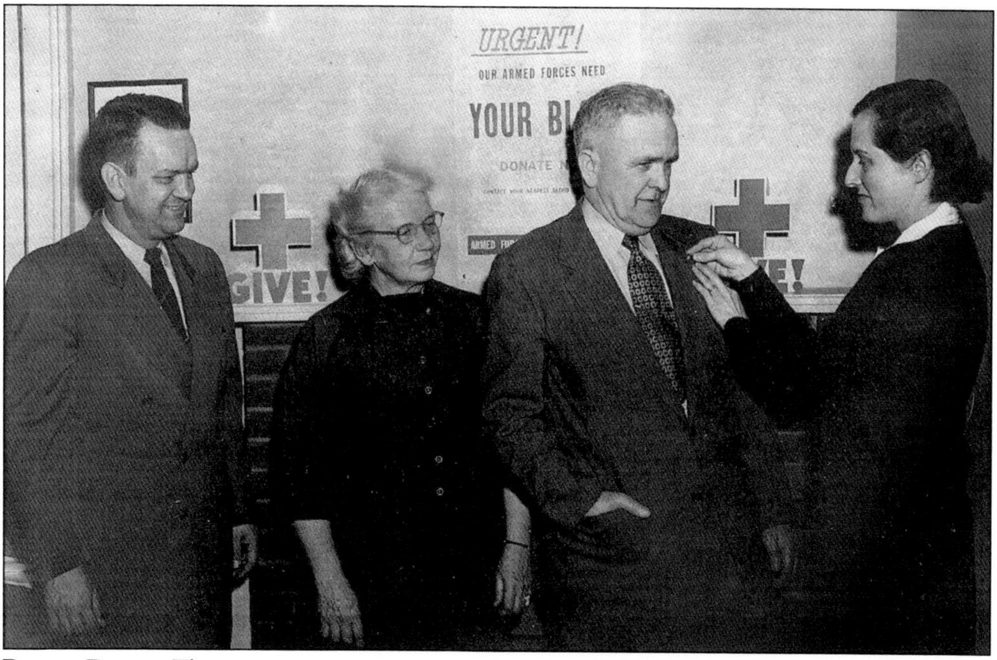

BLOOD DRIVE. These patriotic citizens are answering the call to donate blood for the armed forces as heralded in the poster on the bulletin board. During World War II, the Red Cross, which sponsored this drive, was located in the basement of the Warren County Courthouse.

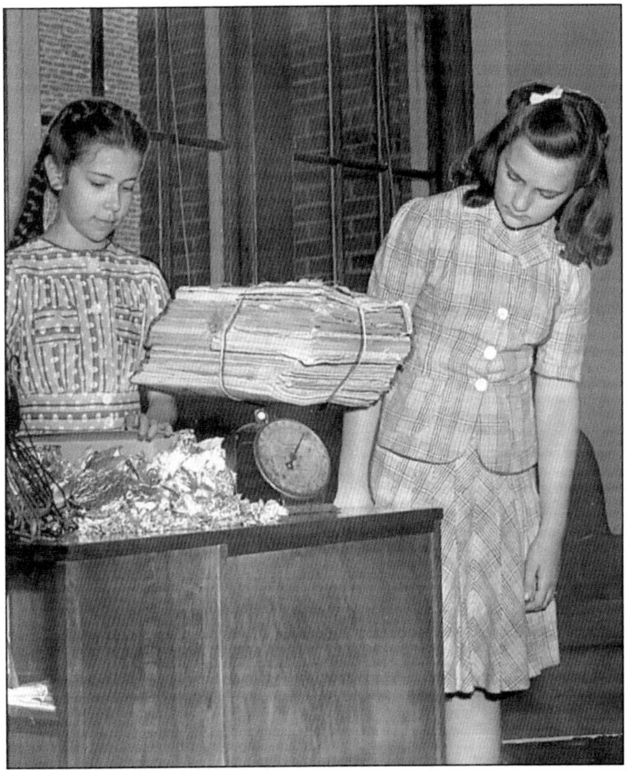

SCRAPPY. Everyone got involved in the war effort during World War II. These students, Betty Byrd and Janette Searcy, are participating in a scrap drive, collecting newsprint, foil, and coat hangers.

V IS FOR VICTORY. Only four days after the attack on Pearl Harbor, the Victory Club organized. The group distributed approximately 50 "Victory Cups" in businesses throughout the community to receive donations from those wishing to contribute to the war effort. The sole purpose of the group was to solicit cash donations, which were then donated to the Treasury Department. Member dues varied from a dime to $1 a week.

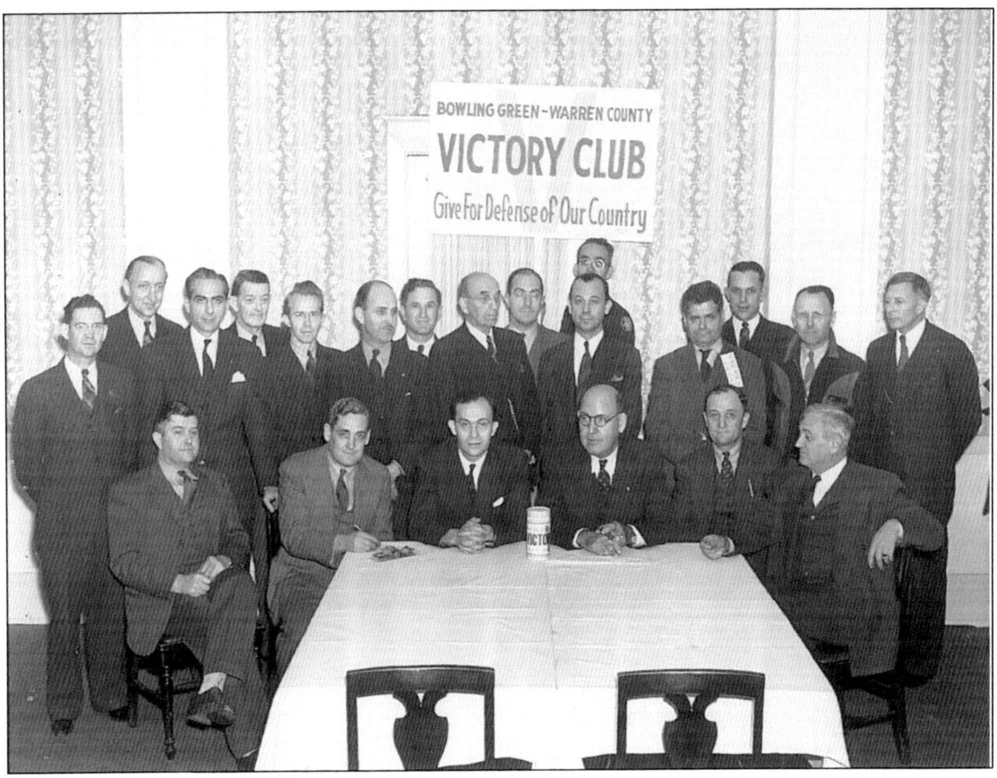

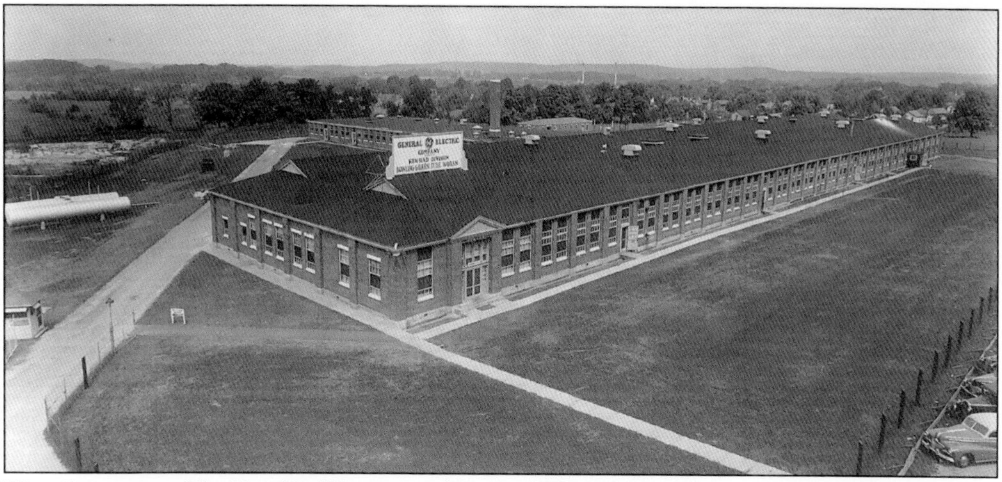

WAR INDUSTRY. The Ken-Rad Division of General Electric operated a vacuum tube production plant in Bowling Green during World War II and employed 200 people. The plant was opened in September 1943 to produce radio tubes for the United States Navy. City officials petitioned the War Production Board in Washington, D.C., in order to have the plant built in Bowling Green.

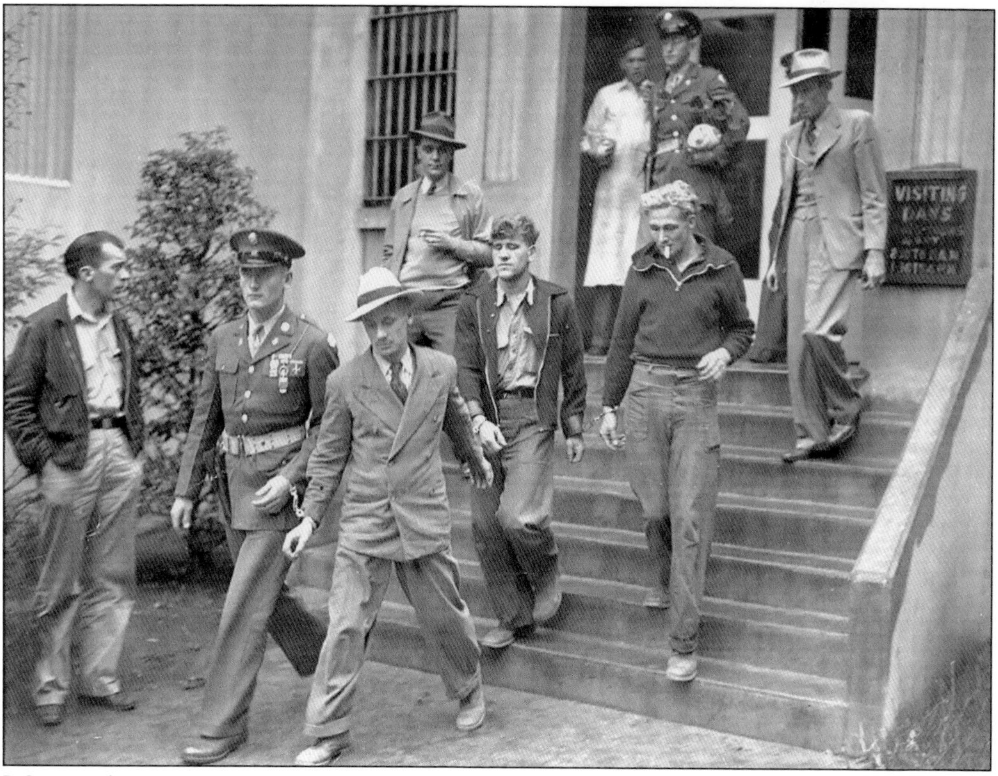

POWs. Three German citizens were arrested six miles north of Bowling Green in November 1942 and placed in the Warren County jail. They had escaped from a train passing through the area. The men asked directions from two Derby Underwear employees who reported the incident to authorities. The arrest caused quite a crowd to gather at the jail. The next day five military policemen moved the Germans to a Tennessee internment camp.

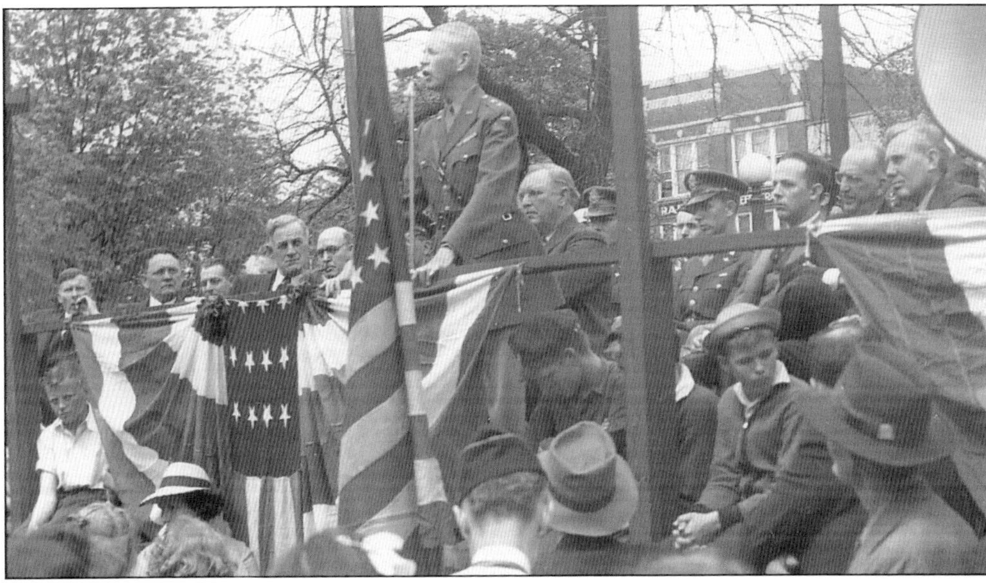

WAR RALLY. Persuading locals to purchase war bonds for financial support of the war effort was the purpose of rallies such as this one held at Fountain Square Park. The building in the background is Pushin's Department Store.

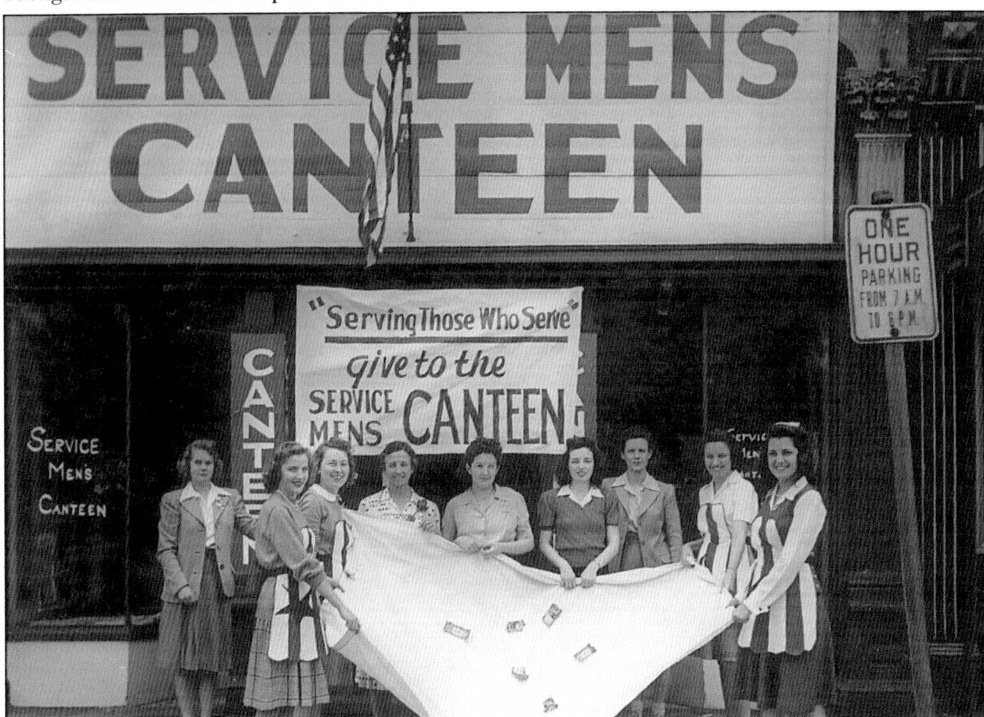

CANTEEN GIRLS. These girls, in their patriotic aprons, are helping raise money for Bowling Green's Service Men's Canteen during World War II. The Canteen was located in the Getty Building on the 400 block of Main Street. The Canteen also operated a free, overnight facility for servicemen on College Street. Thousands of service men traveling through Bowling Green enjoyed the hospitality provided by the canteen.

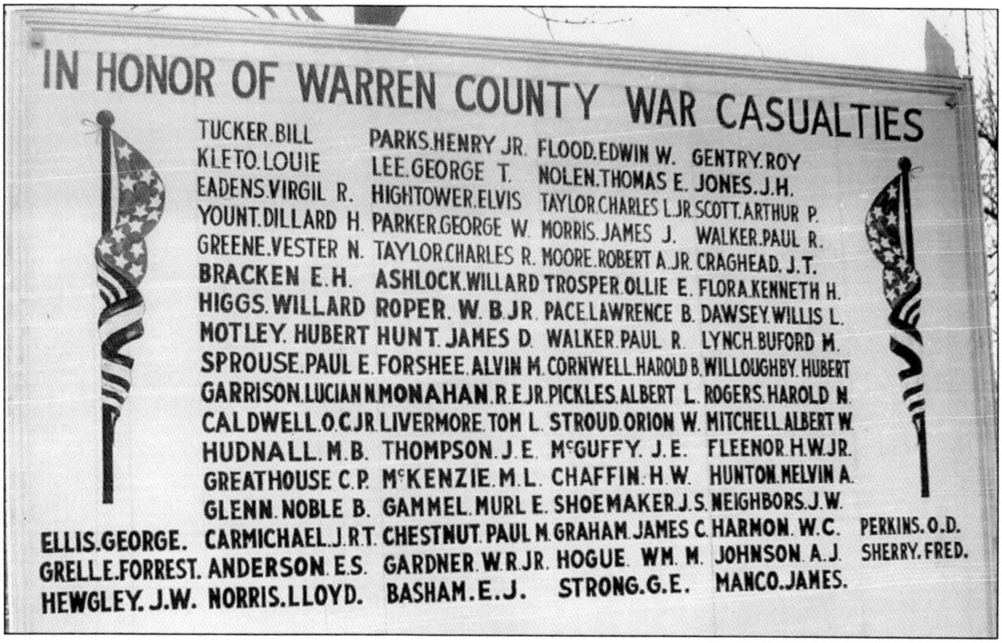

THE WALL. This list of Warren County casualties in World War II stood in Fountain Square Park for months, honoring those who gave the supreme sacrifice for their country.

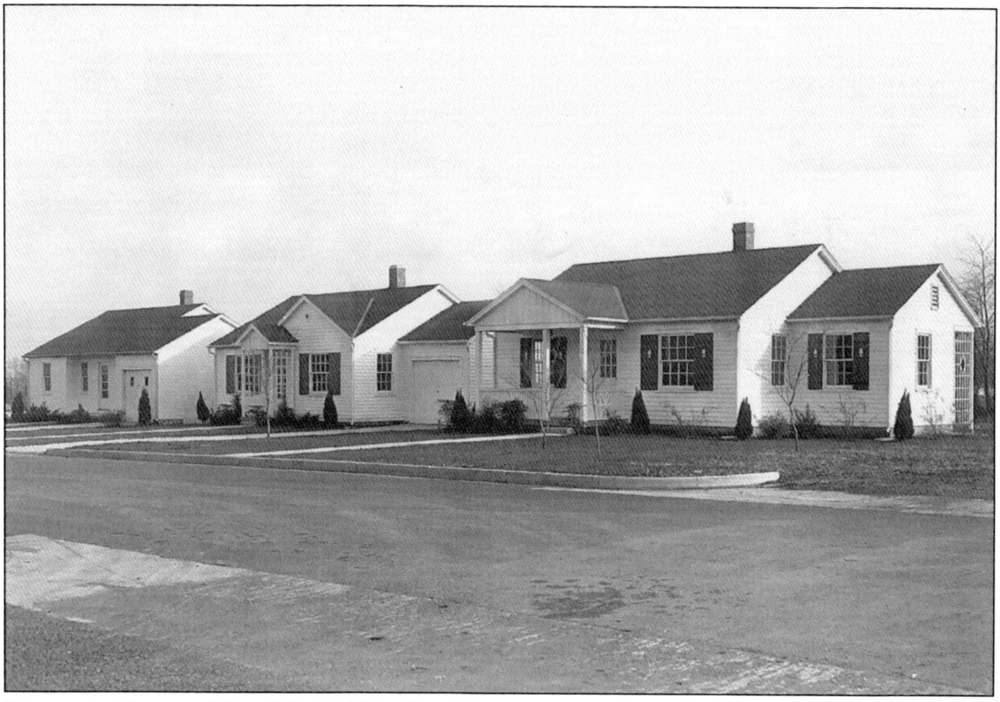

HOUSING BOOM. After World War II, with assistance from the Veterans Administration and with savings from military service, many families were able to purchase homes using the installment plan. These new homes on Lehman Avenue, typical of most post-War construction, were built in 1942. These homes featured attached garages and sold for approximately $3,500 each.

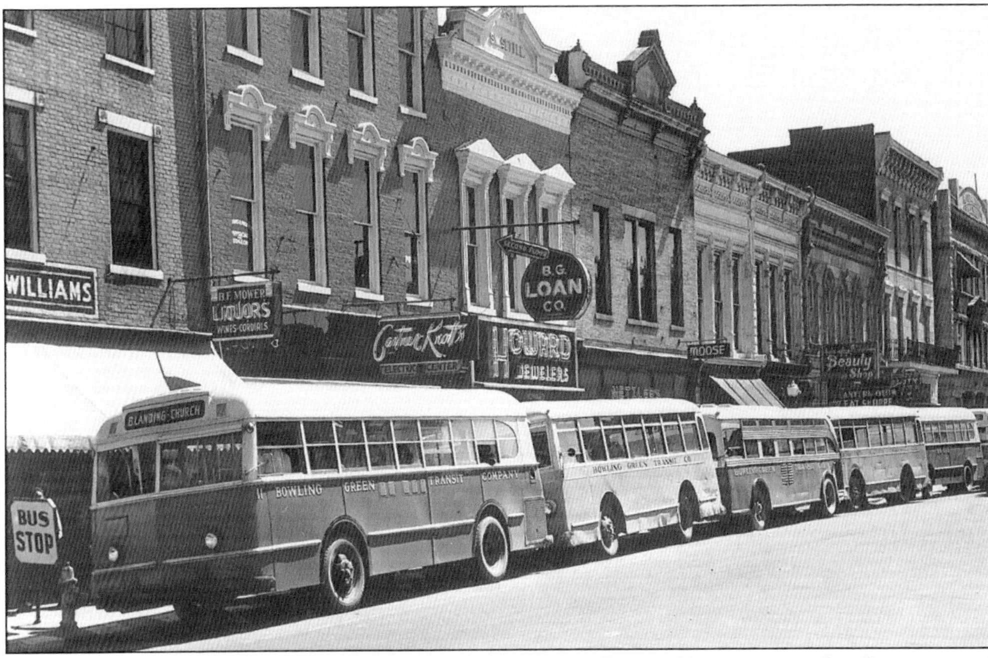

BUSING. The Bowling Green Transit Company was one of several bus systems that has operated in the city. The company started operation in 1945 with three buses. Because this was a city only service, the buses did not use the Main Street bus terminal. Here the buses are parked along State Street in the late 1940s. Fare on the system was a dime. The company discontinued service in August 1956.

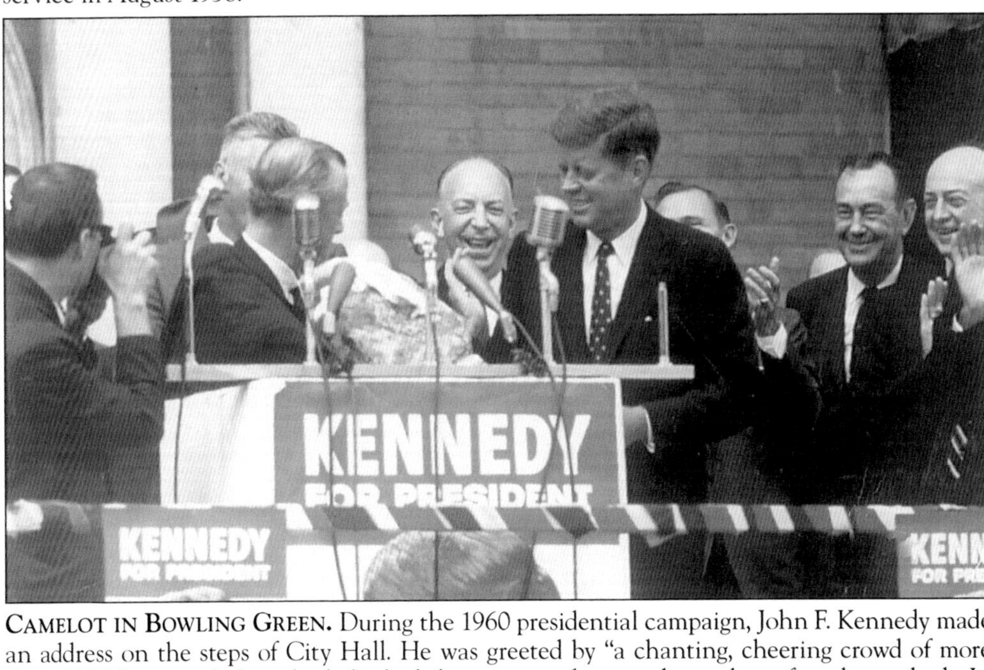

CAMELOT IN BOWLING GREEN. During the 1960 presidential campaign, John F. Kennedy made an address on the steps of City Hall. He was greeted by "a chanting, cheering crowd of more than 5000," some of whom had climbed the trees on the courthouse lawn for a better look. In the photograph Kennedy is handed a genuine hickory-smoked country ham complete with a nice layer of mold.

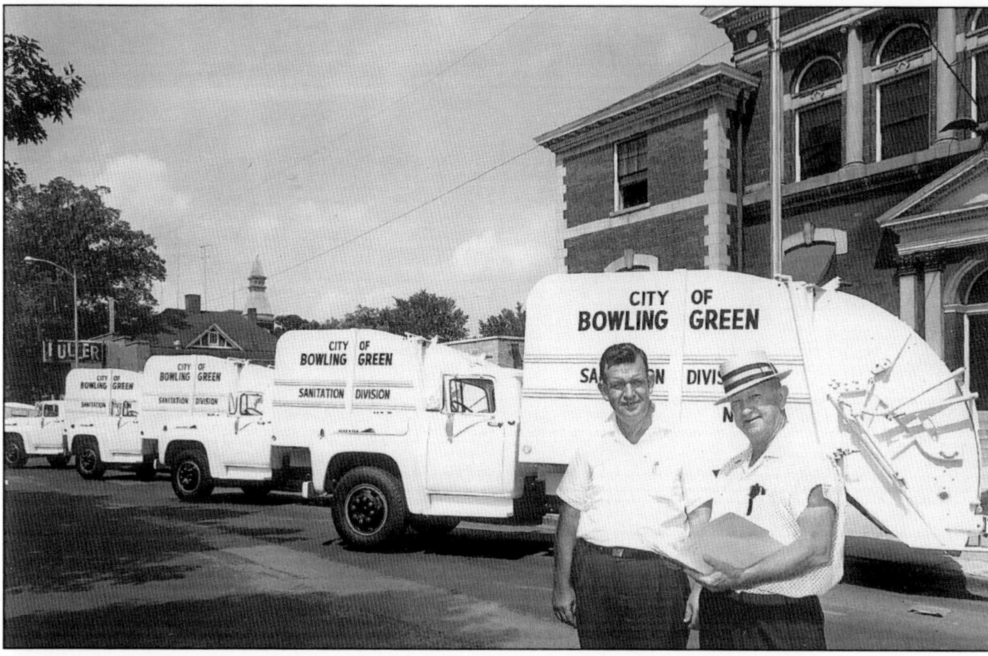

TRASH TALKING. Trash pick-up became mandatory in Bowling Green on June 1, 1960. Mayor Robert Graham considered this action a signal achievement of his administration.

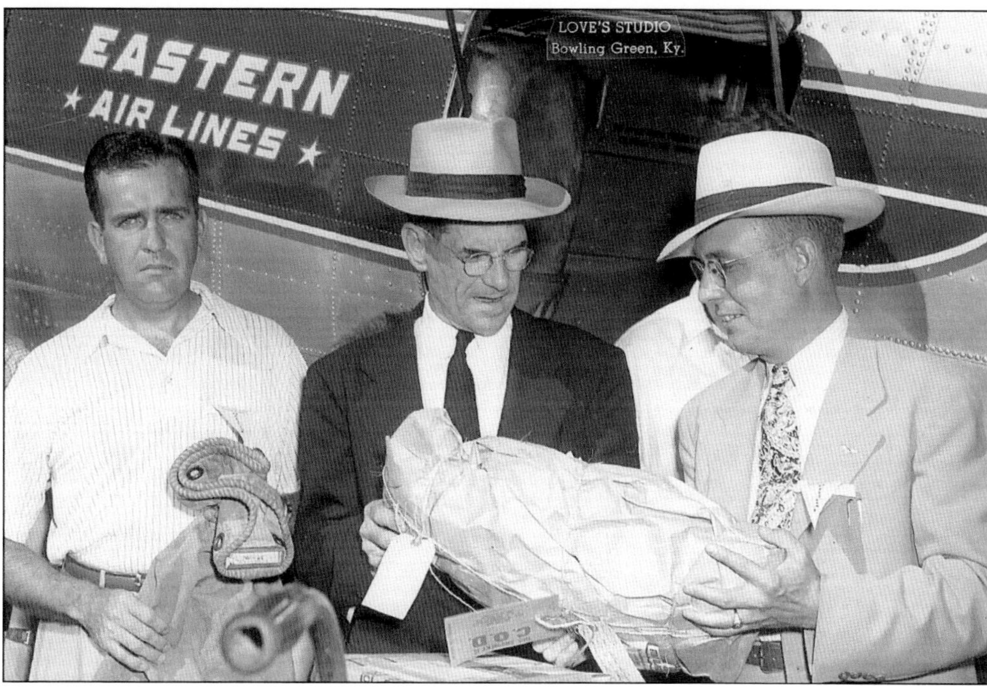

AIR MAIL. Here Bowling Green officials handle one of the first pieces of air mail to leave the city via Eastern Airlines in 1968. The men are, from left to right, O.W. Dotson Jr., mayor Henry Potter, and Garland Stinson of Railway Express. When Eastern inaugurated passenger service from the airport on August 1, 1948, over 15,000 local citizens swarmed around the city airport. (Photo by Love Studios.)

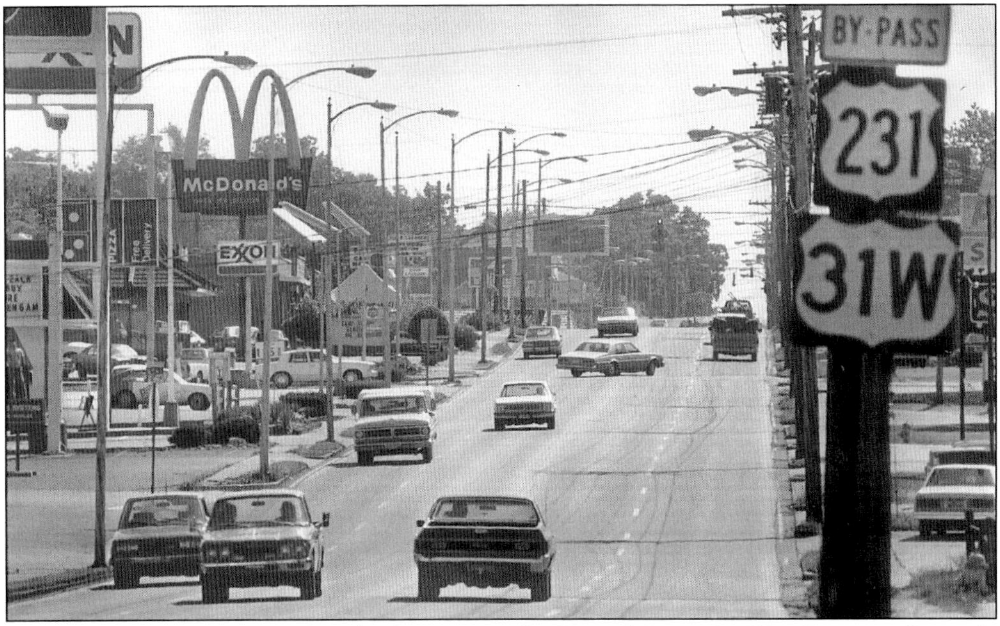

URBAN SPRAWL. Completed in the late 1940s, the United States 31 West By-pass effectively detoured travelers away from downtown Bowling Green and allowed for a business boom around the city's eastern periphery. The highway soon became peppered with court motels, car washes, service stations, strip malls, and restaurants-all catering to the convenience and needs of the traveling public.

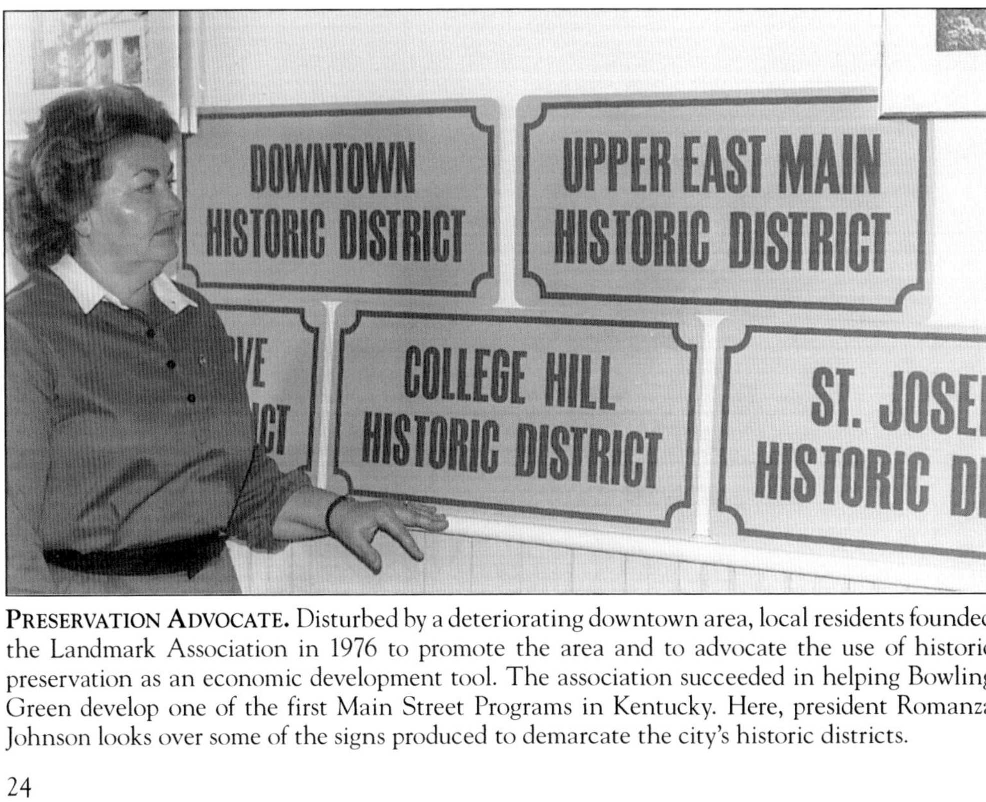

PRESERVATION ADVOCATE. Disturbed by a deteriorating downtown area, local residents founded the Landmark Association in 1976 to promote the area and to advocate the use of historic preservation as an economic development tool. The association succeeded in helping Bowling Green develop one of the first Main Street Programs in Kentucky. Here, president Romanza Johnson looks over some of the signs produced to demarcate the city's historic districts.

Two

Bowling Green Faces and Places

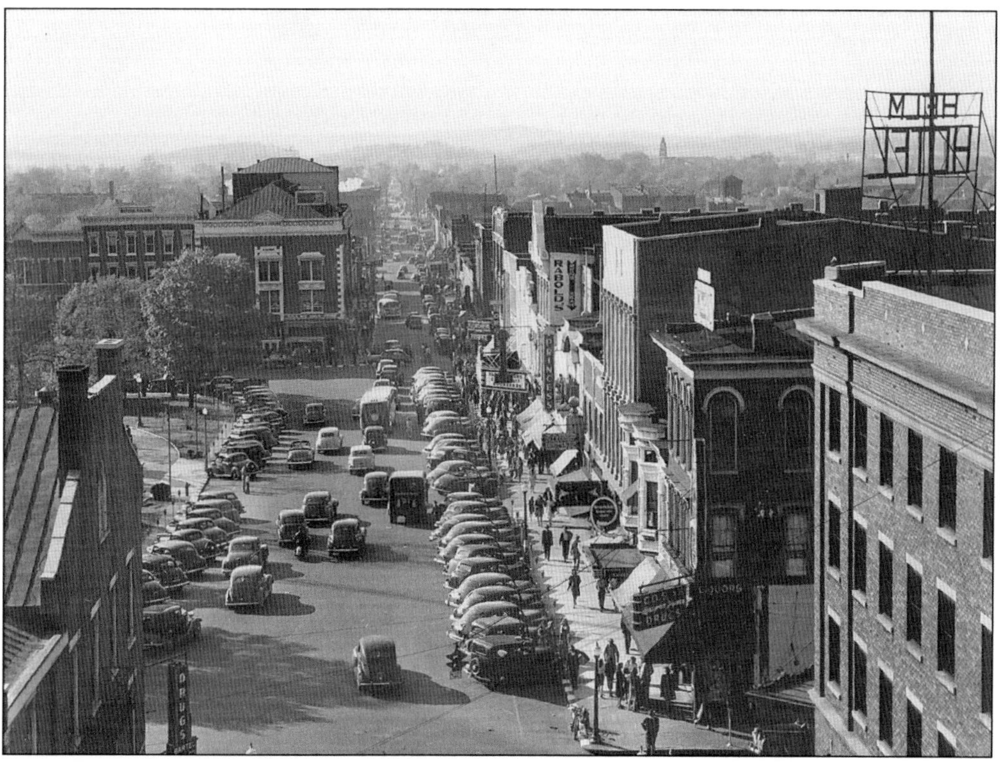

Main Street USA. This photo documents Bowling Green's busy Main Street in the 1940s. To the right is the Helm Hotel. The large building with the hipped roof at the corner of Main and College Streets is the old Opera House with its large windows and stone corner quoins. And we think finding a parking place downtown is difficult today!

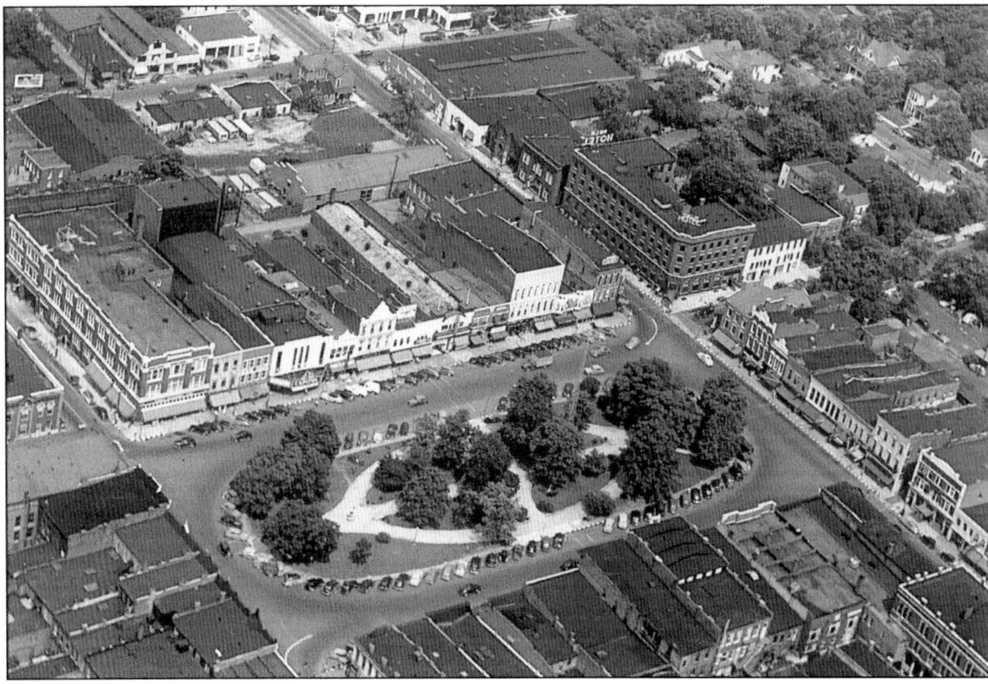

AERIAL VIEW OF FOUNTAIN SQUARE. This photograph of downtown Bowling Green's Fountain Square was taken in the mid-1950s. It shows the footprint of the city's central park and the buildings along Main and State Streets.

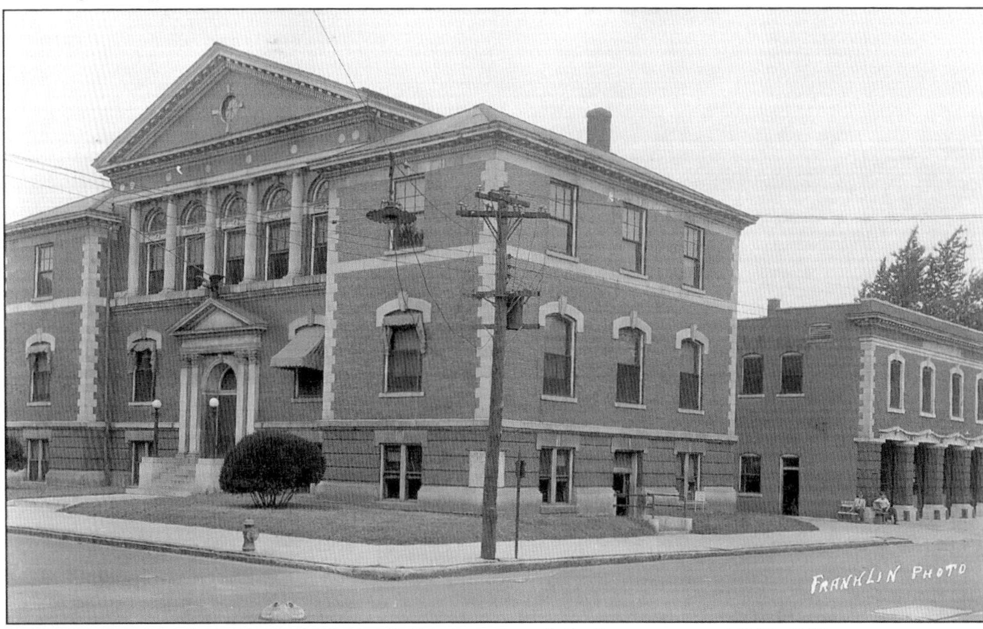

CITY HALL. Bowling Green's City Hall was opened for business in 1907. Offices were moved from the McCormack Building on State Street. Directly behind City Hall was the Central Fire Station, completed in 1908. Both buildings, designed by Louisville architect Brinton B. Davis, are of masonry construction with attractive limestone detailing. The fire station was razed in the 1980s and City Hall went through an extensive renovation in 1986.

Riverview at Hobson Grove. Atwood Gaines Hobson began construction of his home Riverview in 1857, but the Civil War halted construction. The Italianate house, which stands on a small promontory north of downtown, was completed in 1872. After becoming a rental property in the 1950s, the house went into decline. Local citizens banded together to restore the structure in the late 1960s and opened it for tours in 1972.

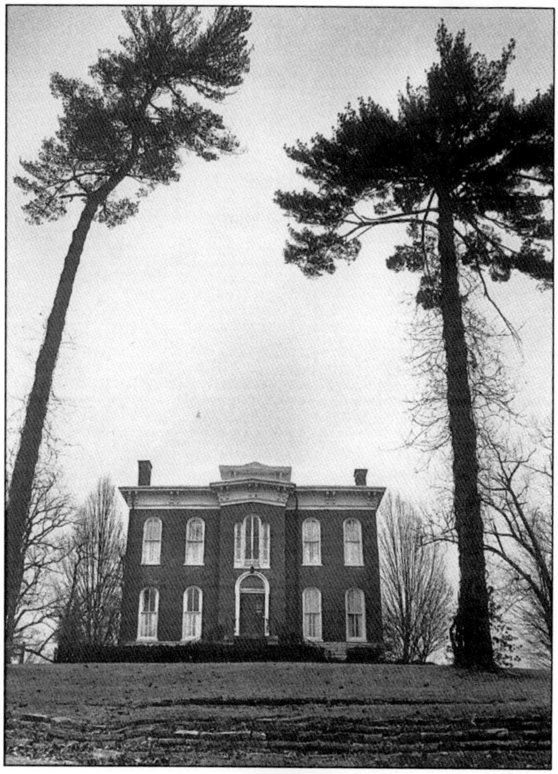

Oldest House in Town. The Mariah Moore House was built around 1818 for Elizabeth and Mariah Moore, widow and daughter of George Moore, a Bowling Green pioneer who died in 1819. The masonry structure is known as the oldest building in Bowling Green. It was converted into a restaurant in the early 1980s. After a 1995 fire, the facility was rebuilt using what was left of the basement and standing walls.

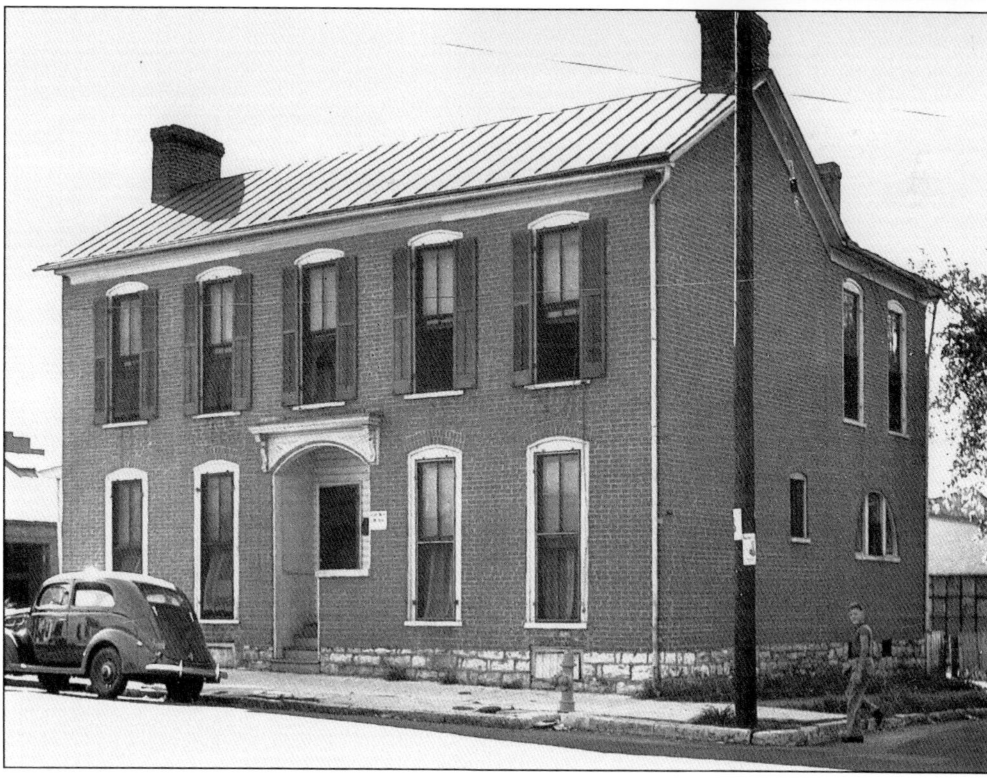

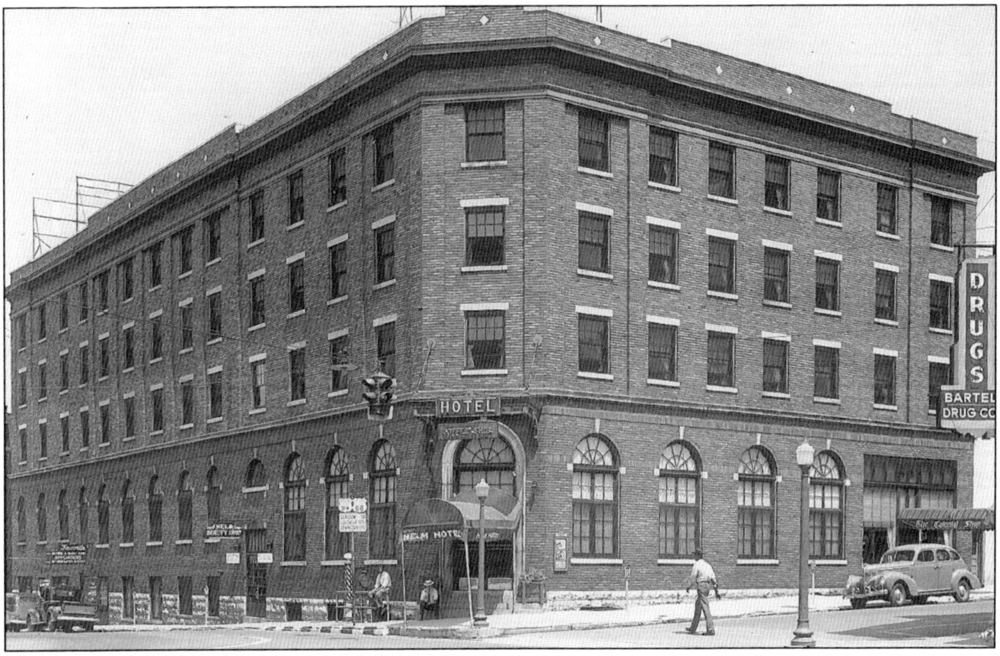

HELM HOTEL. Dr. T.O. Helm had this hotel built in 1923. It was designed by Cincinnati architect C.C. Weber and was built for $300,000. It contained 110 rooms that boasted steam heat, hot and cold running water, and telephones. The Helm family sold the facility in 1969, and it was razed in January 1970 to make way for Citizens National Bank's new building.

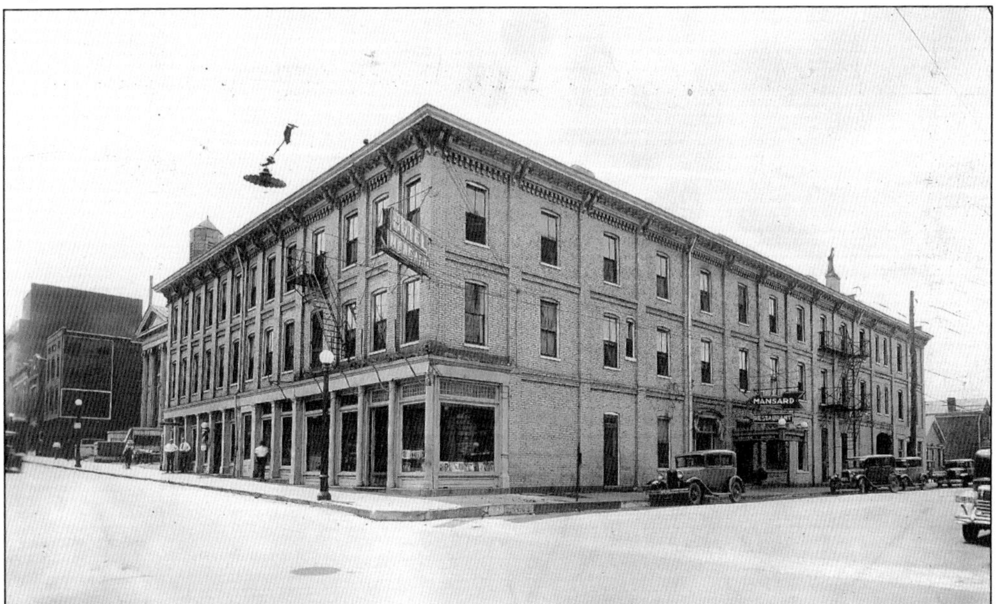

MANSARD HOTEL. The Mansard was considered one of Bowling Green's premier hotels when this photo was taken in the early 1930s. The hotel occupied this building from 1891, when Joseph Winans purchased it, until it burned in 1969. The building with the columns, to the left of the hotel on Main Street, was the old First Baptist Church building, which was used as the oil exchange during the oil boom period, 1917–1921.

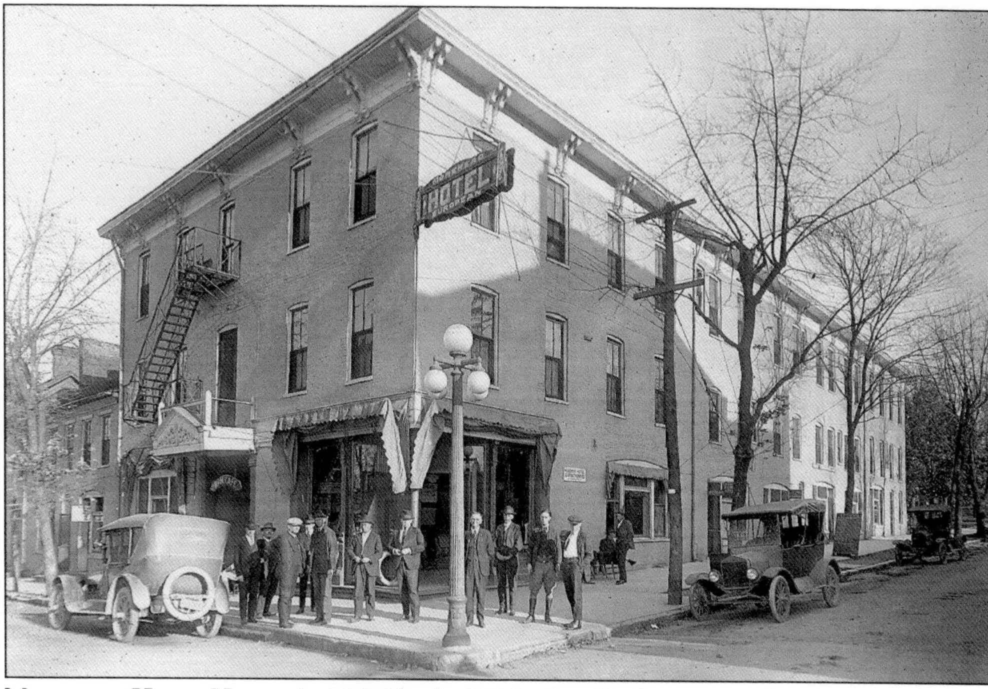

Morehead House Hotel. In 1847 Charles D. Morehead had a two-story hotel built in a pattern that replicated the Quigley-Younglove Building across Main Street. The hotel was extensively remodeled in 1883 and an additional story was added at that time. The exterior photo (above) was taken in 1921 only two years prior to the destruction of the hotel for the new Helm Hotel. The interior photo (below), taken around the turn of the century, is the only known image of the hotel lobby. There are two women in the photo at the left, and it is obvious that the lady on the right has lost a family member, because she is wearing a mourning veil.

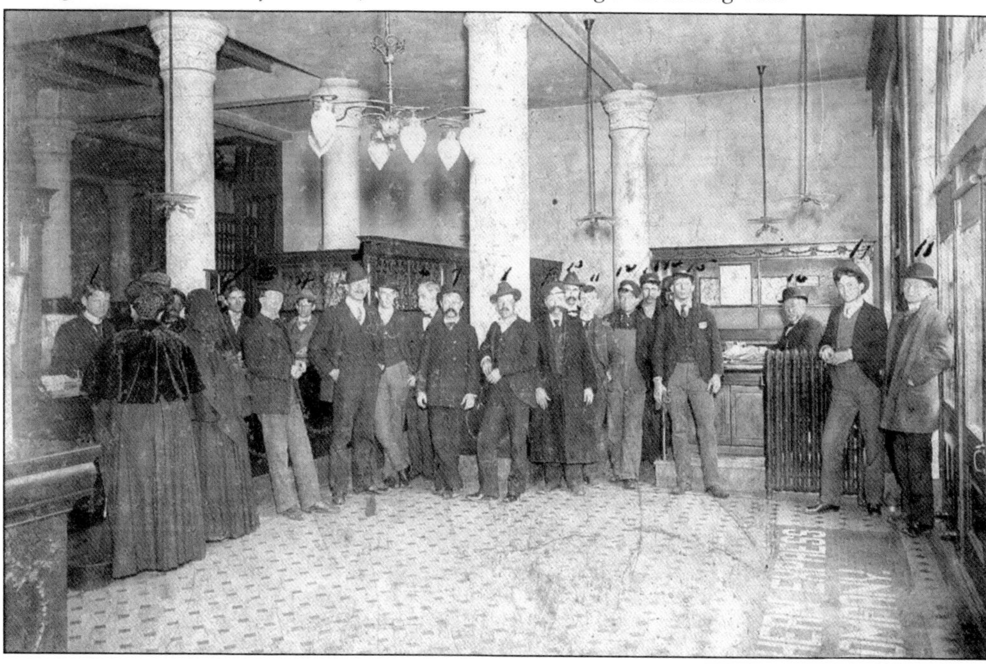

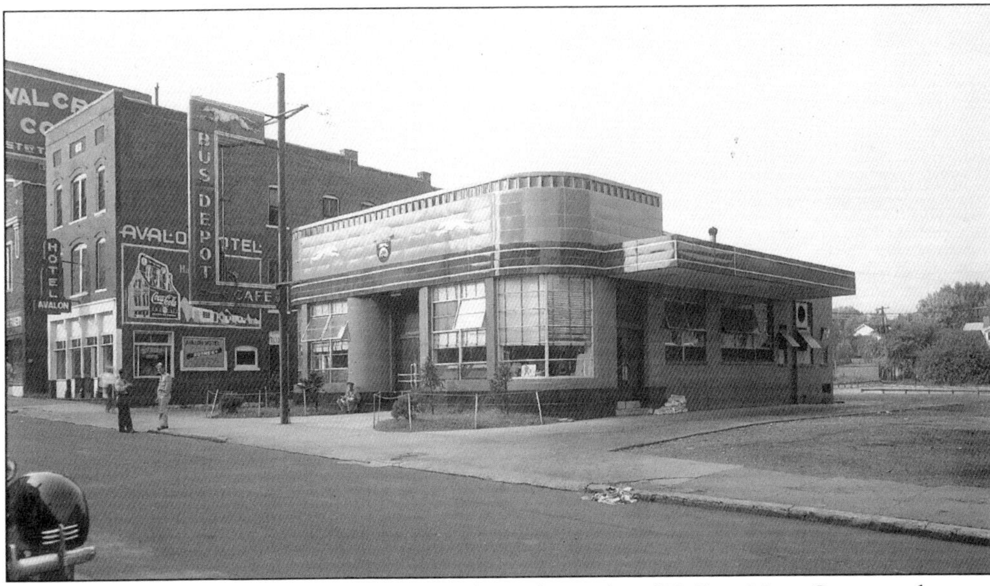

BUS STATION. Bowling Green's bus terminal was located at 311 East Main Street and served up to five different bus lines. The Streamline Moderne building was designed by the Arrasmith architectural firm of Louisville, which created many of these distinctive bus stations across the southeast. The station was razed in 1957 for a parking lot.

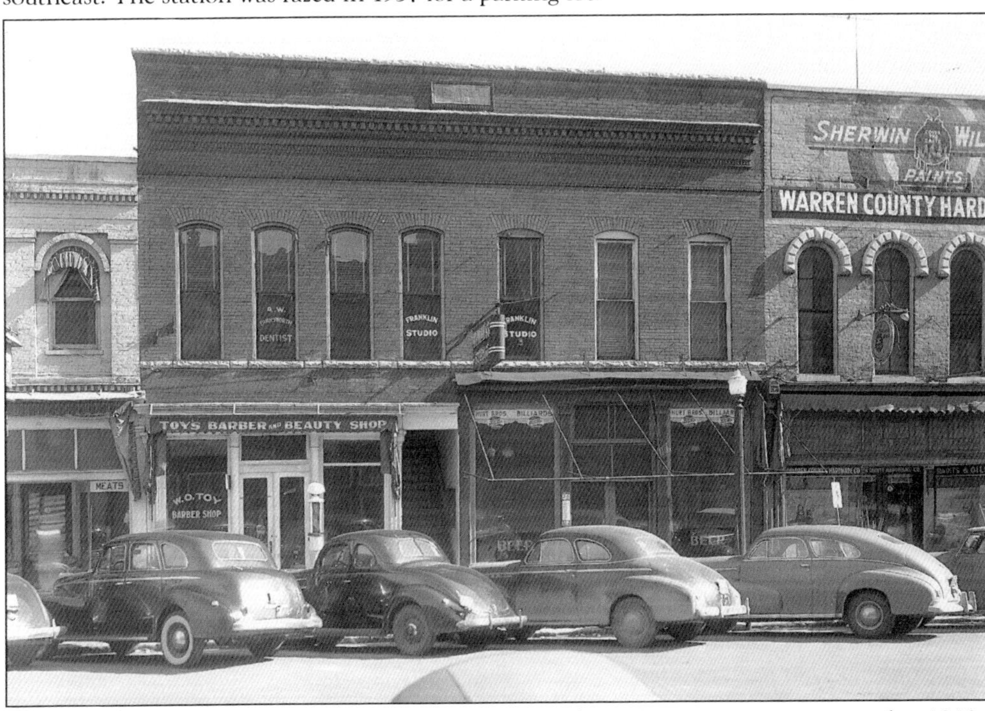

STATE STREET BUILDINGS. This is a typical Bowling Green streetscape in the 1940s. T.C. Mitchell erected the Mitchell Building, the center structure at 930 State Street, in 1903 as a mercantile store. Its façade is typical of period buildings with two storefronts divided by a stairway to the second story. Eugene Franklin's photography studio occupied a portion of the second floor; he took many of the photos seen in this book.

CITIZENS NATIONAL BANK. This longstanding Bowling Green bank opened for business on July 15, 1901. The institution was housed in a substantial three-story building at 439 Park Row. In 1920 that building was razed, and this beautiful Beaux Arts structure was erected. The bank stayed in this location until 1972. Although the building burned in 1984, this beautiful façade was allowed to stand on the square until 1992.

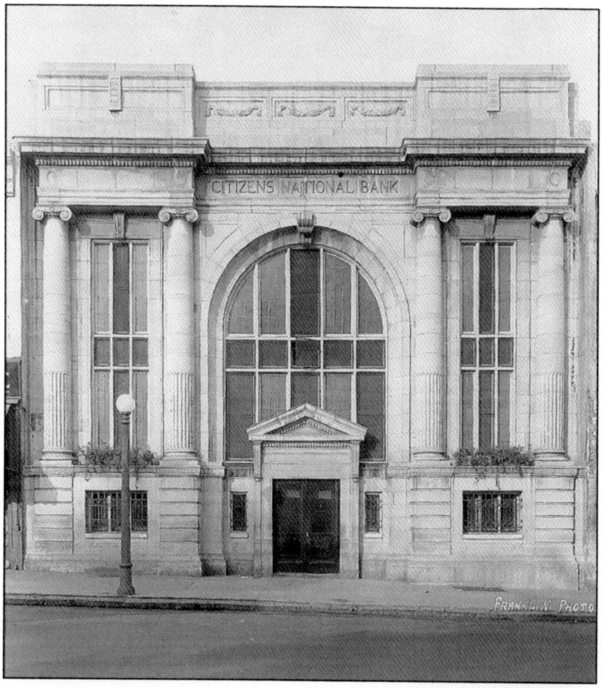

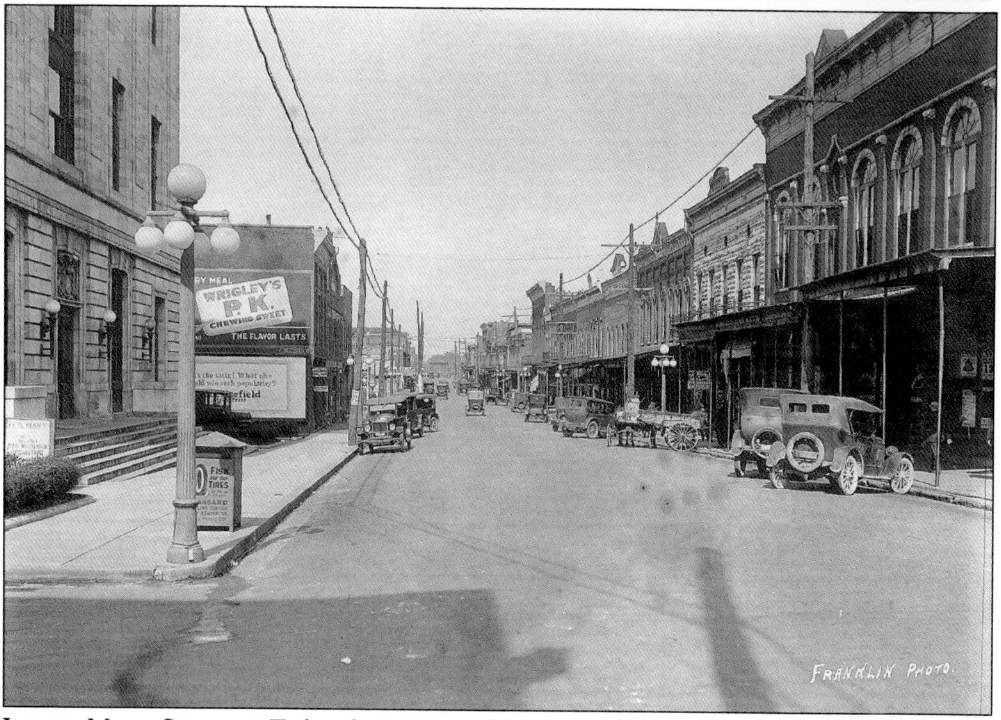

LOWER MAIN STREETS. Today the 100 and 200 blocks of East Main Street look bare, but it was once a thriving commercial area. The stone building on the left is the old post office, now the William H. Natcher Federal Building. Every other structure in the photo is now gone. The 100 block ended at the railroad tracks. West Main Street was residential. Notice the unique lampposts that line the sidewalks.

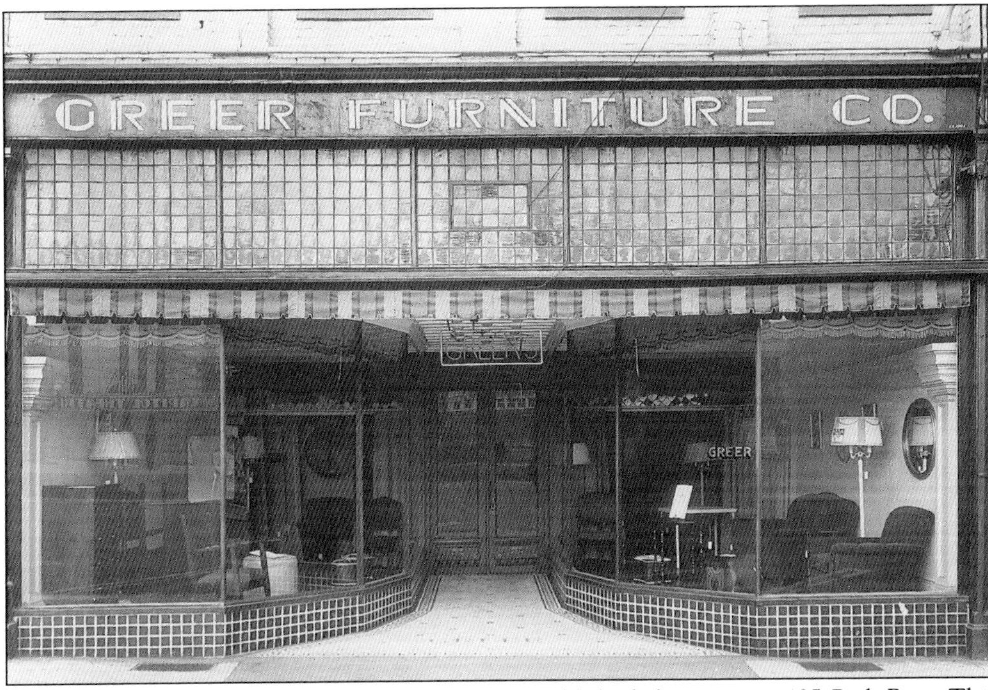

GREER FURNITURE STORE. In 1879, Lee Greer established this store at 405 Park Row. This photograph shows the newly remodeled storefront in 1930. Some history buffs will remember that shortly after the plate glass windows were installed, a stray bull crashed through the glass, ran through the store, and burst through the rear show windows on 10th Street.

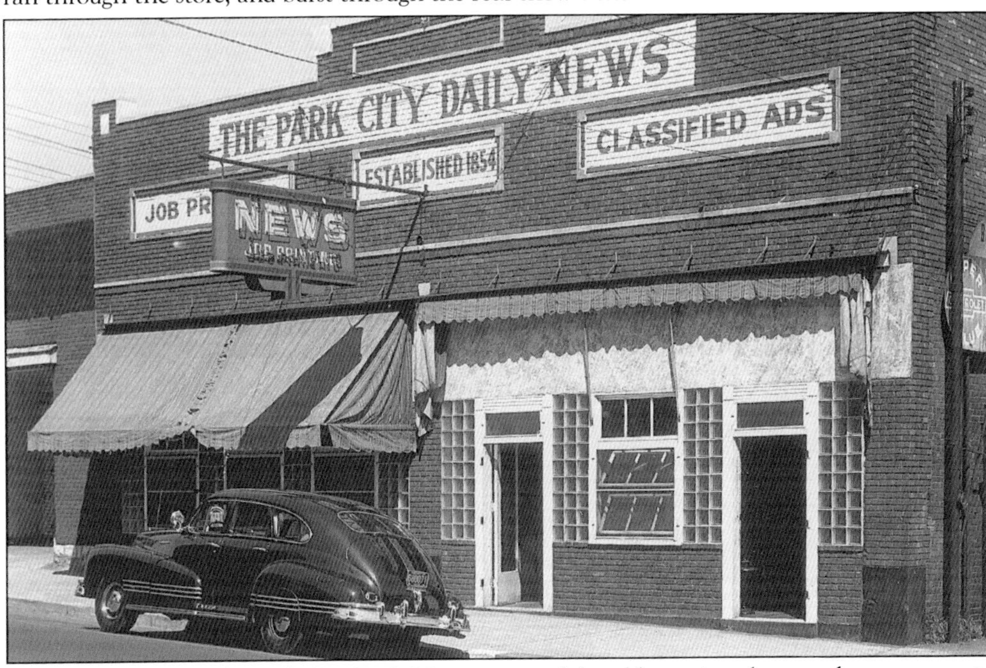

THE DAILY NEWS. The *Park City Daily News* is one of the oldest privately owned newspapers in the Commonwealth. The Gaines family has had ties to the newspaper since the late 1800s. It is now Bowling Green's only daily newspaper.

NOTED POLITICIAN. William Huston Natcher (1909–1994) began his political career in Bowling Green serving as County Attorney from 1938 to 1950 and Commonwealth Attorney from 1950 to 1953. Elected to the U.S. House of Representatives in 1953, Natcher was re-elected continuously until his death. Natcher was known for his outstanding ethics, his refusal to accept campaign contributions, and his record for consecutive roll call votes in the House, which remains unchallenged at 18,401.

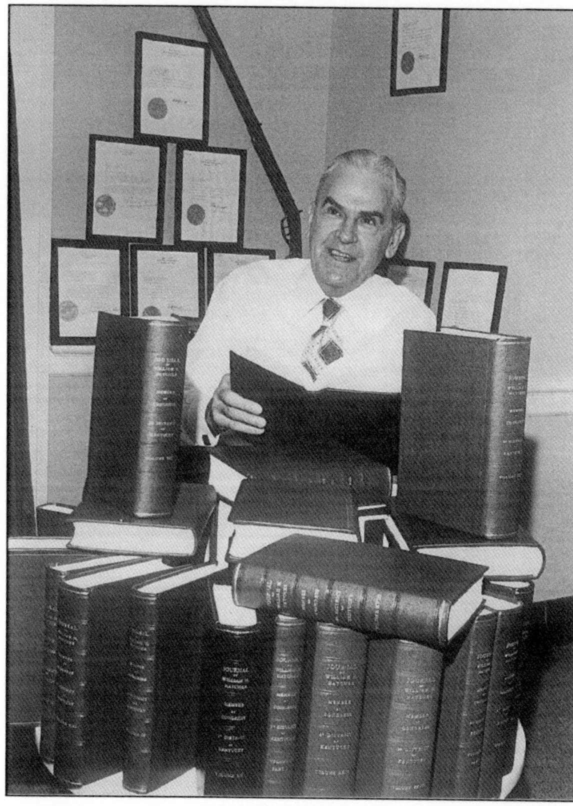

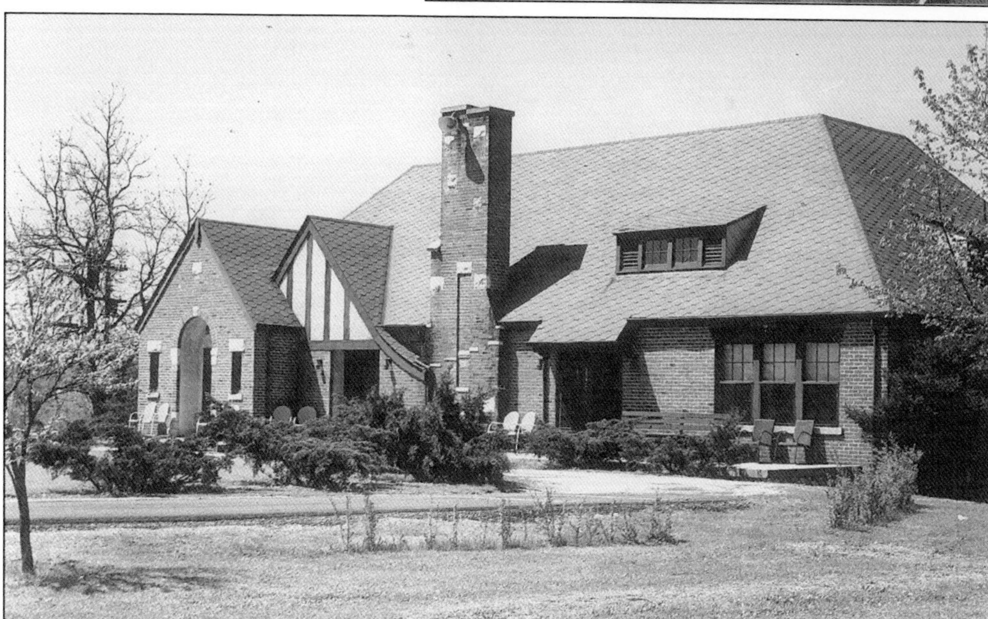

COUNTRY CLUB. The Bowling Green Country Club was organized in October 1913. When its old clubhouse burned in 1929, this structure was built. The club used a natural beach on the Barren River for swimming and maintained a golf course and tennis courts. The club remained here until 1963, when the present country club off Beech Bend Road was built.

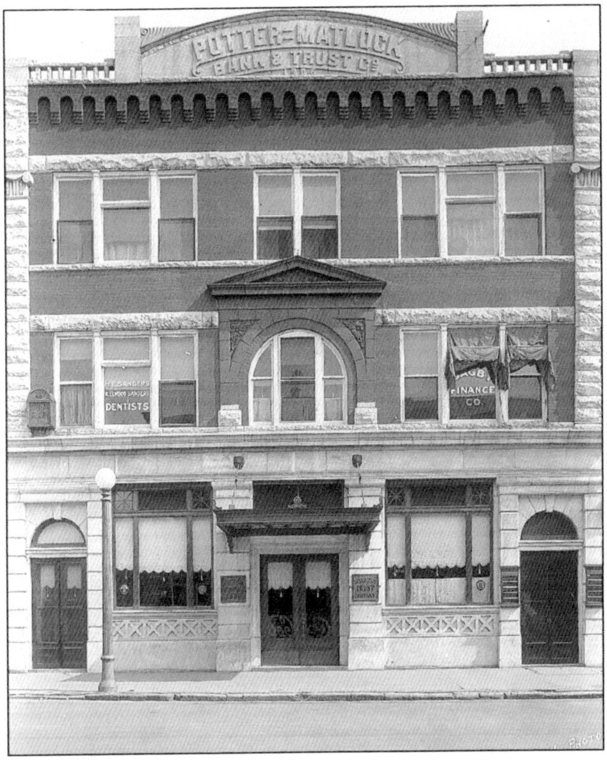

HOUSE OF BILLS. The Potter Matlock Bank was one of the oldest banking institutions in Bowling Green. It merged with American National Bank in 1958. This building, constructed in 1906, still exists under a façade of glass and marble at 922 State Street. Notice the boxed burglar alarm found above the left entrance. The central doors were used by the bank and the flanking entrances were used for the upper floors.

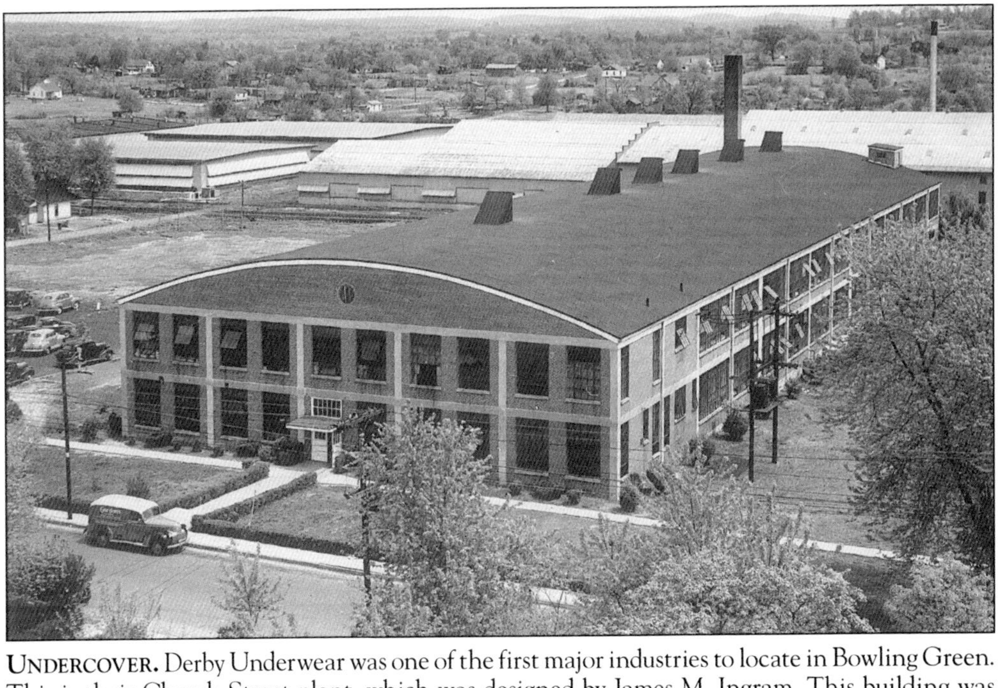

UNDERCOVER. Derby Underwear was one of the first major industries to locate in Bowling Green. This is their Church Street plant, which was designed by James M. Ingram. This building was eventually used by Fruit of the Loom, which sold it in the late 1990s to Houchens Industries. The metal buildings in the background housed the operations of the Burford Tobacco Company.

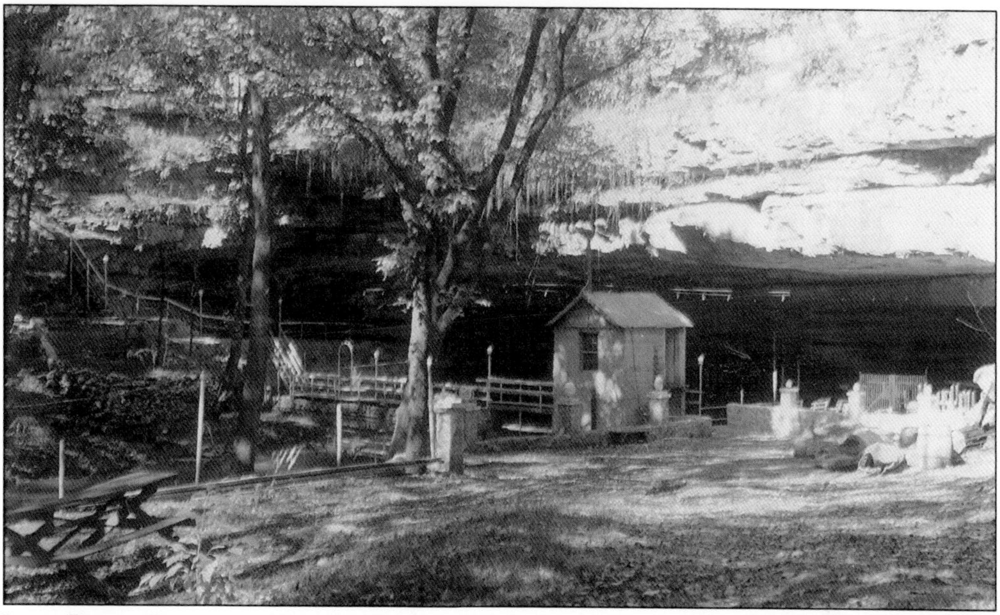

Lost River Cave and Valley. Bowling Green sits atop one of the largest series of caves in the world and is within half an hour of Mammoth Cave National Park. This karst topography is both a blessing and a curse. Lost River Cave is one of the city's most unusual tourist destinations. The cave's mouth, shown above, is the second largest east of the Mississippi River. Lost River has been dammed at the entrance, near the small stone structure in this photo. The power at this location was once used to generate electricity and to run a gristmill at street level. The attractive stone fence and entrance gate to the cave at street level, shown below, was completed in 1934 when the underground "Nite Club" was at it zenith.

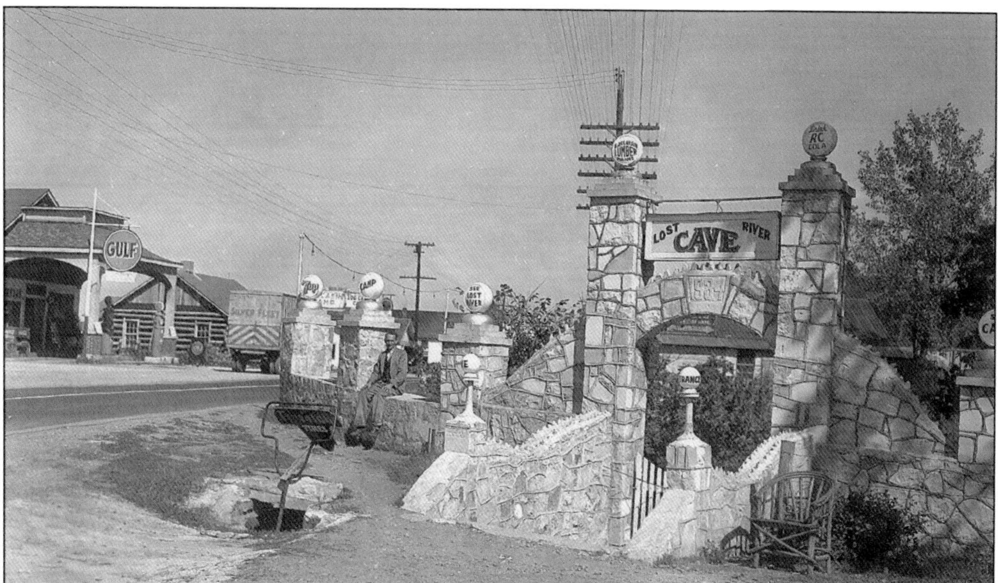

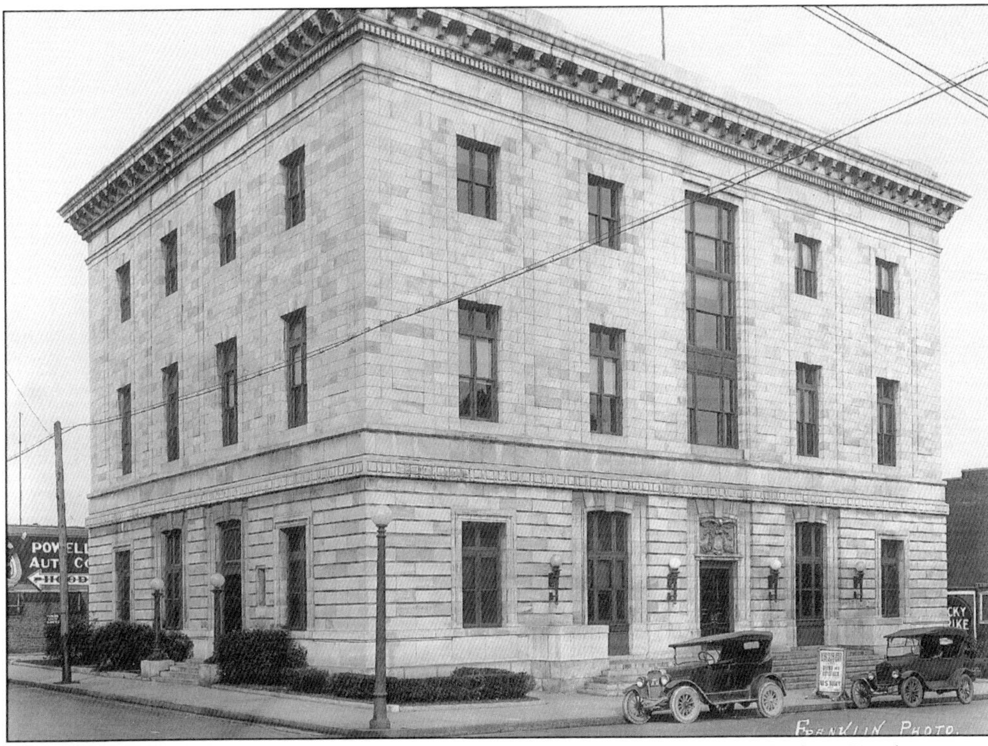

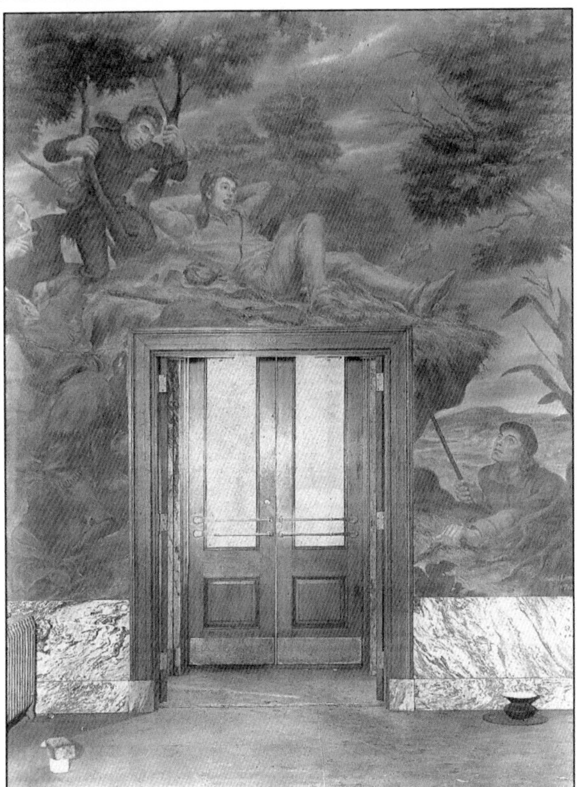

POST OFFICE. Built as Bowling Green's post office in 1912, the building (above) was constructed of Bowling Green limestone. It features a rusticated base and an attractive bracketed cornice. The post office moved in 1963, and the building was extensively renovated. The structure was renamed the William H. Natcher Federal Building in the late 1990s and contains courtrooms and offices. The building's lobby boasts a magnificent mural (left) by Edward Laning, a New York artist working under the auspices of the Fine Arts Section of the Treasury Department. The painting depicts Daniel Boone singing in the wilderness, which was popularized by Boone biographer John Edwin Bakeless.

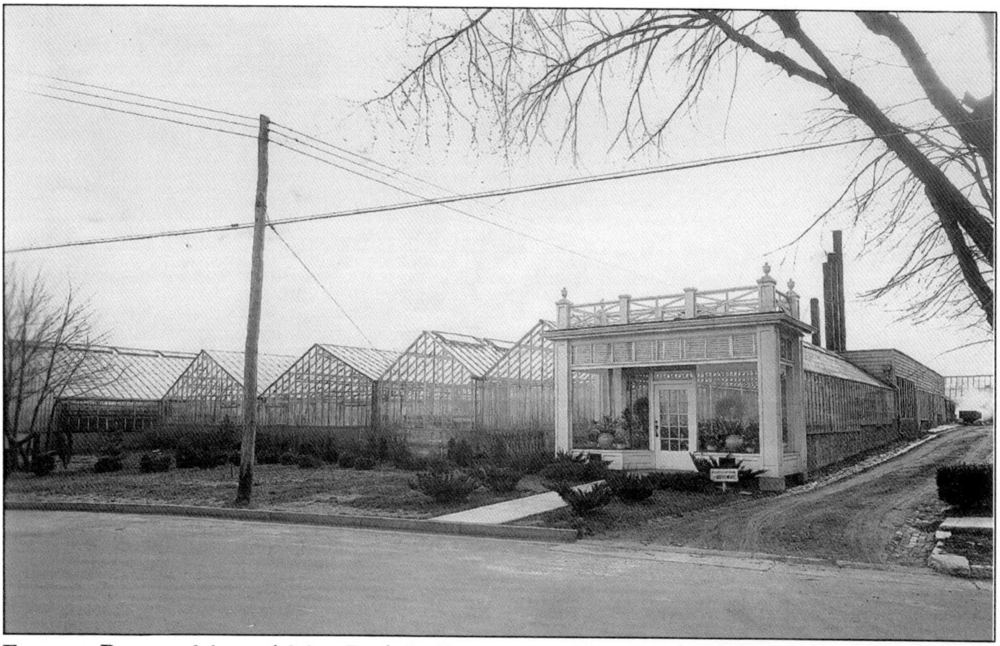

FLOWER POWER. Mr. and Mrs. Paul C. Deemer purchased the Burdell Floral Company and established Deemer Floral Company in December 1922. Located on Fairview Avenue, Burdell had already been in business for 20 years. With extensive greenhouses (below) the Deemers operated a large-scale nursery and floral shop (above), shipping flowers and plants throughout southcentral Kentucky via truck and rail.

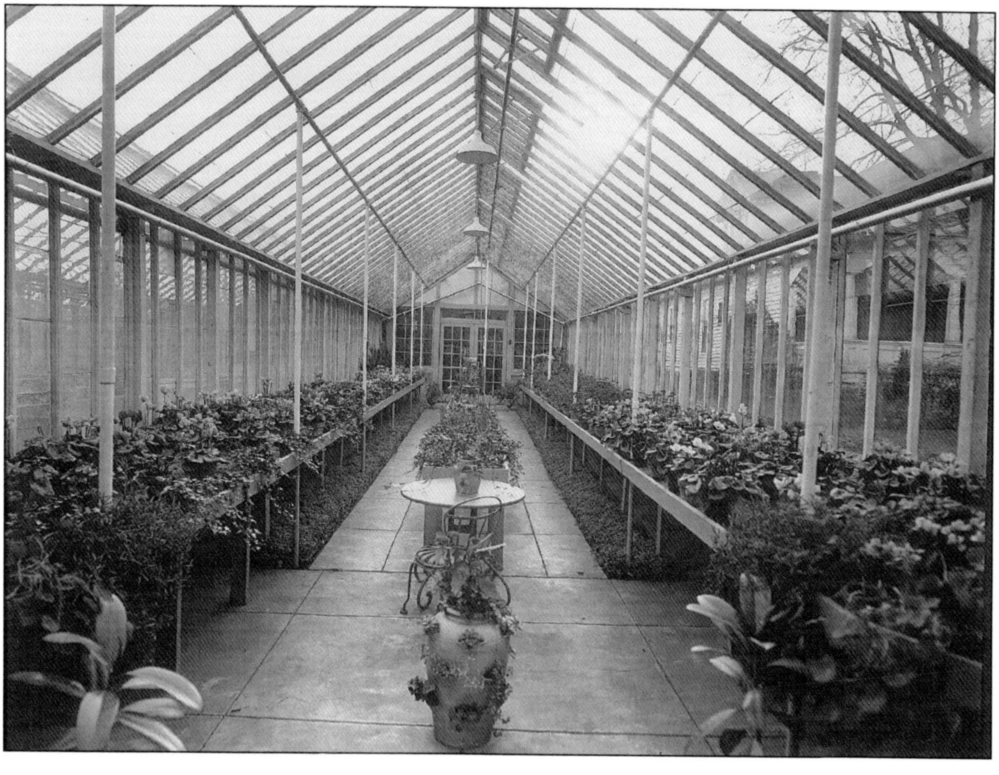

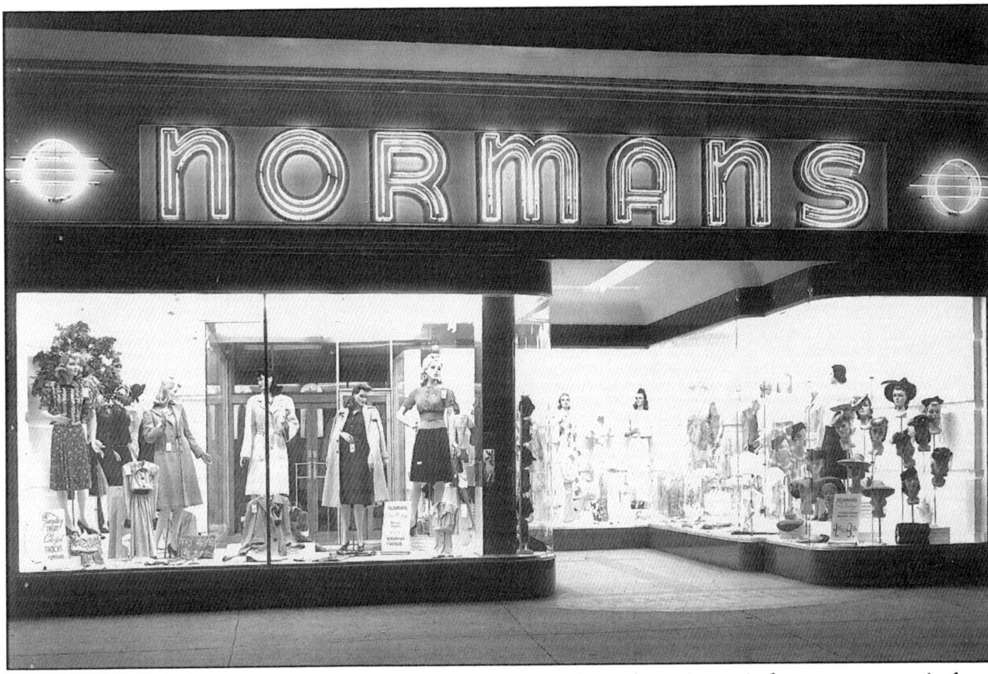

The Store All Women Know. Norman's was one of Bowling Green's favorite women's dress stores. Mr. Ely Norman opened the store in the early 1930s with money that he borrowed from his mother's life insurance policy. When enlarging his facility, Norman employed local architect, James Maurice Ingram, who designed the arresting Art Deco storefront (above.) At the opening, the local paper called the new store "brightly colorful yet restful, combining exquisite taste in restraint with contemporary treatment in both the interior (below) and exterior." Norman's was located at 918–920 State Street until 1991. In its heyday it was "the store all women know," and, as one local disc jockey added, "all men owe."

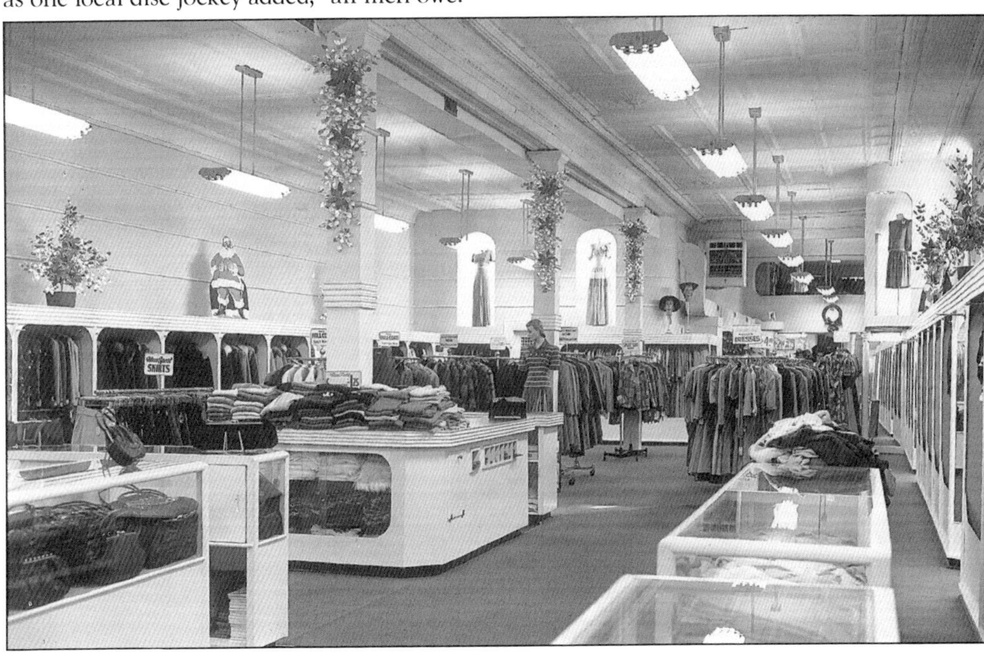

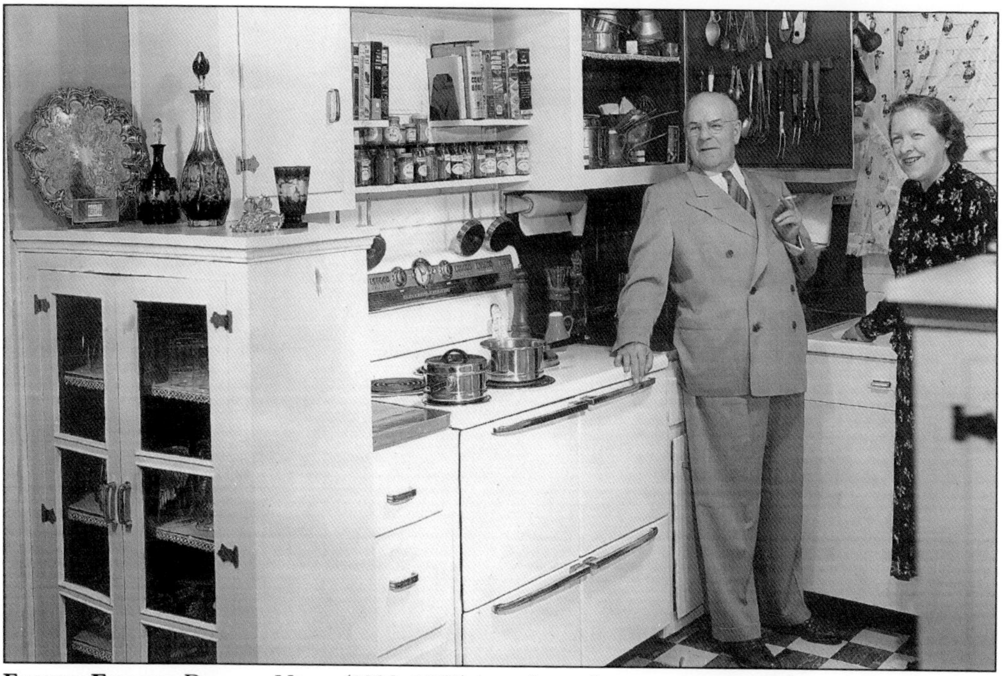

Eatery Expert. Duncan Hines (1880–1959) is perhaps the most recognized name that Bowling Green has ever produced. Hines worked for printing companies in Chicago for 33 years before producing his popular *Adventures in Good Eating* guides that listed restaurants that offered "standout attractions in the culinary department." Here Duncan and Clara Hines enjoy a cigarette in their kitchen.

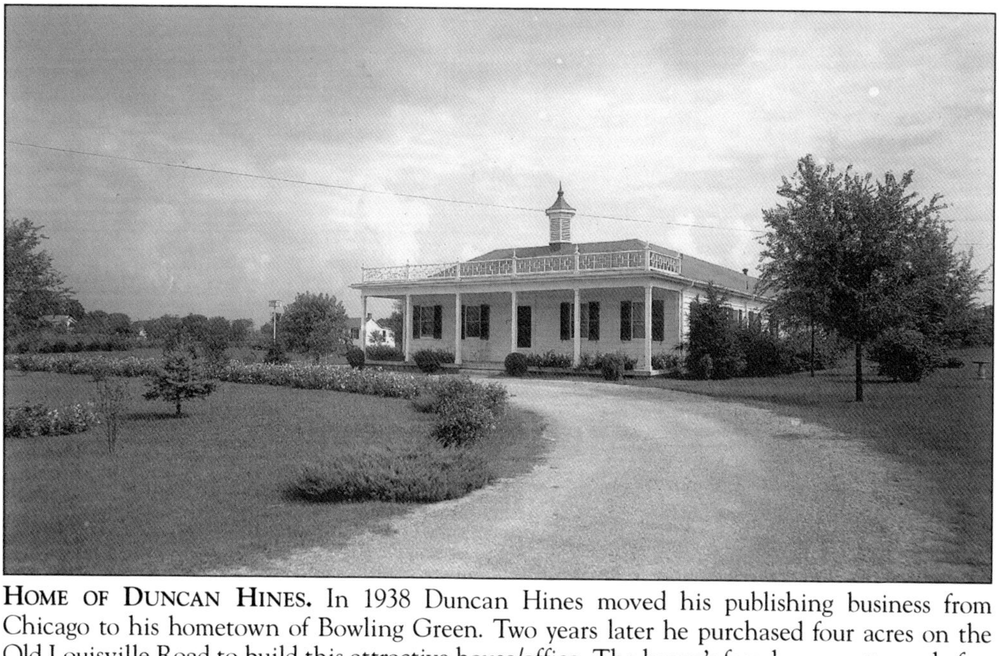

Home of Duncan Hines. In 1938 Duncan Hines moved his publishing business from Chicago to his hometown of Bowling Green. Two years later he purchased four acres on the Old Louisville Road to build this attractive house/office. The house's façade was patterned after the back portico of Mount Vernon, George Washington's Virginia home. The house is now a funeral home.

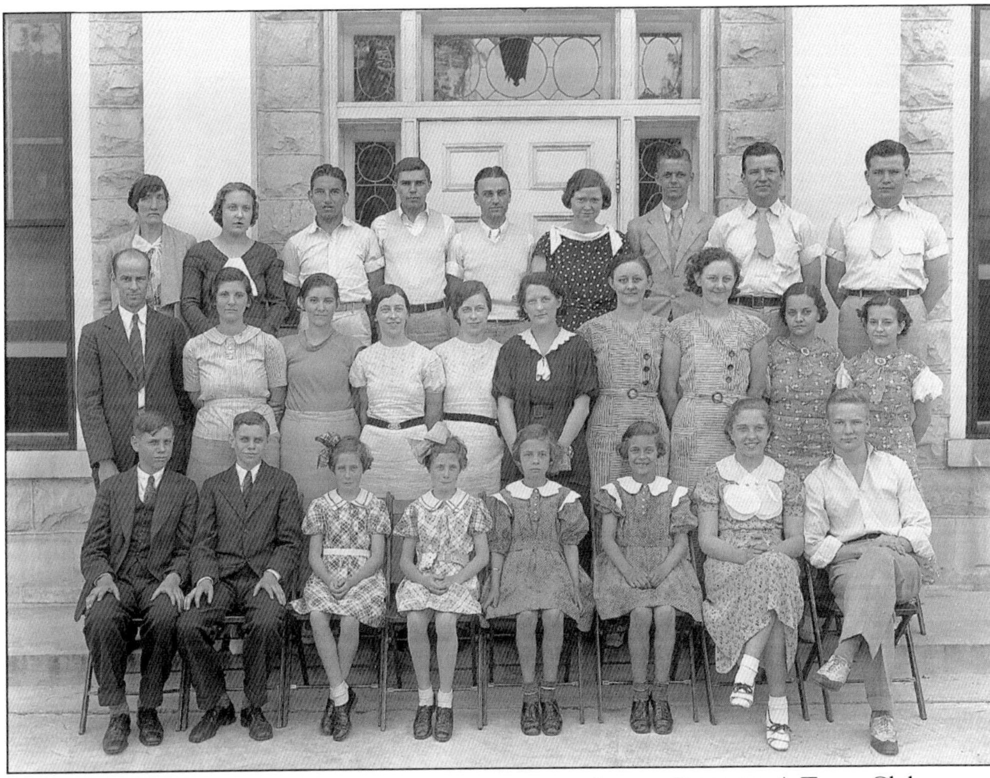

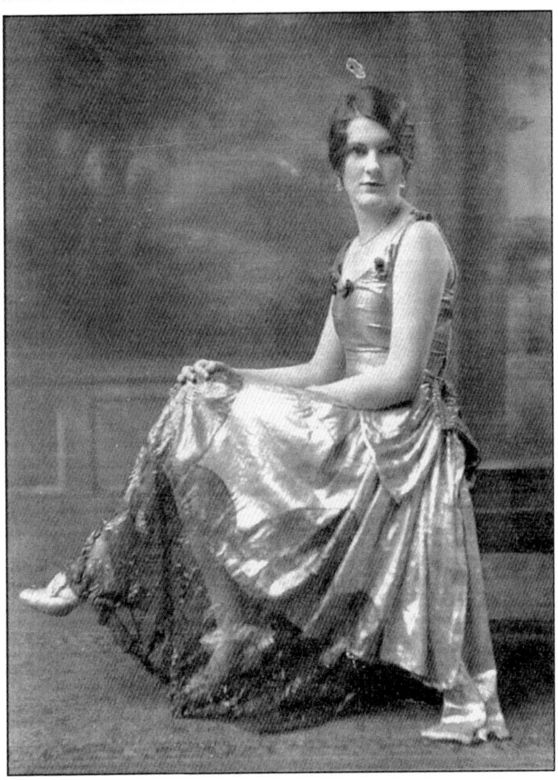

SEEING DOUBLE. A Twins Club was established and maintained in Bowling Green for a brief number of years in the 1930s. This photo undoubtedly is one depicting that group. Taken on the steps of Western Kentucky University's old Home Economics Building, this photograph contains three sets of triplets and nine sets of twins. Can you match them up?

EXERCISE GURU. Josephine Cherry Lowman (1899–1983), the attractive and vivacious daughter of Henry Hardin and Elizabeth (Frisbie) Cherry, literally grew up on the campus of Western Kentucky University. After collegiate training, she briefly headed the Department of Physical Education at WKU. In the 1930s Josephine began writing a daily beauty and physical fitness column, "Why Grow Old." The column was syndicated and appeared in 1,200 daily newspapers in more than 30 countries.

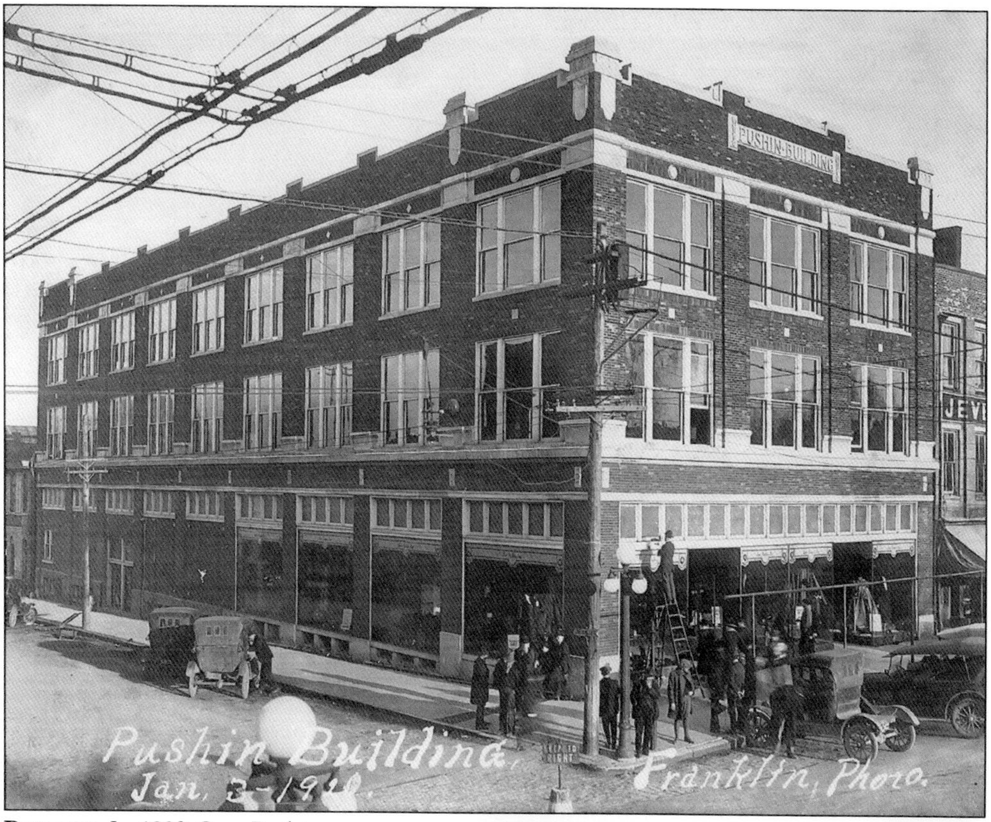

PUSHINS. In 1893, Sam Pushin, a Lithuanian immigrant, opened a dry goods store in Bowling Green. He operated in several locations before building this behemoth structure, which opened in 1921. Creedmore Fleenor, a talented local architect, designed this building, and it was constructed at a cost of $250,000. Pushins was one of the first buildings in Bowling Green to have a public elevator. It remained a department store until 1980.

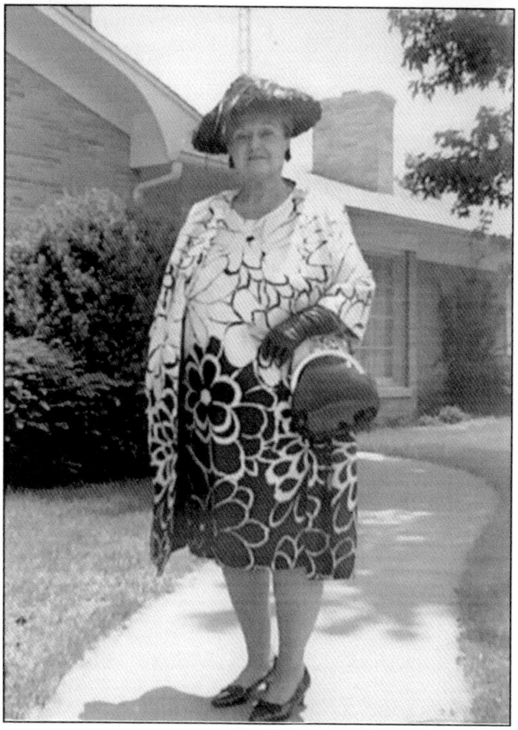

LOCAL MADAME. Pauline Tabor Webster (1905–1992) is one of Bowling Green's most recognized names. Ms. Webster kept a house of ill repute on Clay Street. If a milk can appeared in the driveway, Pauline's was open for business. Urban renewal caused her business to be razed, but interest in Pauline's life piqued with the publication of an autobiography and several national television appearances in the early 1970s.

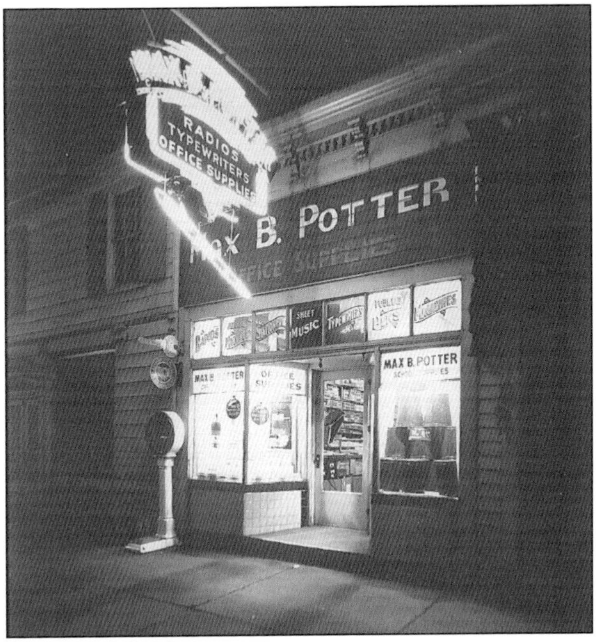

OFFICE SUPPLY. Max B. Potter (1900–1968) ran a popular office supply store on College Street next to Gerard Funeral Home. This attractive night photo indicates some of the products carried by Potter: school supplies, radios, sheet music, adding machines, typewriters, and magazines. Notice the ubiquitous scales to the left of the entrance, the display of office trash cans in the right picture window, and the hanging fountain pen aglow in neon.

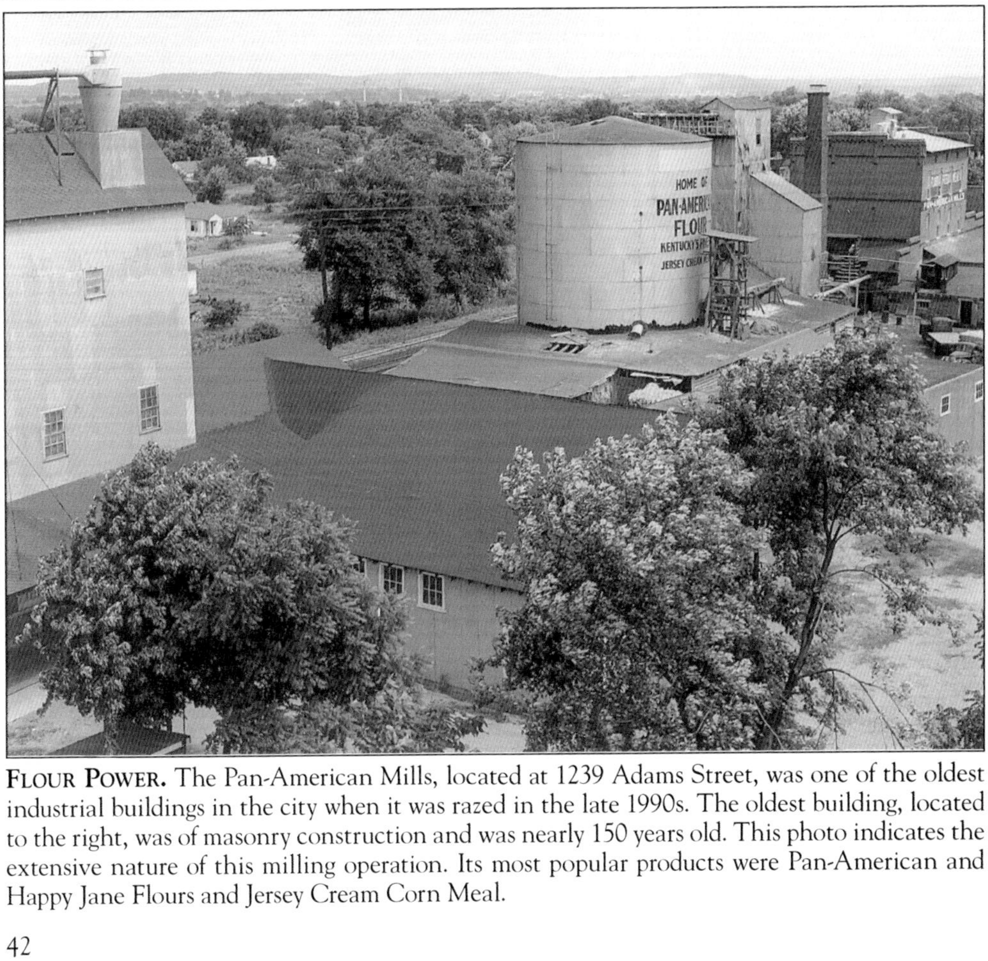

FLOUR POWER. The Pan-American Mills, located at 1239 Adams Street, was one of the oldest industrial buildings in the city when it was razed in the late 1990s. The oldest building, located to the right, was of masonry construction and was nearly 150 years old. This photo indicates the extensive nature of this milling operation. Its most popular products were Pan-American and Happy Jane Flours and Jersey Cream Corn Meal.

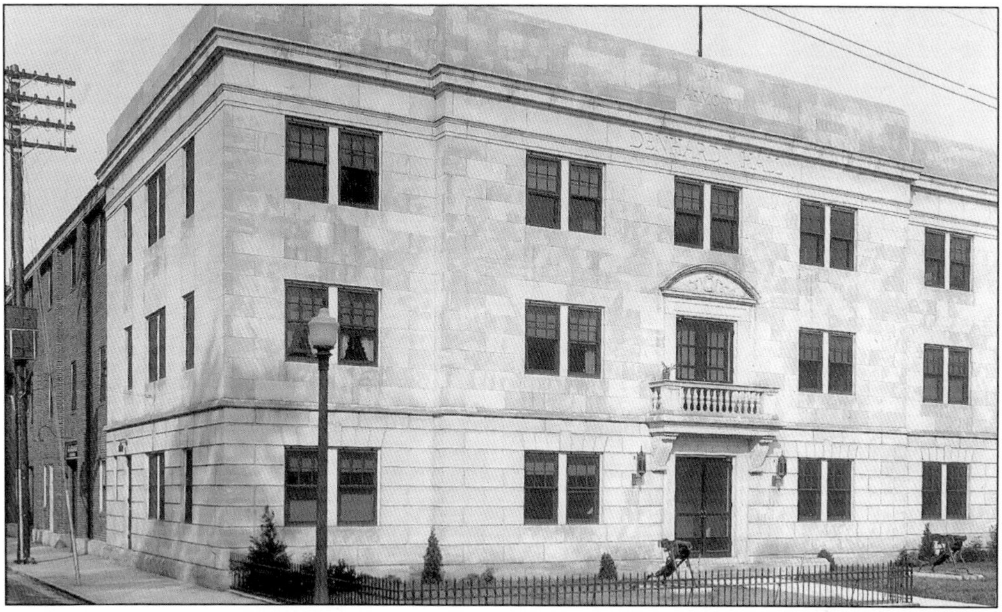

ARMORY. The Denhardt Armory is named for Henry Hardin Denhardt, who served as Warren County Judge, adjutant general, and lieutenant governor. He also had one failed gubernatorial campaign. Louisville architect Brinton B. Davis designed the building in 1927. It burned in 1946, but fortunately the front façade was retained. Today the structure serves as an office building.

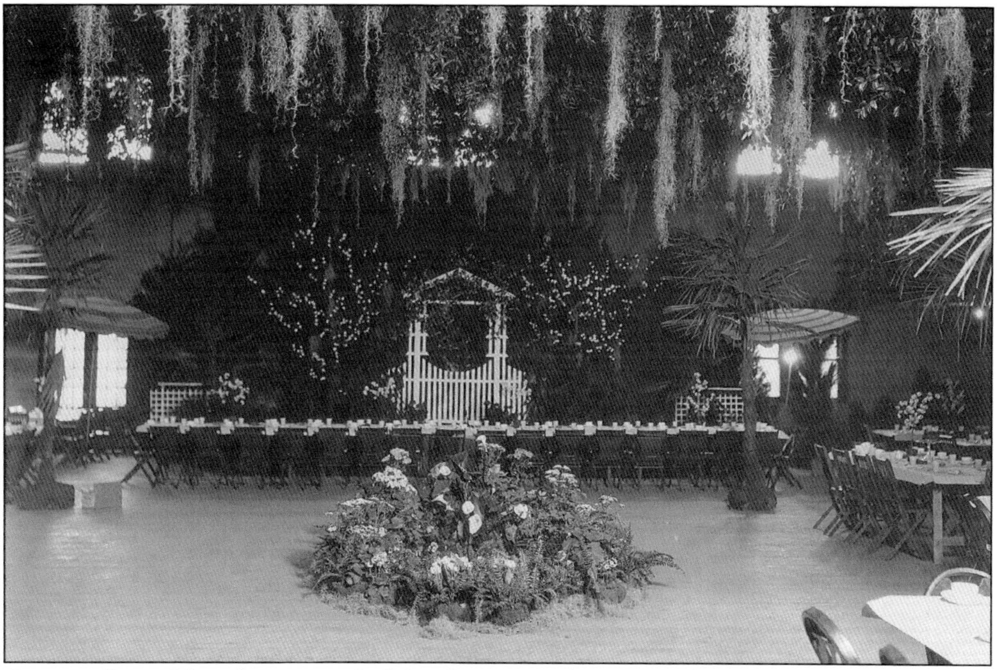

GARDEN SPOT. Here the armory hall has been turned into an Edenic garden dining room for a Rotary Club function. This building served an important role as a drill site for the State and National Guard, but most natives remember it as the location for hundreds of dances, large scale events varying from convention meetings to wrestling matches, and the public library.

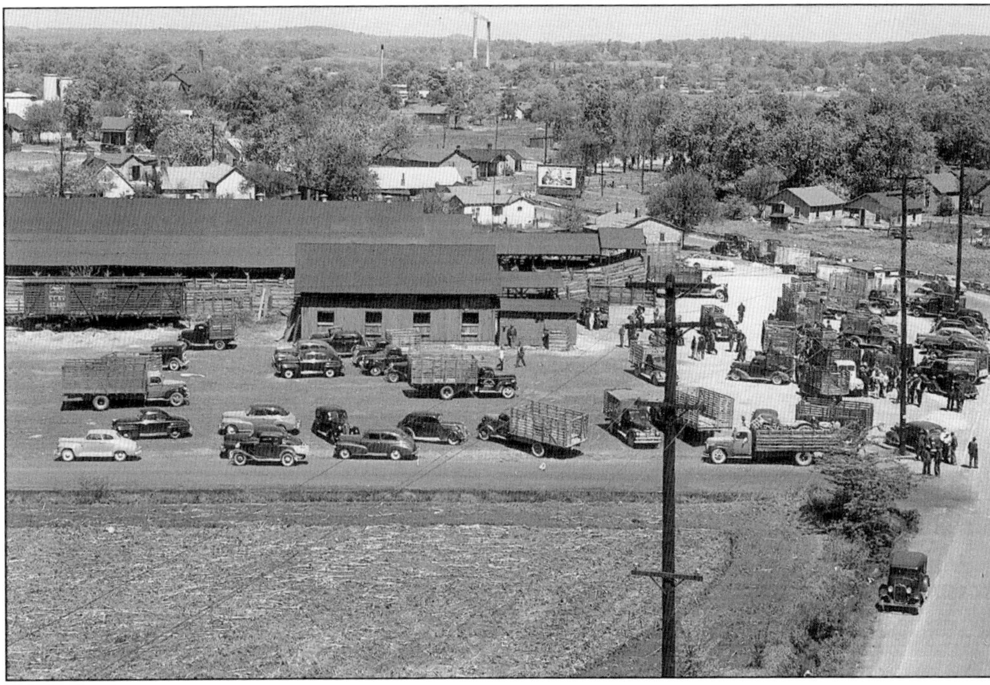

"MOOOVING" BUSINESS. The Bowling Green Livestock Market, at 600 Clay Street, was opened in 1931. Bowling Green has long been a state leader in livestock production and even today trucks line up to deliver cattle. In 2002 over 38,000 head of cattle were sold here.

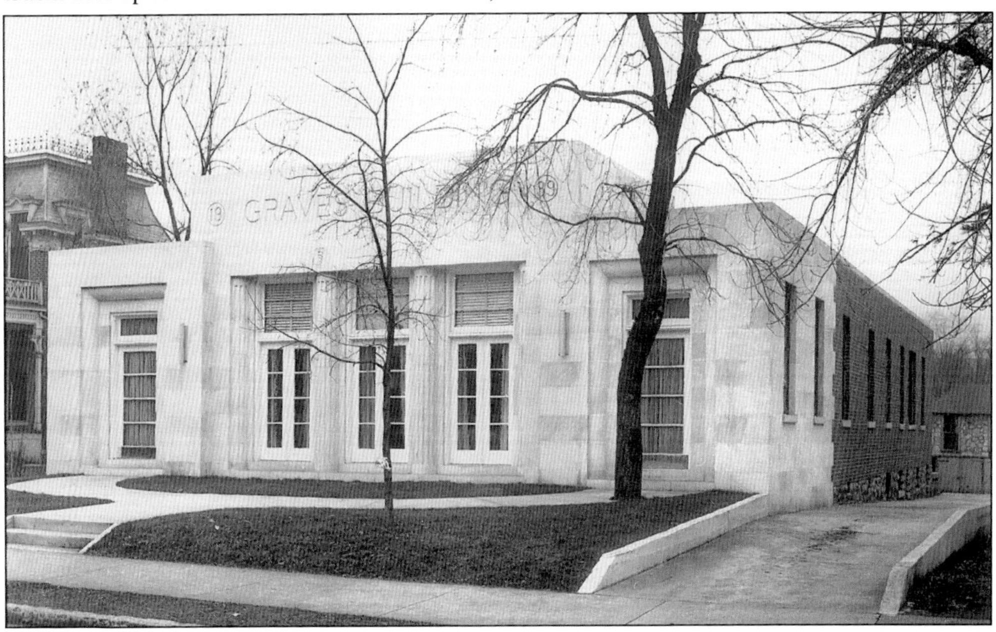

GRAVES GILBERT CLINIC. Dr. Guthrie Yoehlee Graves (1903–1967) received his medical training at Vanderbilt University and began practicing medicine in Bowling Green in 1930. Seven years later he formed a partnership with Dr. J.T. Gilbert. Their first clinic, designed by James M. Ingram at 1100 State Street, opened in 1939. The clinic now occupies a large modern building near the Medical Center.

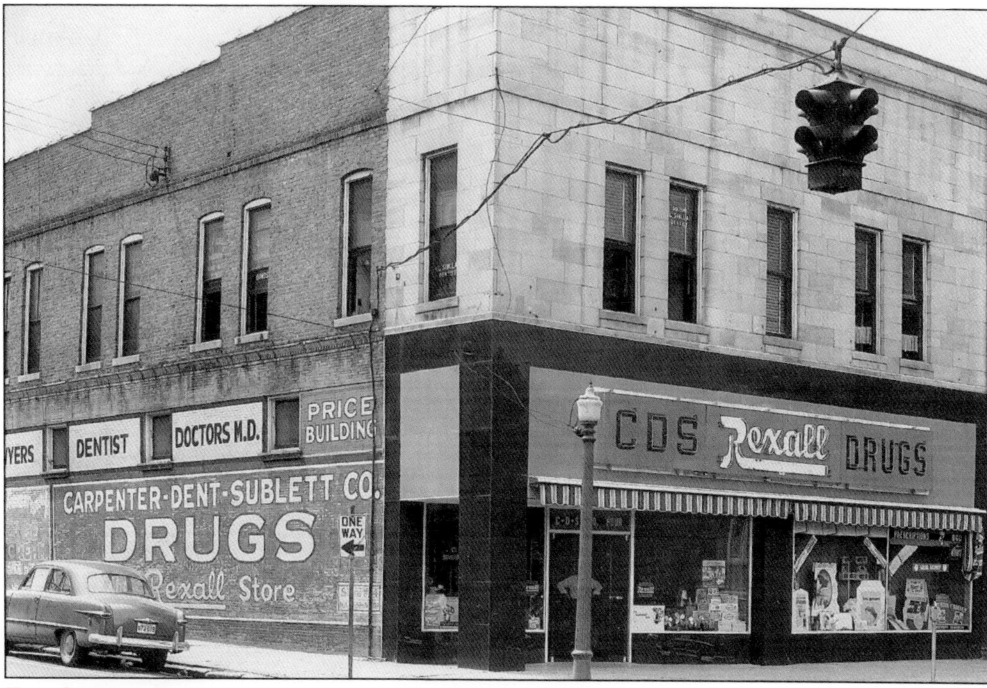

THE CORNER DRUGSTORE. The Price Building has held a drugstore since it was re-built in 1912 upon the ruins of the old McCormack Building. Mr. Willis operated the first drugstore at that location. The Carpenter Dent Sublett (CDS) drugstores, a local chain which started in 1912, purchased Willis's store in 1928. This site became the location for CDS #4. The exterior photo (above) shows a typical CDS storefront after it was remodeled in the 1940s using Carrara glass tiles on the store front and a prominent sign. Notice the two-colored traffic light. Part of the popular lunch counter can be seen in the interior photo below. The remodeled interior featured a checkered tile floor and Art Deco influenced counters and signage. The traditional scales that also told fortunes occupies a prominent location in the room; the side panel reads: "Your wate and fate."

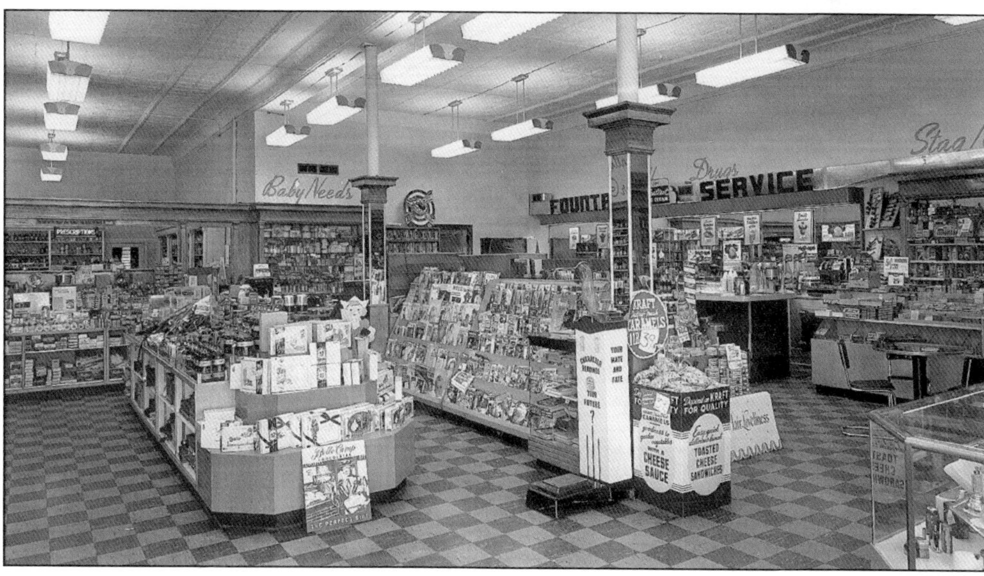

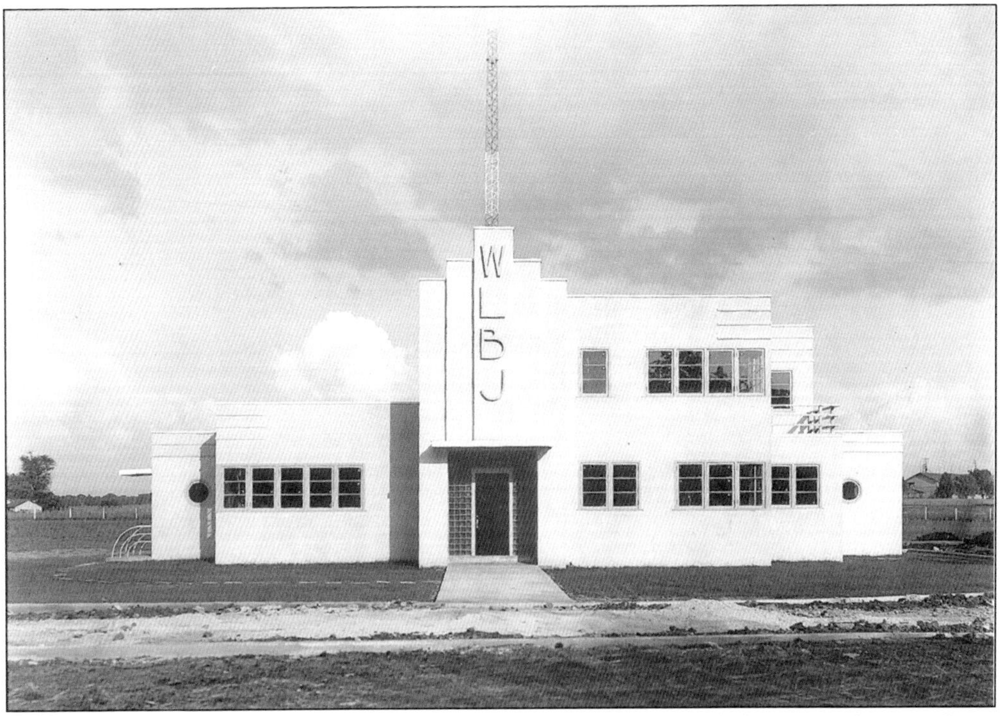

RADIO STATION WLBJ. Local architect James M. Ingram designed the Streamline Moderne WLBJ station. It opened for business at the intersection of Lehman and Fairview Avenues in June 1940. Its call letters were the initials of its first owner, L.B. Jenkins. The stair stepped tower is still visible above the funeral home that currently occupies the property. During the fledgling years of radio and television in Bowling Green, local programming proved popular. Below, a local band is ready to "go on the air." The seated radio announcer is Bill Beard.

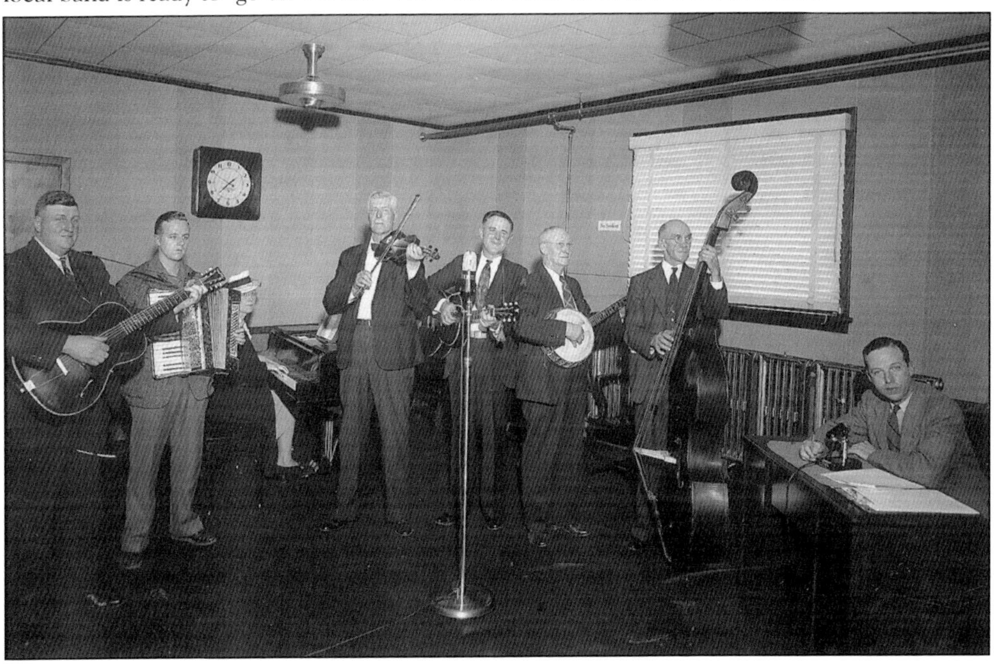

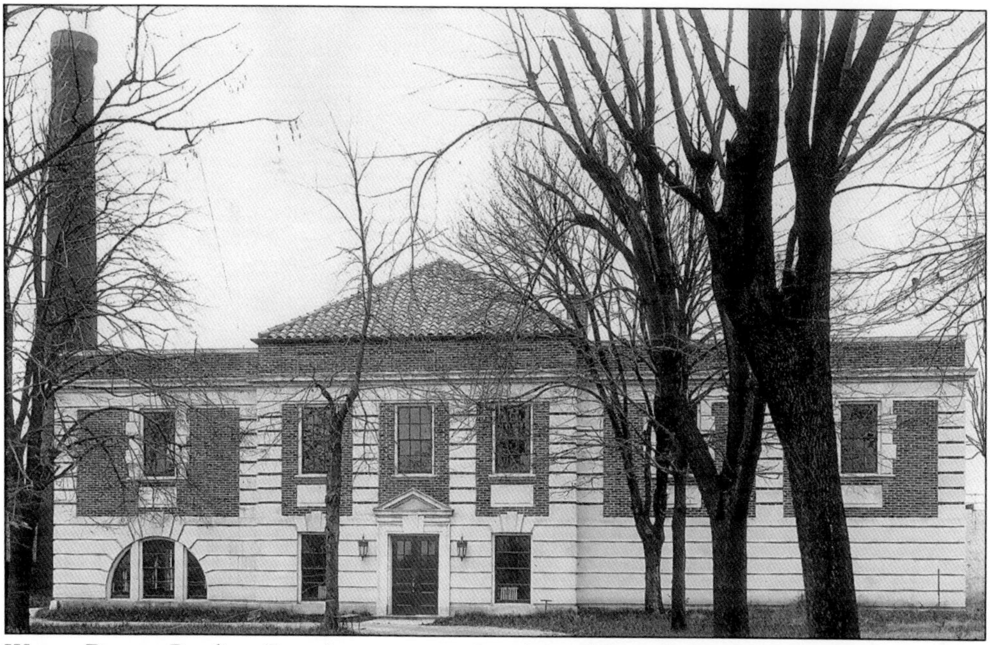

WATER PLANT. Bowling Green's water system has depended on the Barren River since the 1860s when a pumping station was built on its banks. At that time, water was pumped to a holding reservoir at the top of what was then known as College Hill; it was promptly renamed Reservoir Hill. This building and its mechanical systems were designed by the Chester Engineering Company of Pittsburgh.

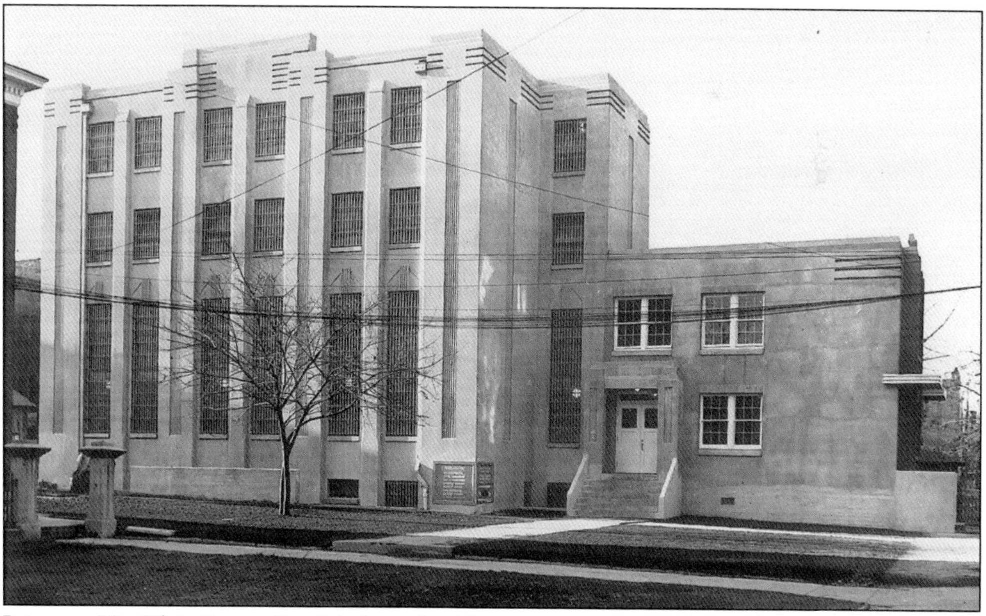

LOCKED UP. This Streamline Moderne building was constructed in 1939 as a Works Progress Administration project. It replaced the old jail on State Street that had been in use since 1860. The new jail was designed by James M. Ingram and has the distinction of being the first jail in the South built with reinforced concrete inner cells. This jail was used until the new jail was completed in the late 1980s.

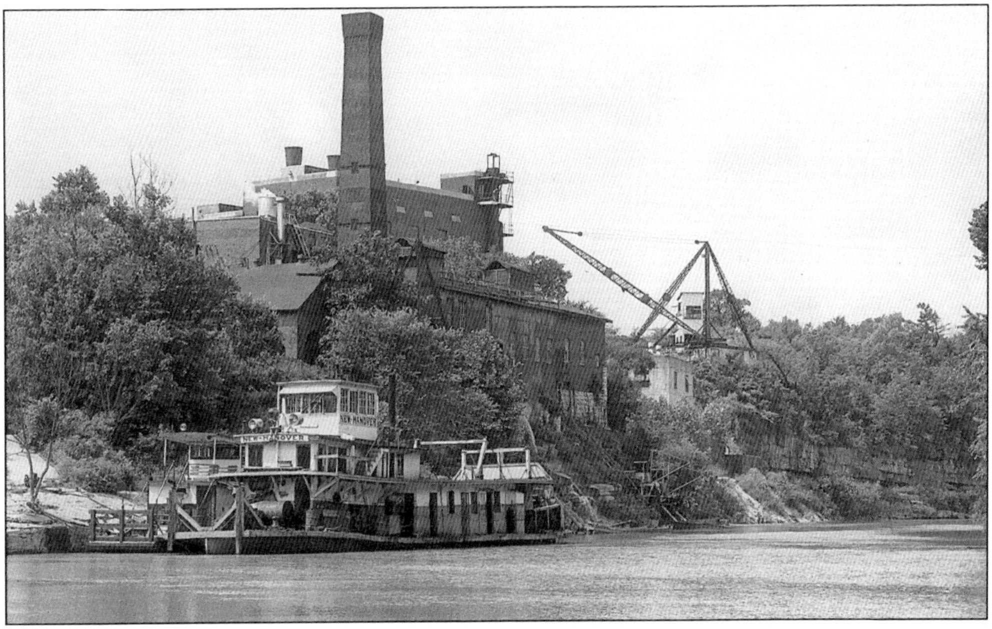

BOATLANDING. Bowling Green's boatlanding, northeast of downtown, was at one time a very busy commercial area. By the 1940s, when this photo was taken, activity began to wane. Still, one can see the steamboat *New Haven* docked and ready to receive freight. The building with the large masonry chimney on the bluff is the old Bowling Green Ice Company. The Delafield electric power plant, opened in 1931, looms in the background.

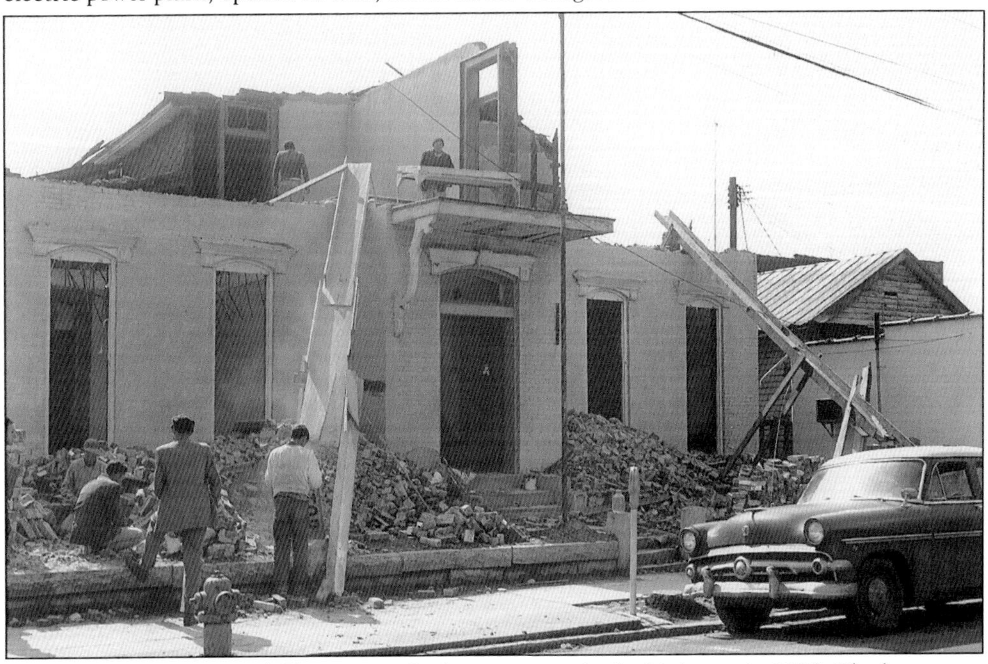

TUMBLING DOWN. Patrick Fleming, an Irish immigrant, built this house in 1883. The house was used as a residence until 1939, when the Bible Presbyterian Church purchased it and added an auditorium at the rear. Later it was used as an annex for the Center Street School. The building was razed in 1962. The small building on the right is the old Burger Basket.

Harmonizing Quartet. All of the Hilltoppers, one of the most popular male ensembles of the early 1950s, were students at Western Kentucky University. The group enjoyed several number one songs and were considered "tops" by swooning young coeds. The men are, from left to right, Billy Vaughan, Jimmy Sacca, Seymour Spegilman, and Don McGuire. Popular Kentucky author, Bobbie Ann Mason, once served as their national fan club president.

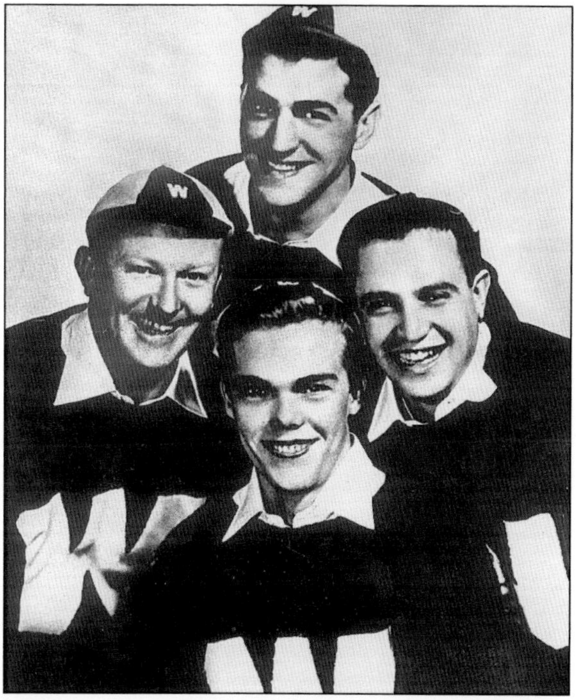

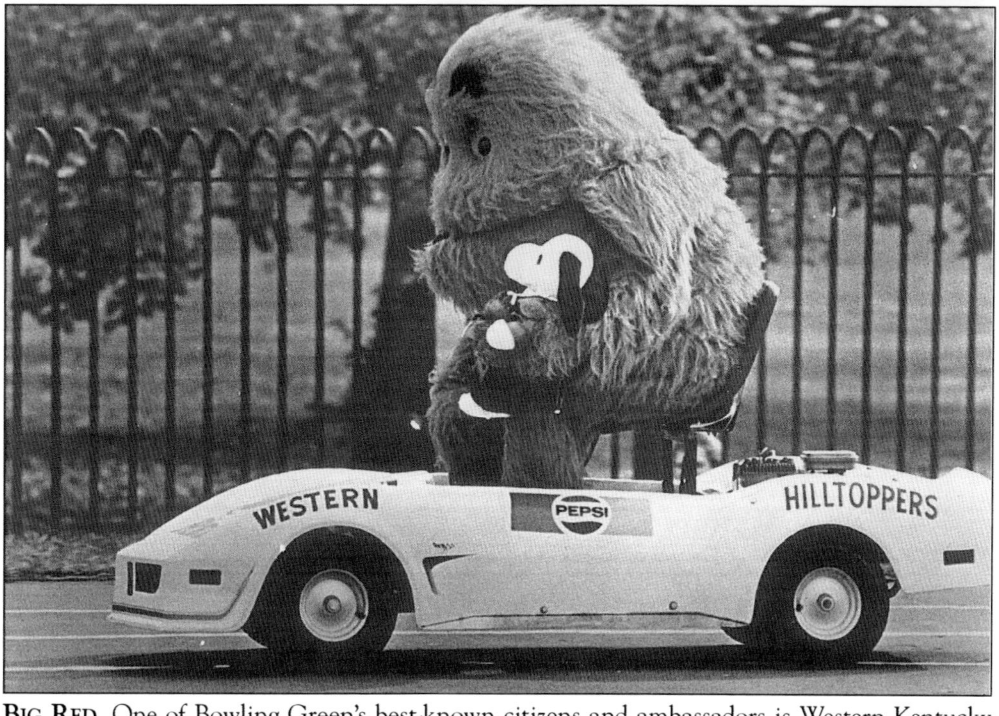

Big Red. One of Bowling Green's best-known citizens and ambassadors is Western Kentucky University's mascot, Big Red. He is loved by children of all ages and his antics are known throughout collegiate sports. Big Red made his debut at a December 1979 basketball game. This 1980 photograph shows the eternally grinning Big Red atop another Bowling Green icon, the Corvette.

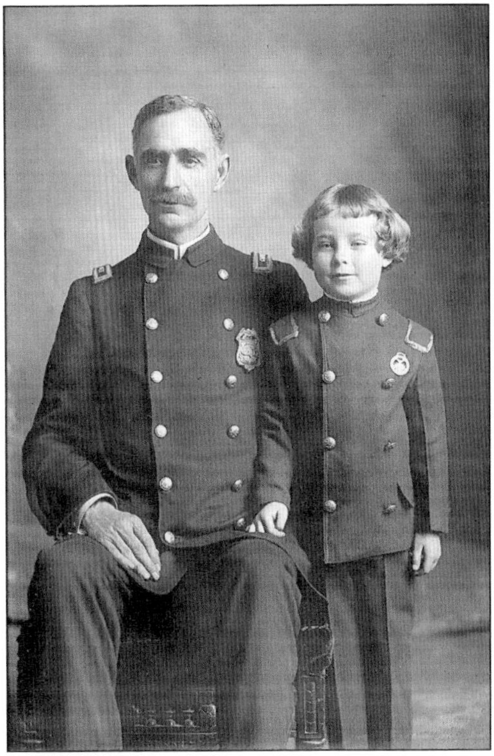

FIRE CHIEF. John G. Moltenberry (1864–1941) became Bowling Green's first paid fireman in 1898 and became fire chief in 1904. He served in that capacity for 33 years. Moltenberry remained a bachelor until he was 53, when he married his younger brother's widow. She had three sons and the couple later had three daughters. This child obviously wants to become a fireman.

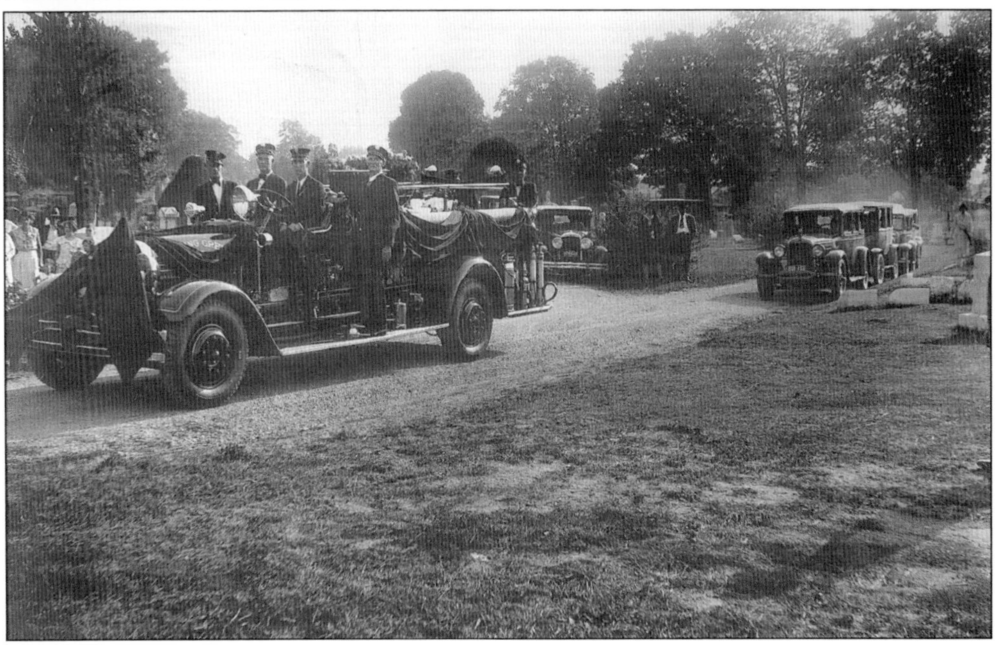

PAYING RESPECTS. This photo documents the graveside service of fire department employee Bluford Yates on October 4, 1931, at Fairview Cemetery. Yates was the driver for the fire department's engine #2, so his body was taken from his home at 303 College to the cemetery atop that vehicle. Over 100 cars were in the funeral procession. The engine is appropriately attired in black crepe.

STYLISH MODISTE. Carrie (Burnam) Taylor (1855–1917), a native of Bowling Green, started a small dressmaking business in her home in the 1870s. With hard work and good advertising, Taylor's operation soon became one of the largest of its kind in the state, employing over 300 women in a factory that she operated near the corner of State and 8th Streets. Taylor left an estate valued at more than $250,000.

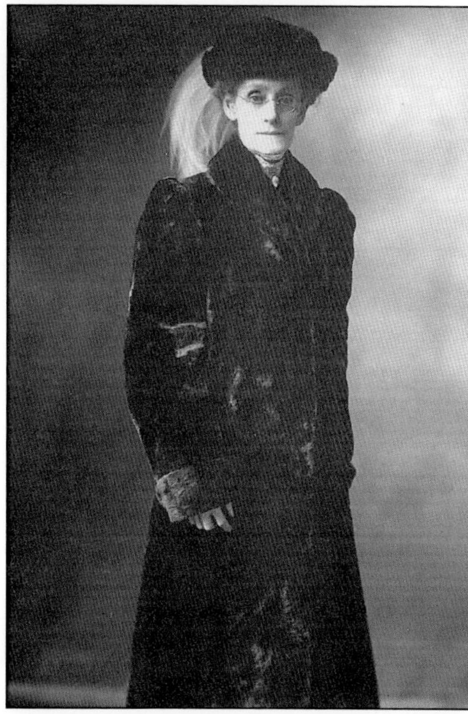

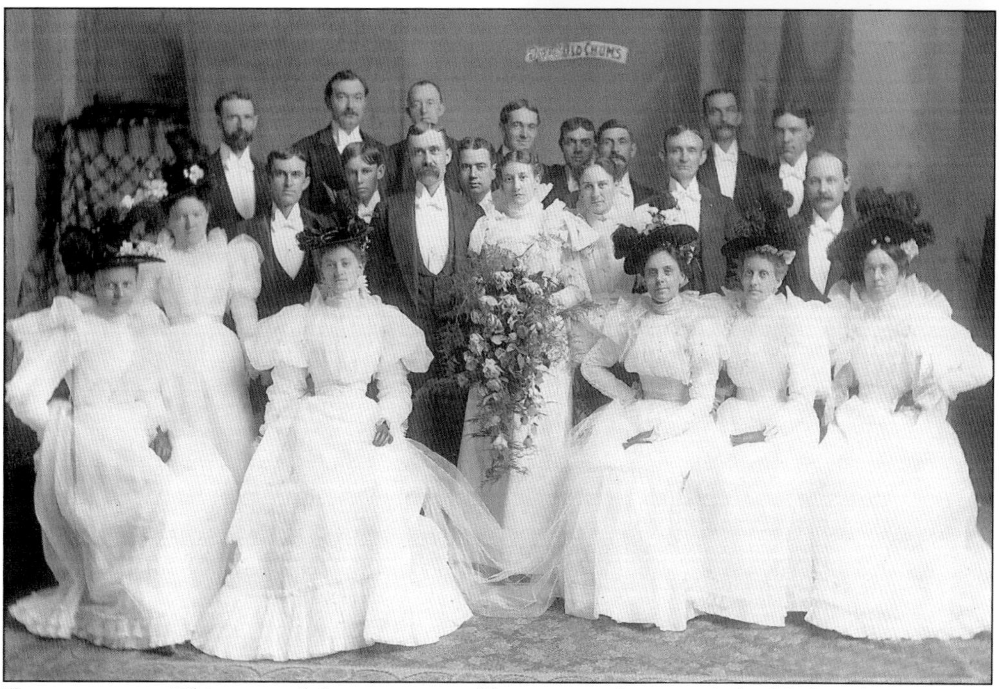

TAYLOR-MADE. This turn-of-the-century wedding party photograph highlights the creativity of Carrie Taylor's dressmaking skills. The ladies are outfitted in the style of the day with leg of mutton sleeves, cinched waists, and full skirts. The bride and groom are Bettie Robertson and Henry T. Hagerman. They were married at the old First Baptist Church building on Main Street.

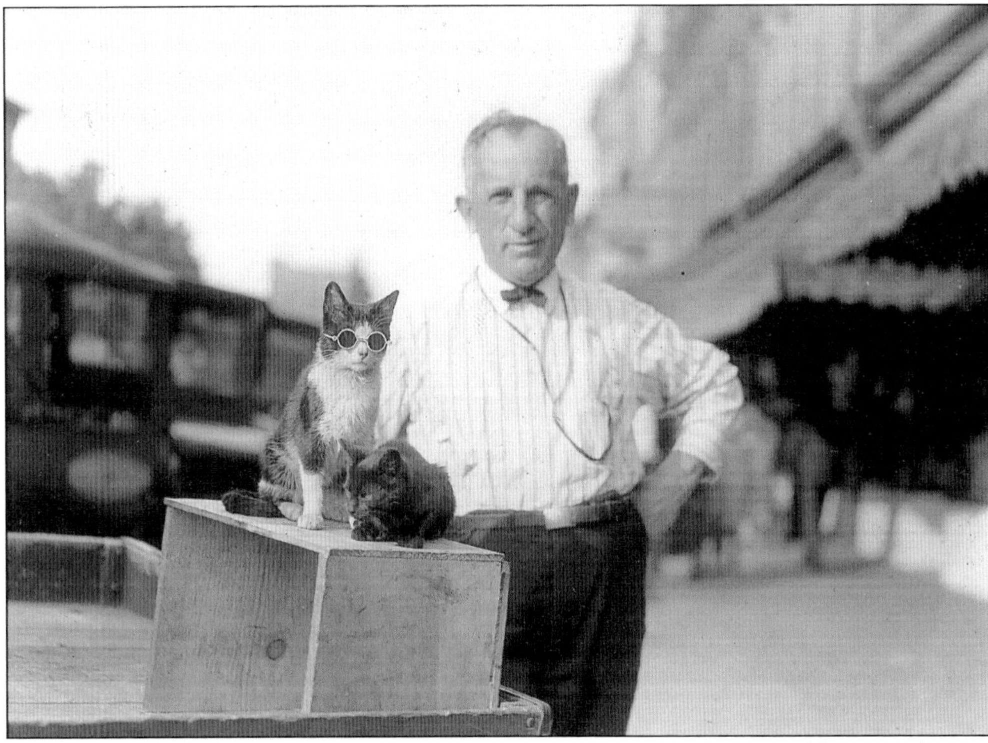

KITTY, KITTY. Lon Dodd managed a grocery downtown. This photo of Dodd and his bespectacled feline friend is one of the most popular photos in the Kentucky Library's collection.

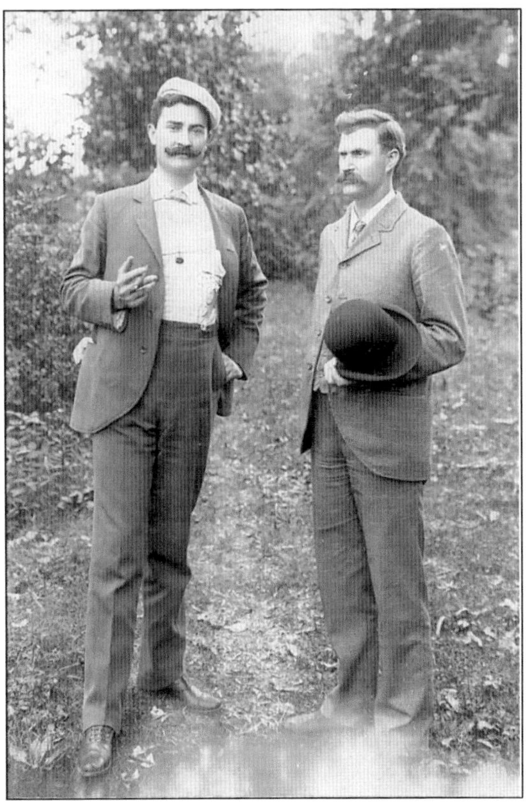

FAMOUS EVANGELIST. The dandy on the left is Mordecai F. Ham (1877–1961), an itinerant, fundamentalist evangelist who preached across the nation in large tents, courthouses, churches, brush arbors, and makeshift tabernacles. He was born near Greenwood in Warren County and maintained a home in Bowling Green for many years. Ham is noted for being the preacher who delivered the message when Billy Graham was converted.

MINSTREL SINGER. Bowling Green hosted many professional minstrel shows over the years and the Elks Club Minstrel was an annual entertainment highlight. The city produced a number of minstrel performers including Allen Settle, Joe Blackwell, Fred Hespin, Baker Rock, and Billy Blackwell (pictured). Blackwell had a short career, joining the J.A. Coburn Minstrels in 1909 and dying of typhoid fever in April 1911.

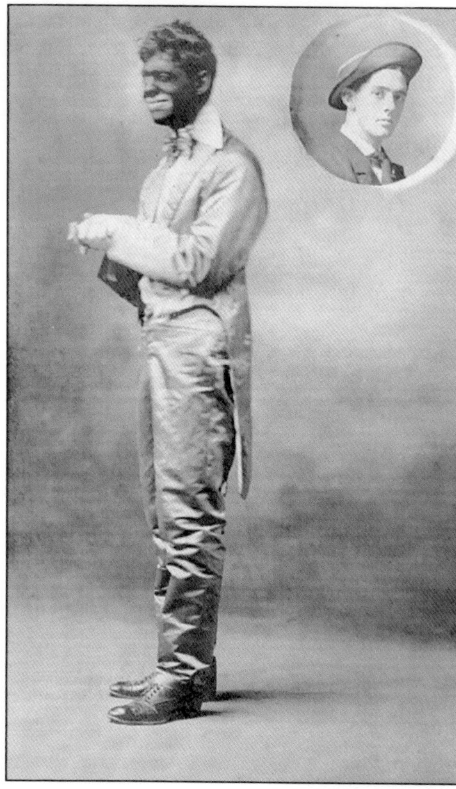

YOUNG FARMER WITH PROMISE. The boy in the buggy below is Lester Bryant, the 1912 state champion corn grower. On one acre near his Rockfield home, Bryant raised 148 bushels of corn. He traveled to Washington, D.C., to participate in a national parade of winners. Unfortunately, he blew out the gas jet in his room's light fixture and suffocated. The home in the background is Cabell Hall on Western Kentucky University's campus.

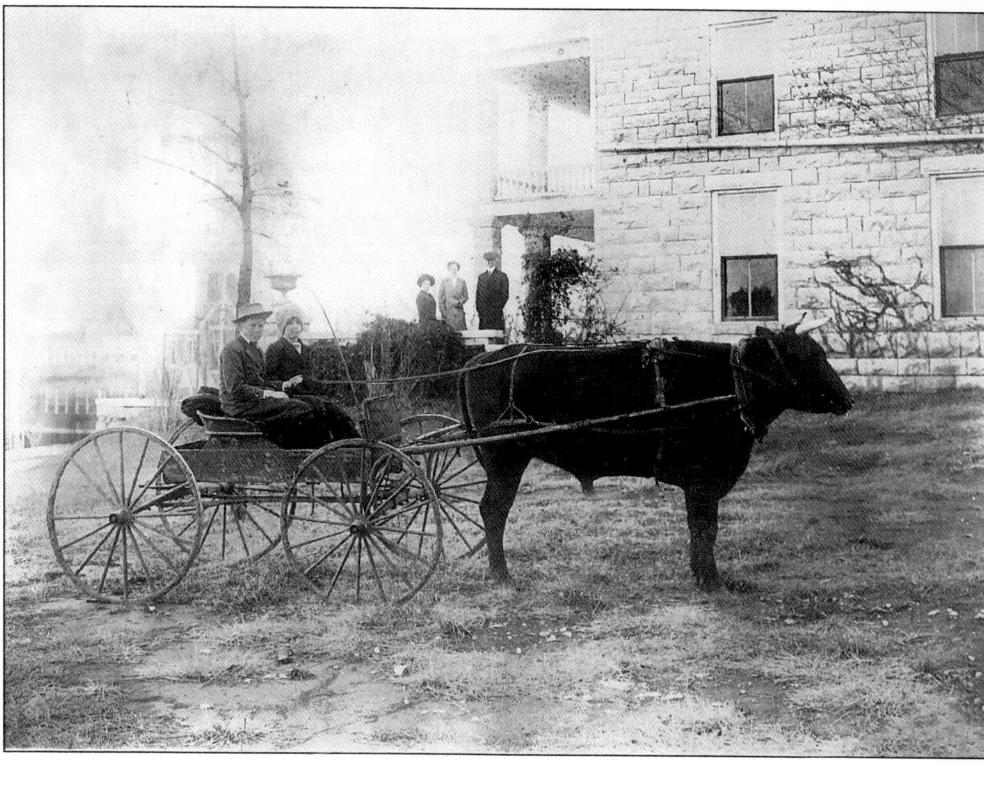

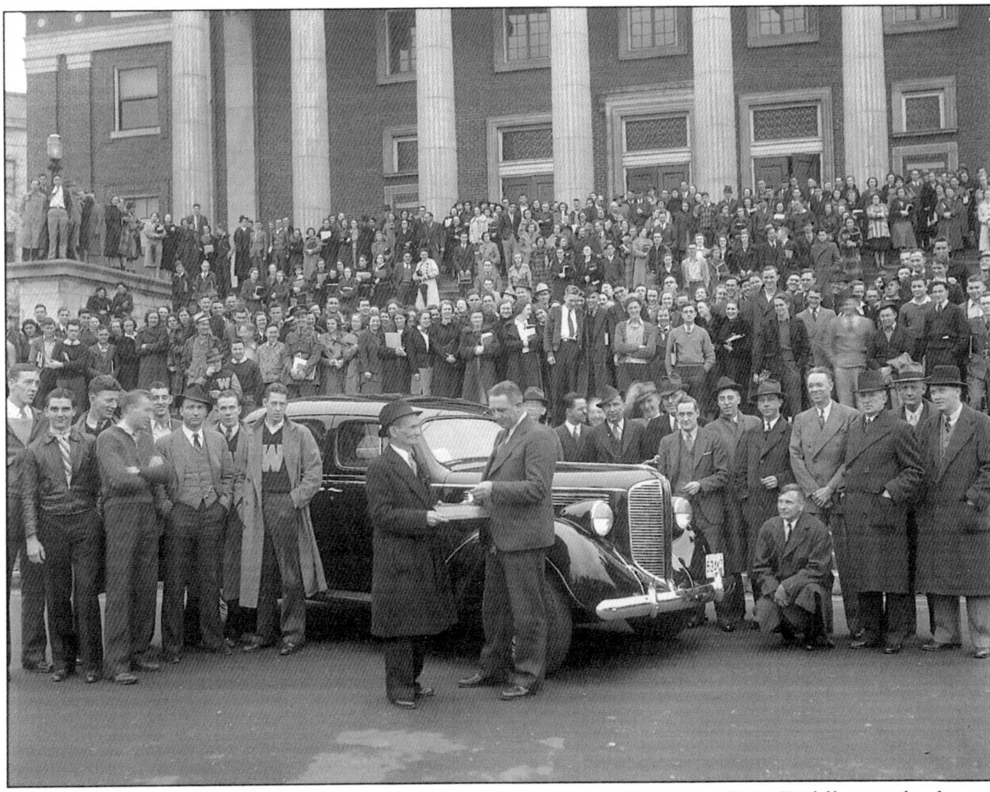

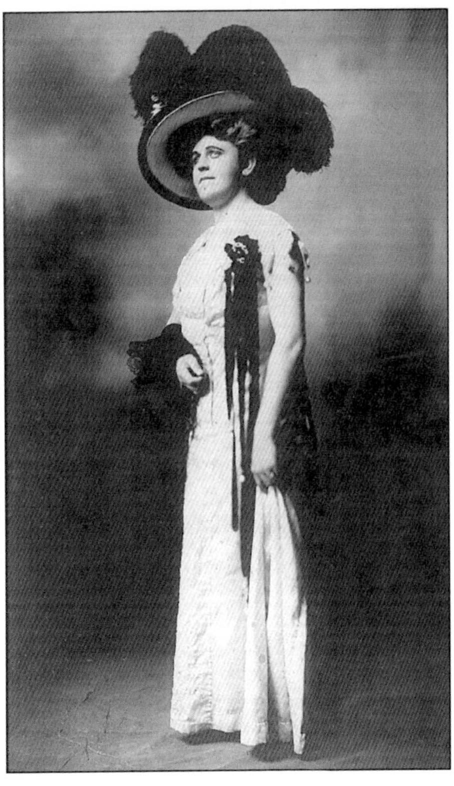

BASKETBALL LEGEND. E.A. Diddle coached several sports for Western Kentucky University during his 42-year tenure, but he is best known as one of the most victorious coaches in collegiate basketball. Diddle posted 755 victories in his career and won many fans with his personable style, humor, and malaprops. The campus basketball arena, built in 1963, is named in his honor. Here he is receiving keys to a new car at Van Meter Hall.

TAKING A DRAG. Will B. Hill (1882–1968) was a popular Bowling Green dandy in the early years of the 20th century. Here, he is dressed for a part in a drama production, when he was director of chapel for the Business University. Hill worked for several downtown mercantile stores before beginning his career as the "publicity man" for Western Kentucky University in 1928. He retired from that position in 1957.

Three

Bowling Green at Play

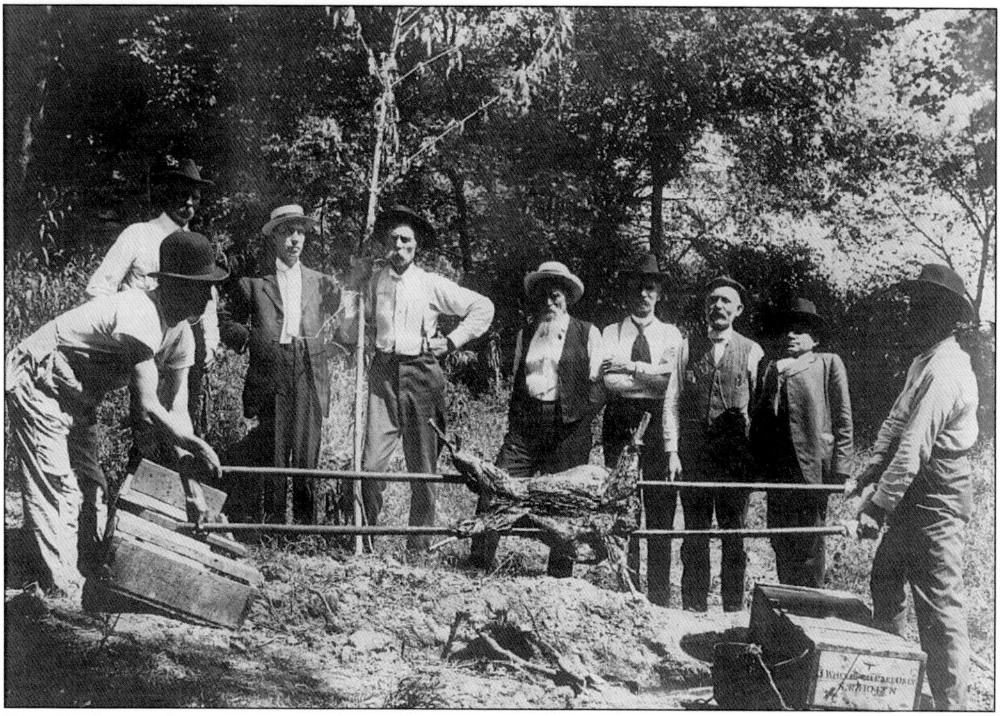

Bar-B-Que. The quintessential outdoor meal in Kentucky is bar-b-que, with the meat slow cooked over an open fire pit. In southcentral Kentucky the meat is usually pork. This photograph from around 1905 features a typical pit bar-b-que with the pig on spits, which were turned periodically to allow for more even cooking. Nearly 80,000 people attended Warren County's largest bar-b-que in 1935 when Tom Rhea announced his candidacy for governor.

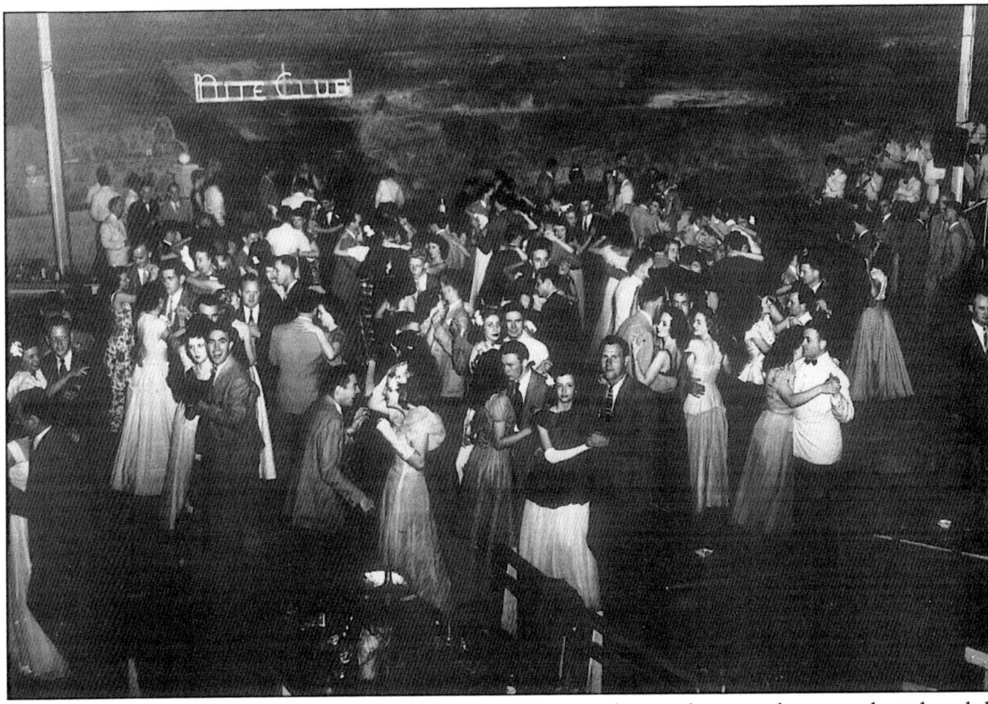

UNDERGROUND BOOGIE. Lost River Cave at one time boasted an underground night club where people came to dance the night away in natural air conditioning. The subterranean "Nite Club" (above), complete with colored lights, a dance pavilion, and dining facilities, played host to such luminaries as Dinah Shore and Francis Craig and his NBC Orchestra. Clubbers reached the facility by a precipitous set of frame stairways known as the "winding stairway" (below.) The Friends of Lost River Cave re-opened the cave to tours in the mid-1990s and a replica of the dance pavilion has recently been built.

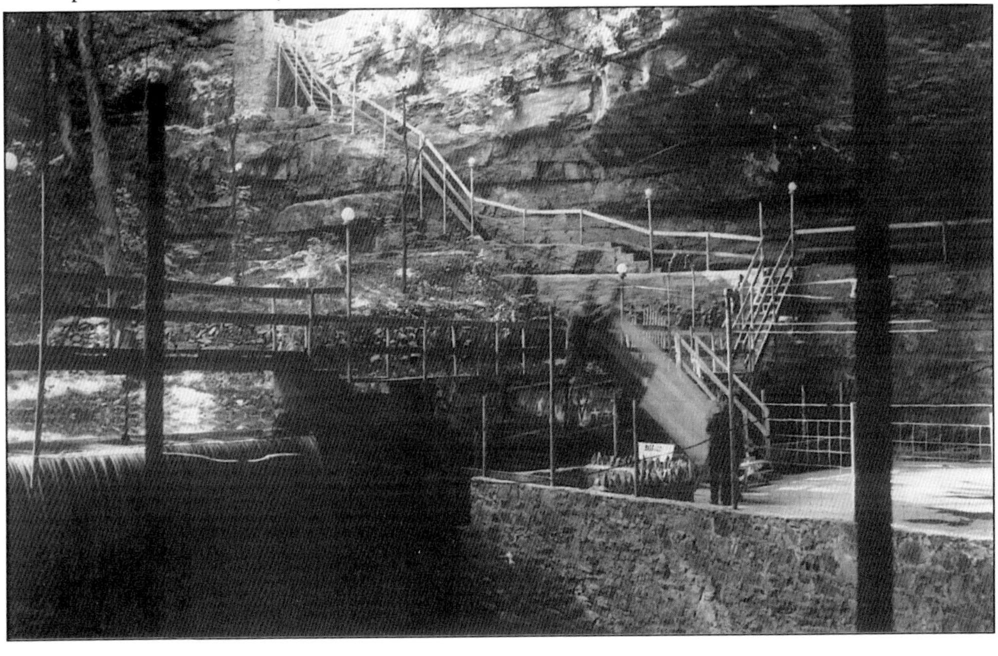

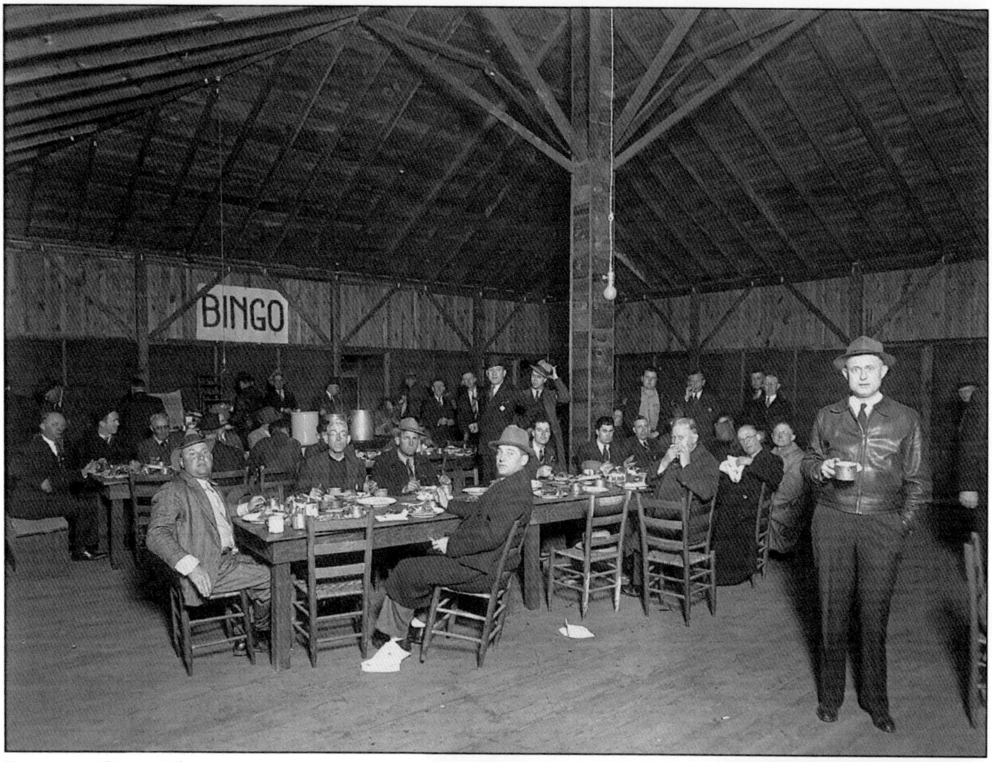

DINNER OUT. These men are enjoying the Black Crow dinner held in the Beech Bend Park pavilion on March 12, 1939. The Pennyrile Conservation Association held the event to culminate the group's annual crow shooting contest. The menu included "black partridge" stuffed with dressing, gravy, baked potato, slaw, and coffee.

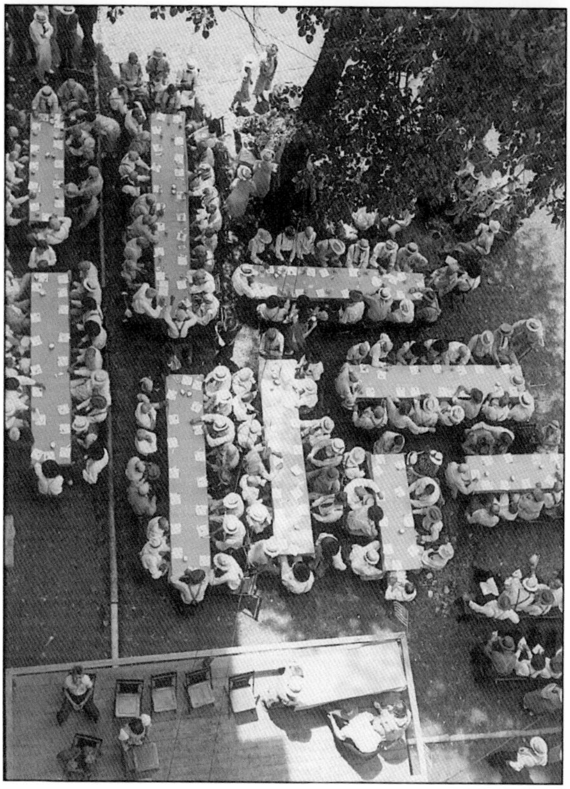

GRAZING. This unique photograph was taken from the second floor of the courthouse to document one of the Old Men's Reunions held on the lawn. About 140 men over the age of 75 attended the first reunion in 1935. William Reynolds Pearson, who was 92 years old, received a commemorative cane for being the oldest man present. A local druggist presented each senior citizen with a corn cobb pipe and a sack of tobacco.

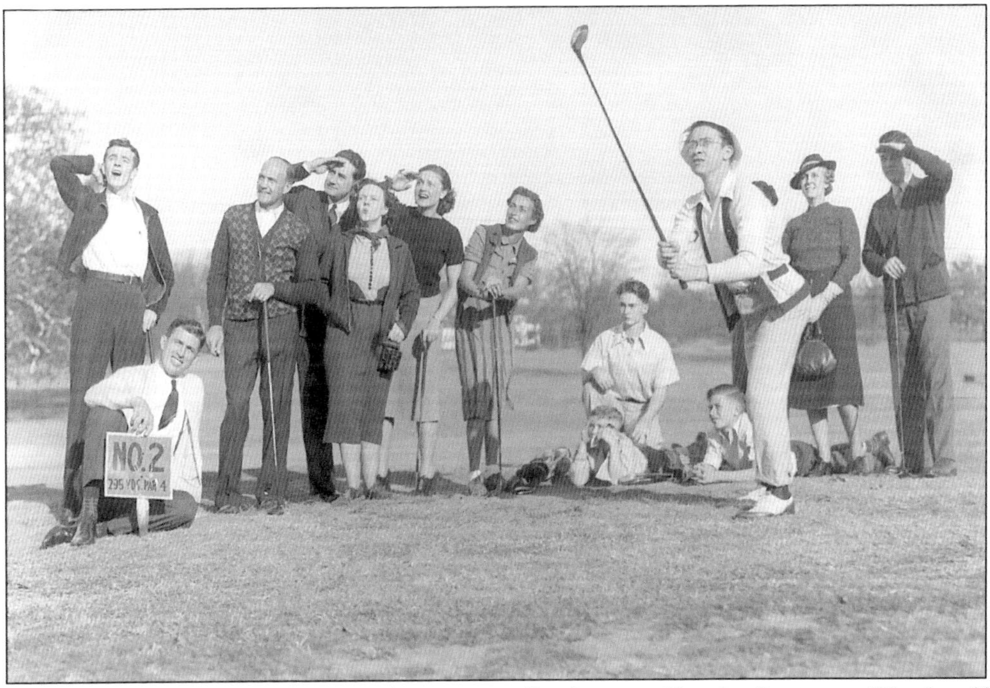

FORE! Don't be deceived. These people are not really playing golf at the Covington Woods golf course. Instead, they are posing for a publicity photograph, which advertised an unnamed play produced by the Bowling Green Players, an amateur drama group.

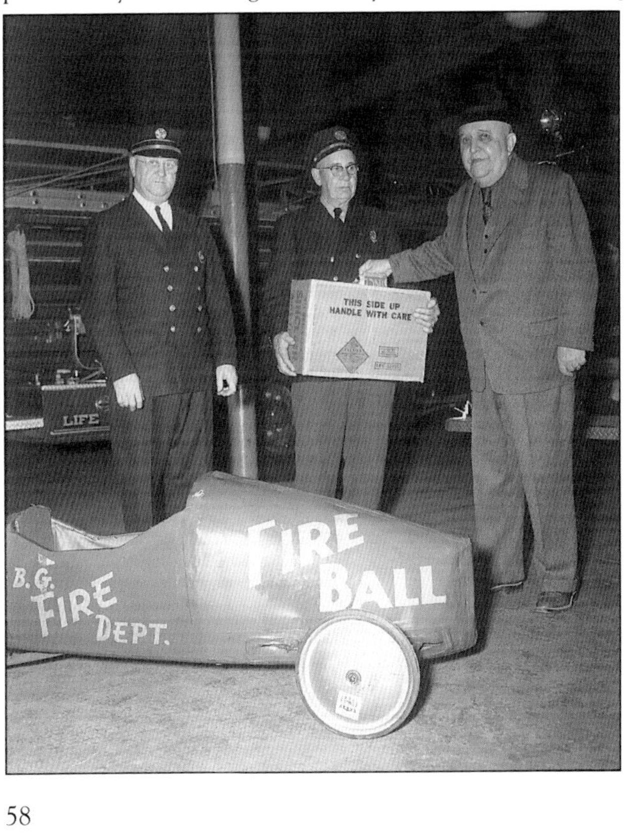

SOAP BOX DERBY. The first All-American Soap Box Derby was held in Bowling Green in 1937 and was discontinued after the 1972 race. Entrants raced down College Street, one of Bowling Green's steepest inclines. The local Kiwanis Club brought the competition back in 1998. This December 1957 photograph shows mayor C.W. Lampkin drawing the winning ticket for the "Fire Ball," the entry for the Bowling Green Fire Department.

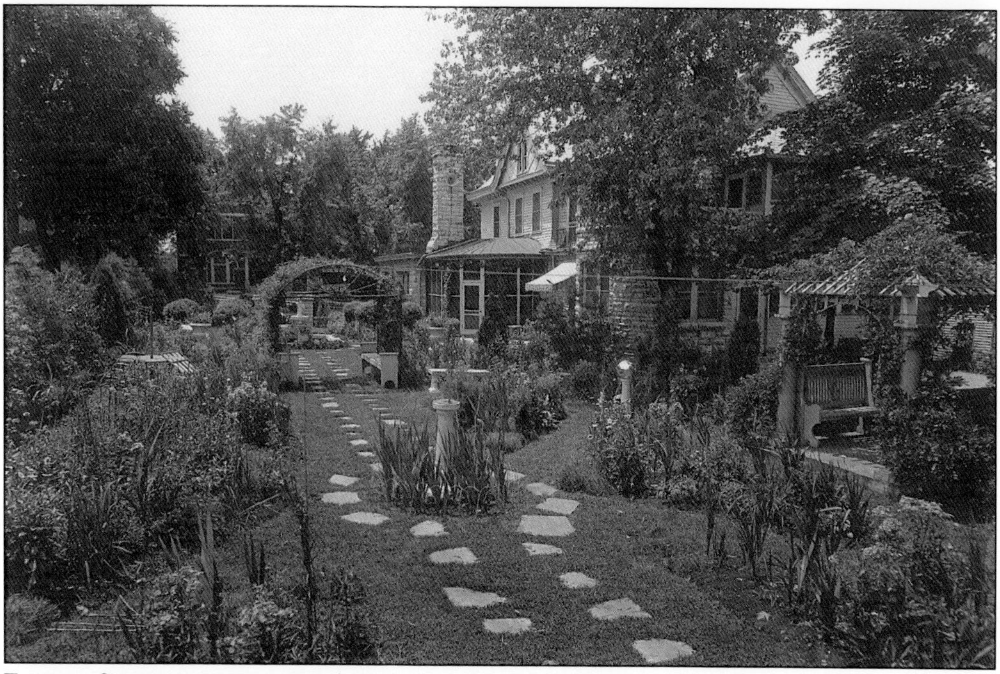

EDENIC SURROUNDINGS. Gardening is one of America's most popular hobbies today and has been a perennial favorite for years. Here you see the garden of Mrs. Mora Sharpe (1860–1942) who lived at 610 East Main Avenue. She creatively used her space, filling it with garden ornaments, arbors, and a rock goldfish pond.

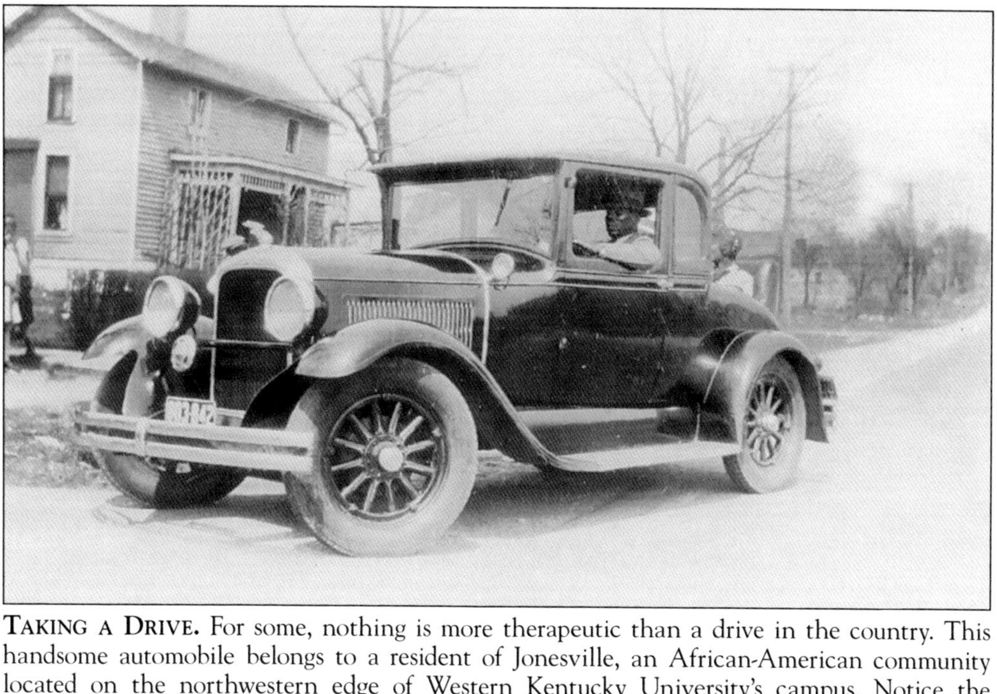

TAKING A DRIVE. For some, nothing is more therapeutic than a drive in the country. This handsome automobile belongs to a resident of Jonesville, an African-American community located on the northwestern edge of Western Kentucky University's campus. Notice the driver has a female passenger in his rumble seat. Jonesville was physically distinguished through urban renewal.

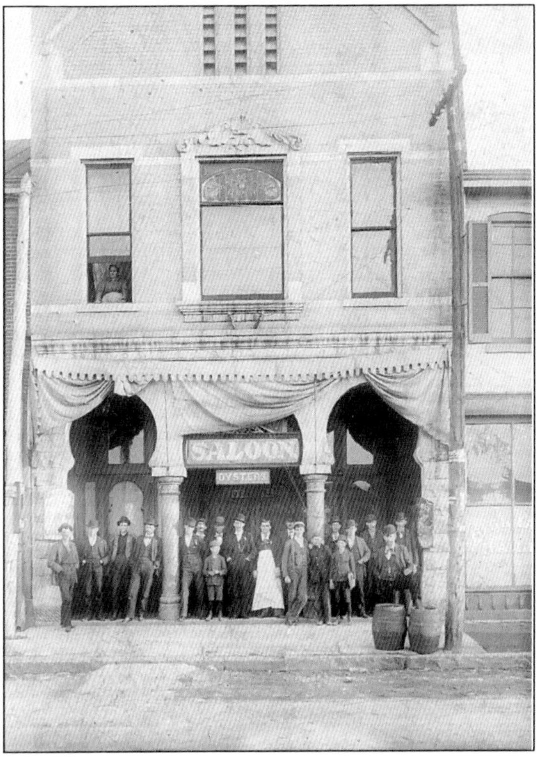

WHERE EVERYBODY KNOWS YOUR NAME. The Kirby Saloon, on lower East Main, was one of Bowling Green's most popular drinking houses. The attractive facade was designed by architect Creedmore Fleenor. It was razed in 1987, but portions of the attractive Moorish style limestone arches were saved. Next door a convenient billiard hall welcomed those who desired additional leisure activity.

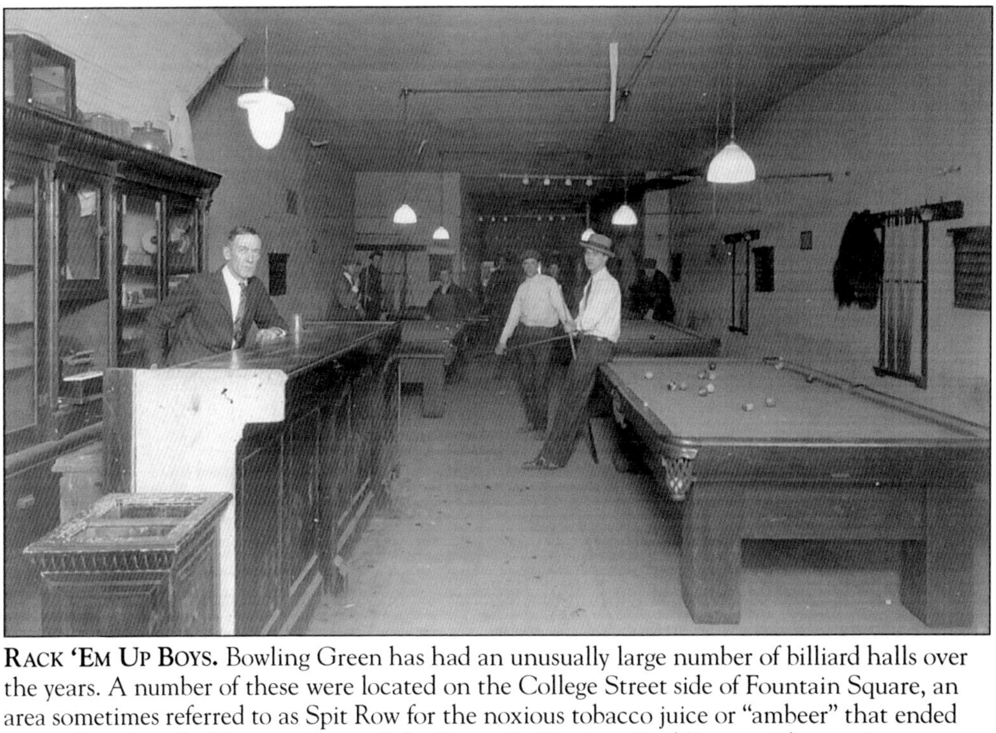

RACK 'EM UP BOYS. Bowling Green has had an unusually large number of billiard halls over the years. A number of these were located on the College Street side of Fountain Square, an area sometimes referred to as Spit Row for the noxious tobacco juice or "ambeer" that ended up on the sidewalk. This is a photo of the Stone & Garrison Pool Room with proprietor Paul Stone behind the counter.

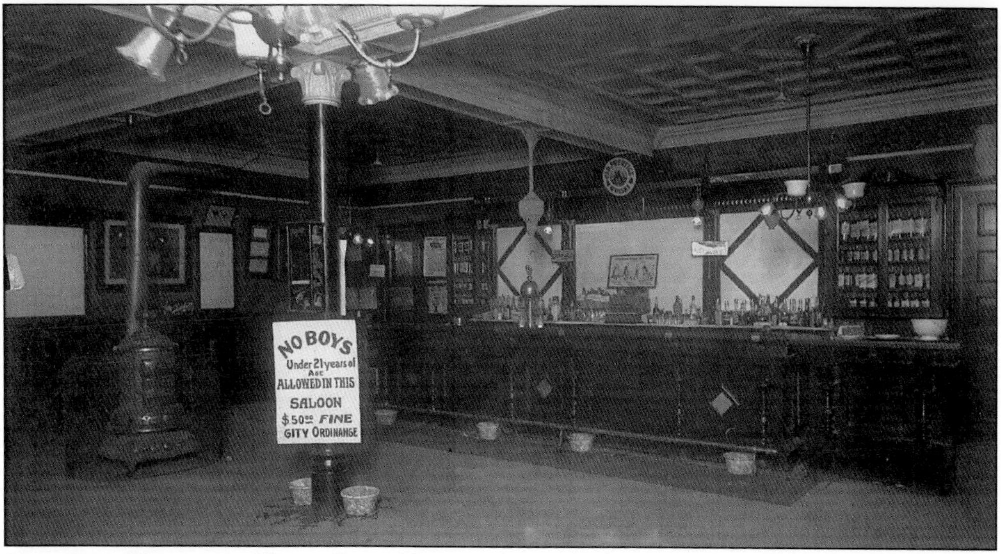

THE OLD WATERING HOLE. Patsy Fitzpatrick, an Irish immigrant who came to Bowling Green as a stone worker, eventually opened a popular saloon at 330 East Main Street. During Prohibition the bar was hastily converted into an ice cream parlor. This room boasted a beautiful tile floor, so Patsy provided plenty of enamel spittoons to make sure people did not soil it.

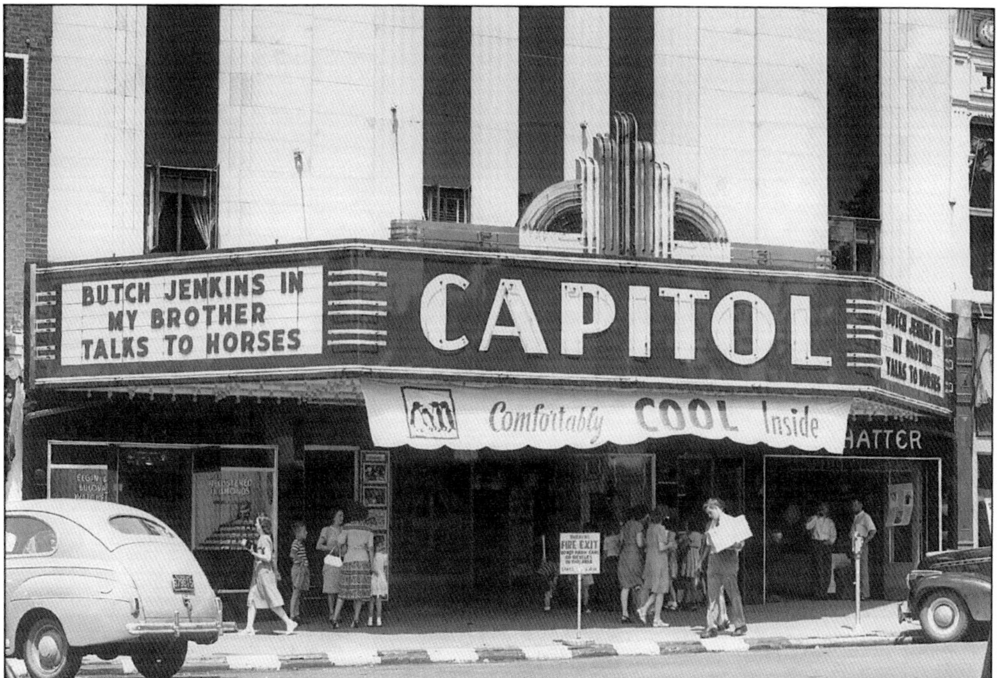

TINSEL TOWN. The first theater at this location was called the Columbia. It went through extensive renovation in 1920 and was renamed the Capitol. That building was razed and a modern structure was erected that opened in March 1939. The theater closed in 1977 and steadily deteriorated. Volunteers helped raise the $1.2 million to restore the building in 1981. Today, the Capitol Arts Center is a community-owned center for the performing arts.

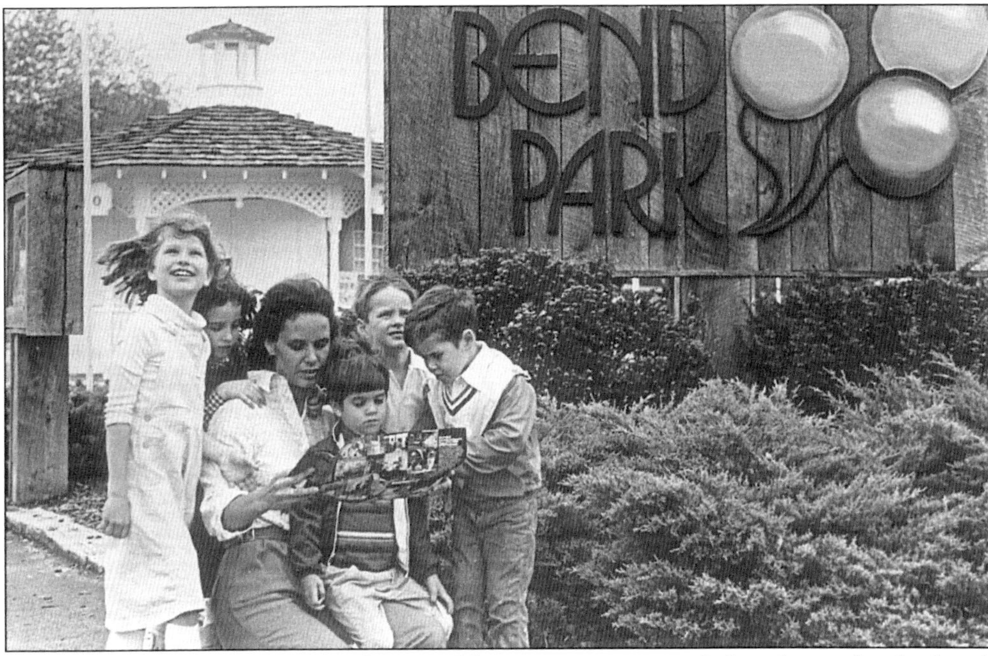

BEECH BEND PARK. Curren Brashear and his two sisters named their home for the beech trees in a bend of the Barren River. They opened a large pavilion facility in 1907 for dancing and skating. From this grew a recreational complex including a fairway of theme park rides, a race track, a large swimming pool and water rides, huge campground, horseback riding, and entertainment venues. One of the park's popular attractions was a large menagerie of animals, including Blondie the elephant (below). Advertisements noted that "animals in the zoo are carefully chosen for their beauty and individuality." Admission to the park was one dime, but rides were an additional charge. In its heyday the park enjoyed a national reputation and is experiencing a revival.

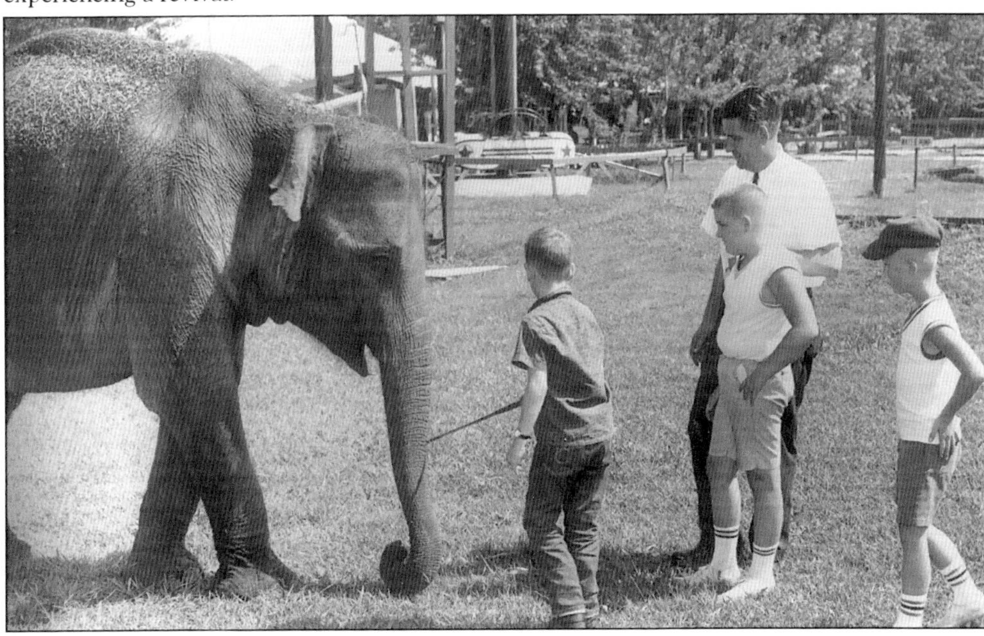

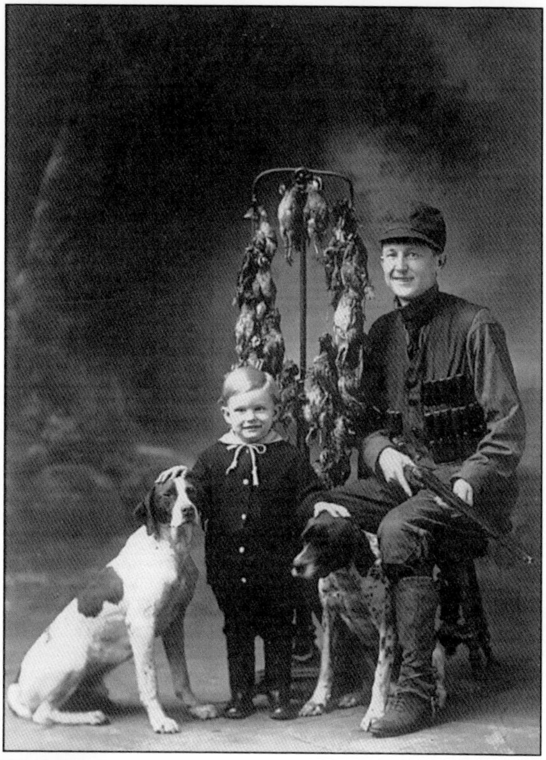

LIKE FATHER, LIKE SON. Phillip Jordan Noel Sr. (1874–1950) and his son Junior believed in recreation. Senior was an eccentric man, a Spanish-American War veteran who began his career as a horse trainer and ended his life as an insurance executive. He wrote poetry, published books, collected guns, invented two types of gun holsters, and was an avid hunter as displayed here.

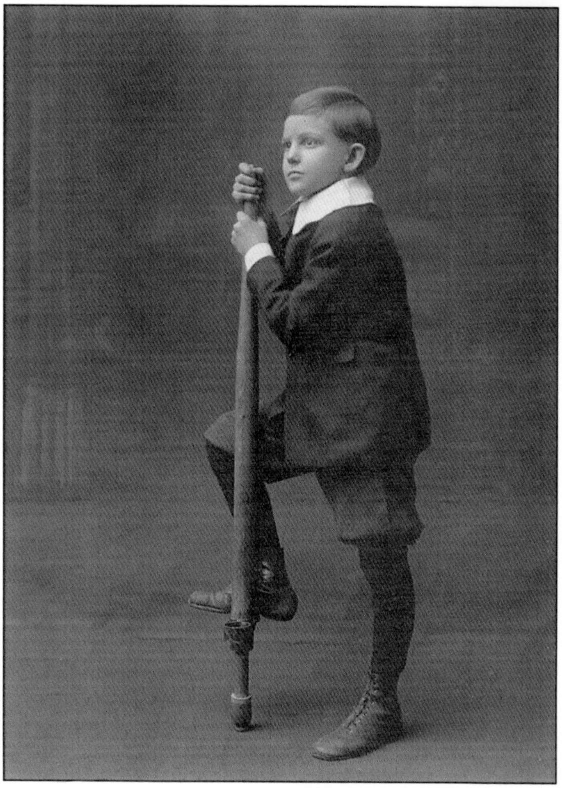

JUNIOR. Senior passed his interest in outdoor sports to his son, who is captured here with his pogo stick. For many years the Noels lived on Park Street and were sometimes seen walking their pet terrapins. Junior later became a physician and worked at Walter Reed Army Hospital in Washington, D.C.

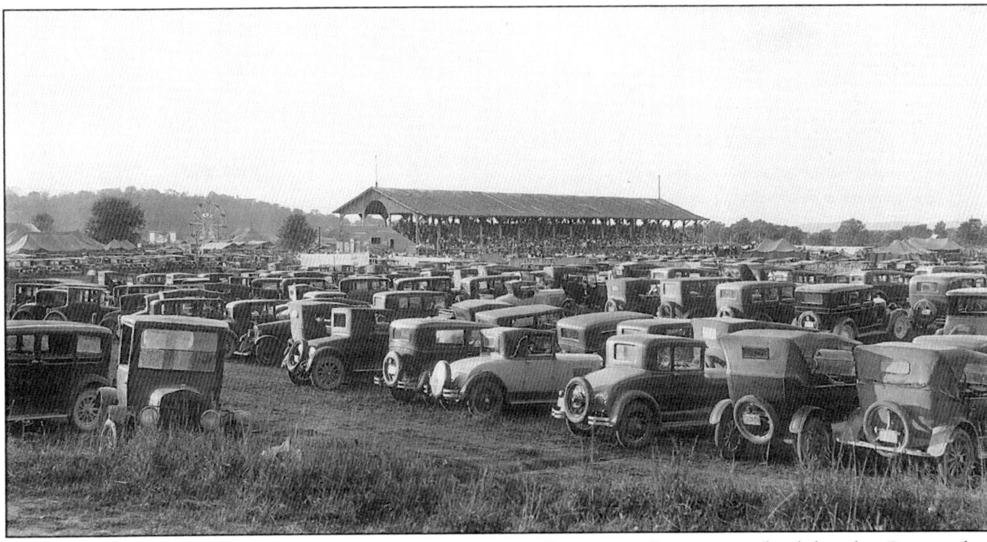

Fair Day. The grandstands at the Warren County Fairgrounds were packed for the September 1929 fair, which had been defunct for several years. The fall event was revived with a generous $1,000 donation from Mr. H.D. Binks, a Chicago businessman who moved to Warren County and purchased a large horse farm in 1929. He went bankrupt shortly after the fair took place.

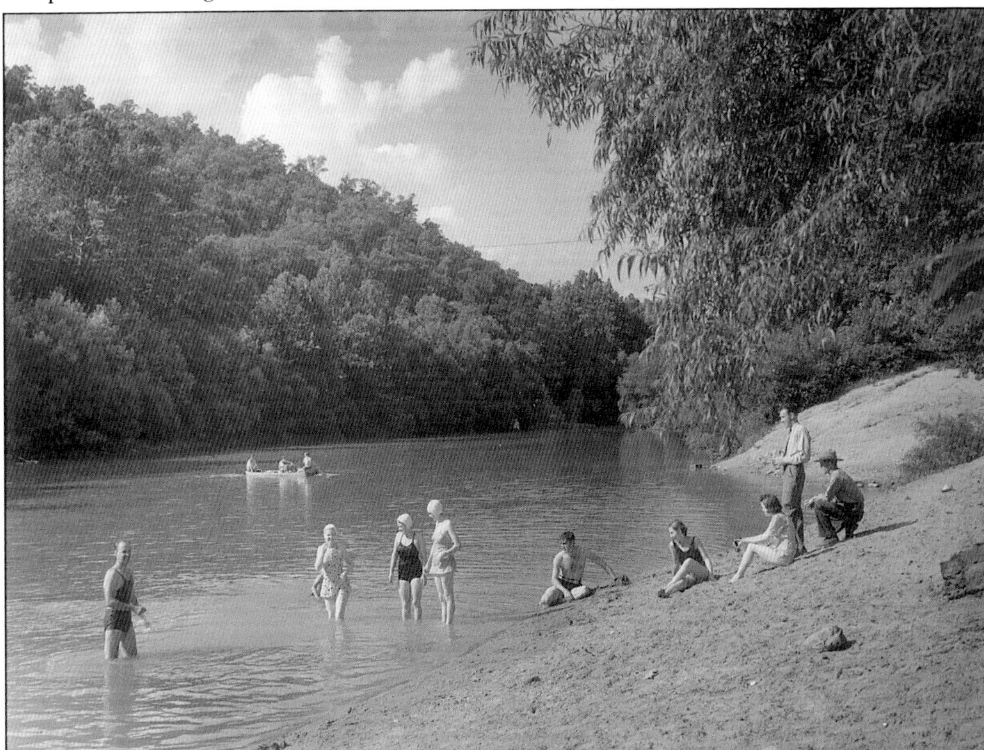

The Old Swimming Hole. Kentucky gets hot and humid in the summer and one of the few ways to cool off is to head to the pool. Fewer people swim in the rivers now, but in days past there was no better way to spend a summer afternoon than frolicking in the Green, Barren, or Gasper Rivers or in Drakes Creek. These waterways remain popular for fishing and boating.

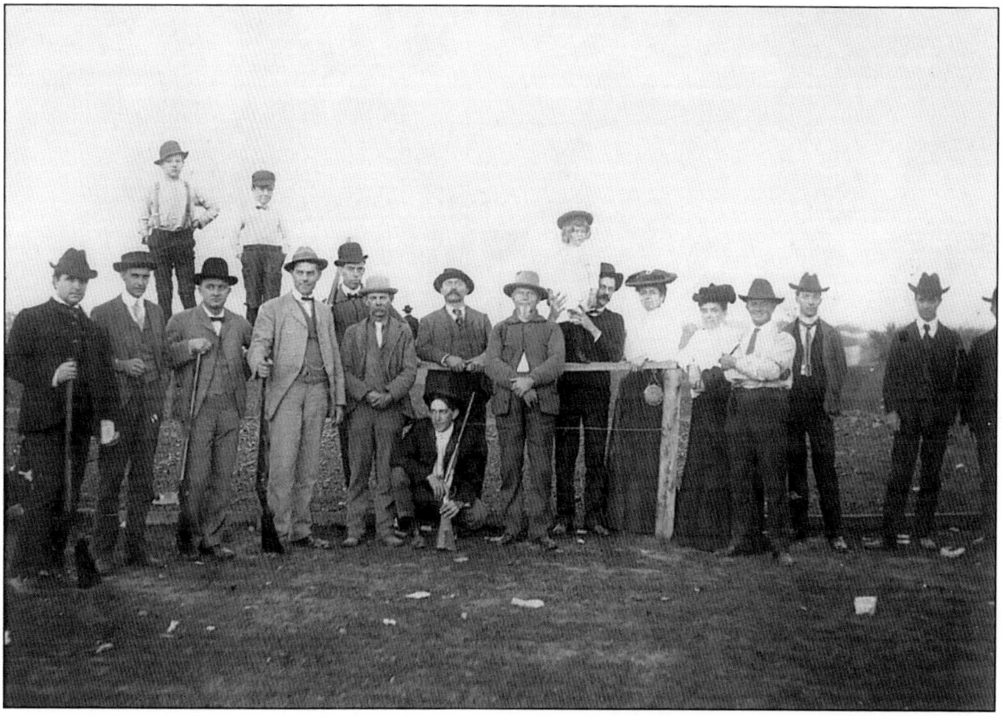

SHOOT! The Bowling Green Gun Club was formed in 1900. The group eventually established a shooting range and club house at Hobson Grove. George Hobson, who managed the club, stands at the center, behind the fence, in a dark hat and sporting a dark mustache.

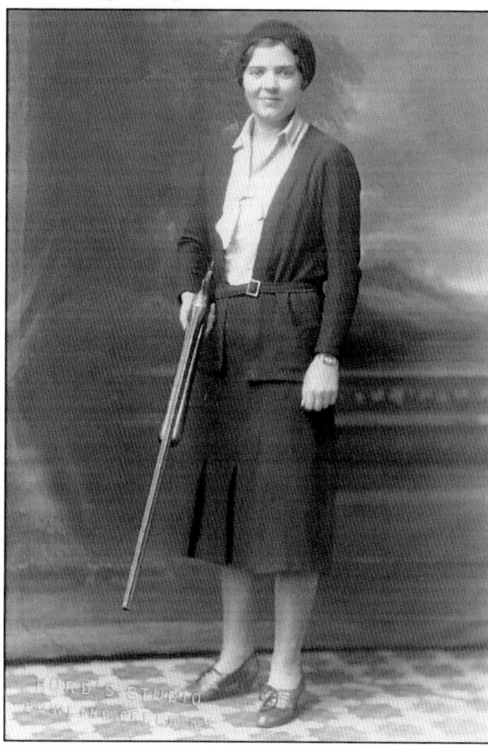

SHOOTING STAR. George Anna Hobson's father, George, taught her how to shoot at an early age. She practiced at the local gun club's shooting range, which was located near her home (today's Riverview at Hobson Grove). Soon the petite Bowling Green youngster became a crack shot and began entering competitive trapshooting contests. In 1924, at the age of 16, Miss Hobson captured the Women's Amateur Clay Target national championship at Vandalia, Ohio.

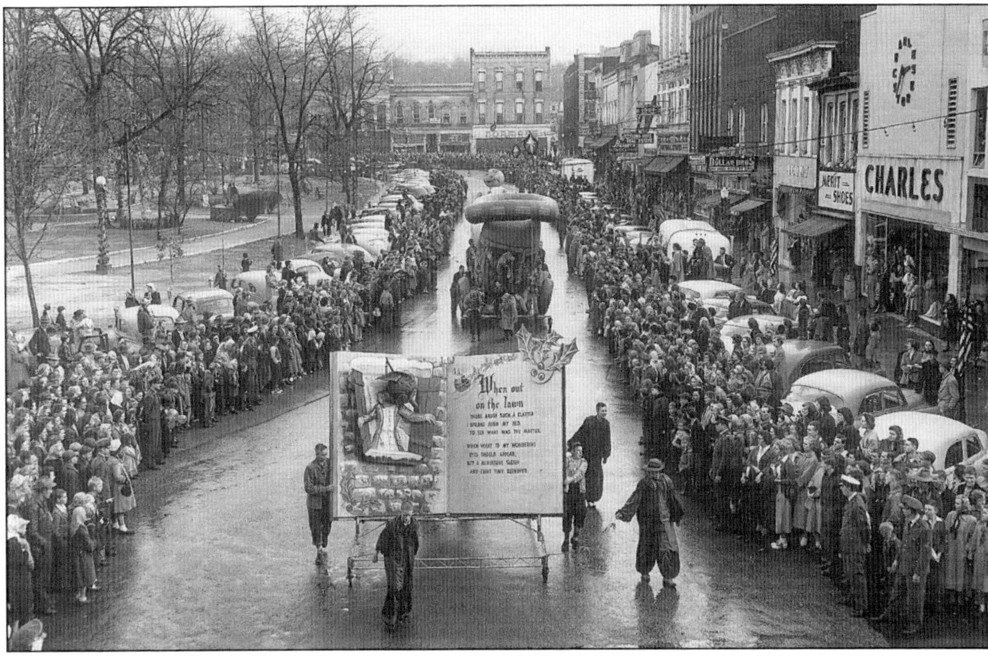

YULETIDE PARADE. The Christmas Parade has been a Bowling Green tradition for well over 50 years. The event was first coordinated by the local chamber of commerce, but that responsibility eventually fell to the local Jaycees chapter. The parade is held the first Saturday in December each year and draws thousands to the downtown area. Officials estimated that the crowd for the 1951 parade, pictured here, was between 45,000 and 60,000 people.

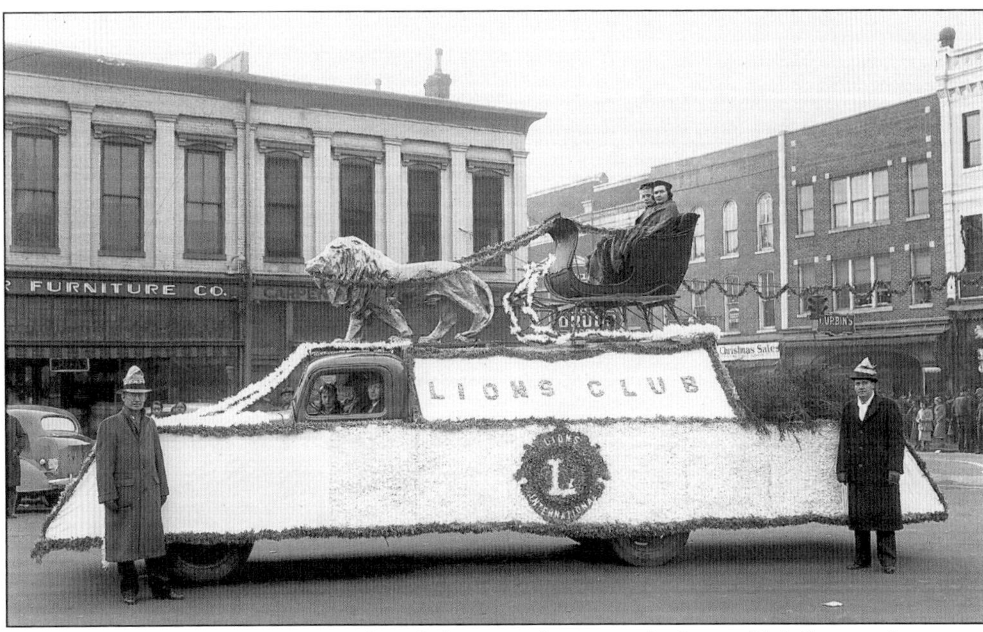

DASHING THROUGH THE SNOW. These ladies are riding atop the Lions Club float in the annual Christmas parade. The float is parked in front of CDS #10 at the corner of Park Row and College Streets. This building, which included the Greer Furniture Company, burned in June 1992.

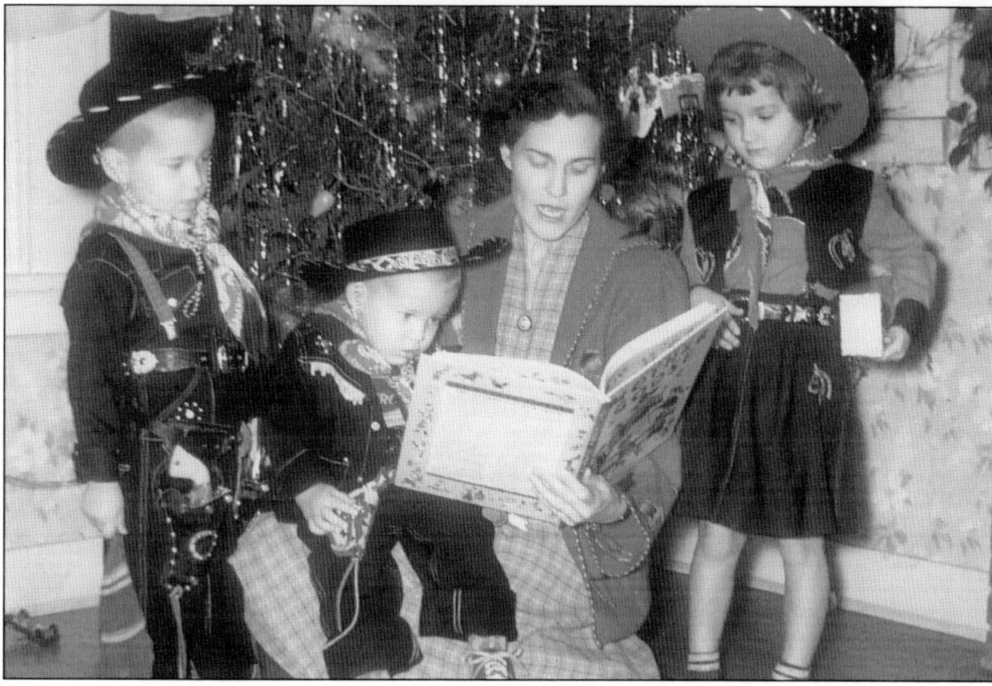

COUNTRY CHRISTMAS. Mildred Collier reads Mother Goose stories to three of her children, James, Kenneth, and Janice, in 1951. The children are decked out in their cowboy and cowgirl outfits that Santa delivered. James, at the far left, has pulled his stocking over to enjoy during story time.

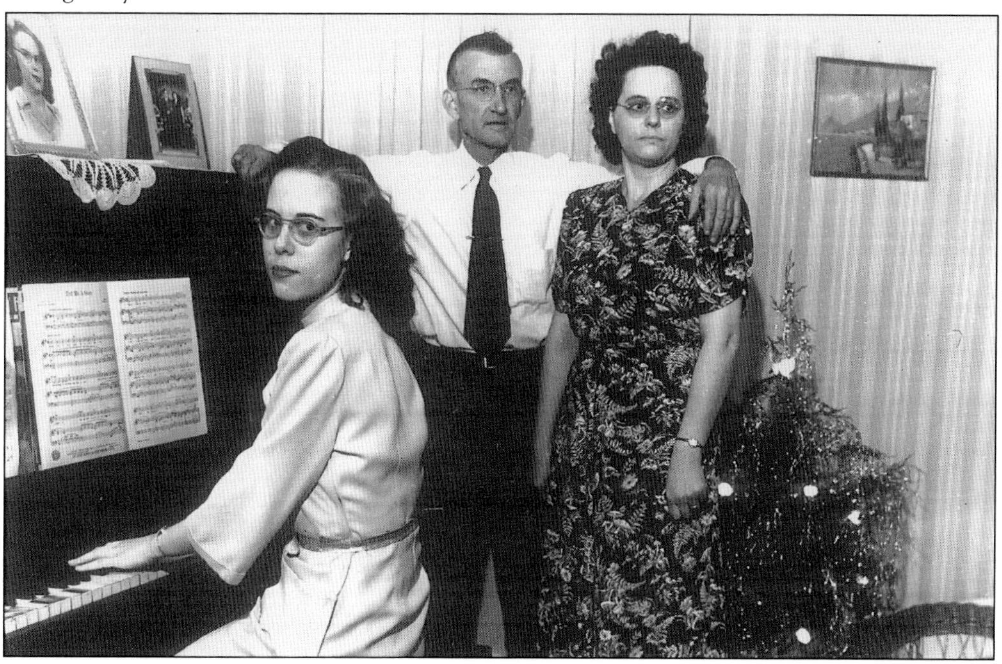

MERRY CHRISTMAS! This family in the late 1940s is taking a few moments from the hectic yuletide season to gather around the upright piano and sing some Christmas carols. Notice the diminutive tree with lights.

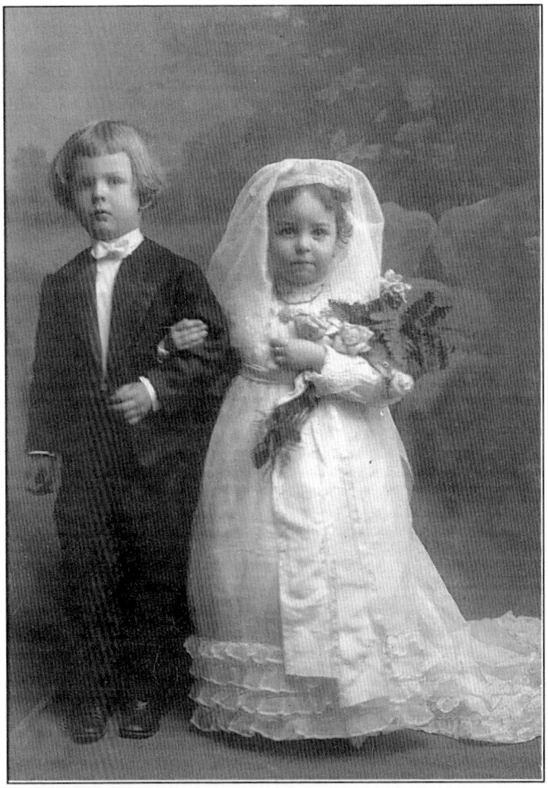

Munchkin Wedding. "Tom Thumb" weddings were popular fundraising events at the turn of the century. Marjorie Mitchell and Jesse Sweitzer were the bride and groom at this 1906 Tom Thumb wedding held at the First Christian Church. In 1922 Marjorie, or Margie, really married Maxwell H. Leichhardt. This photo is one of several in the Kentucky Library collection taken by famed clairvoyant Edgar Cayce, who also attended the First Christian Church.

A Menagerie. These Bowling Green children are surrounded by animals. They're enjoying a ride in their "Tennessee" wagon pulled by a pet goat. Chickens and turkeys gaze in envy at the stuffed rabbit who has his own cart.

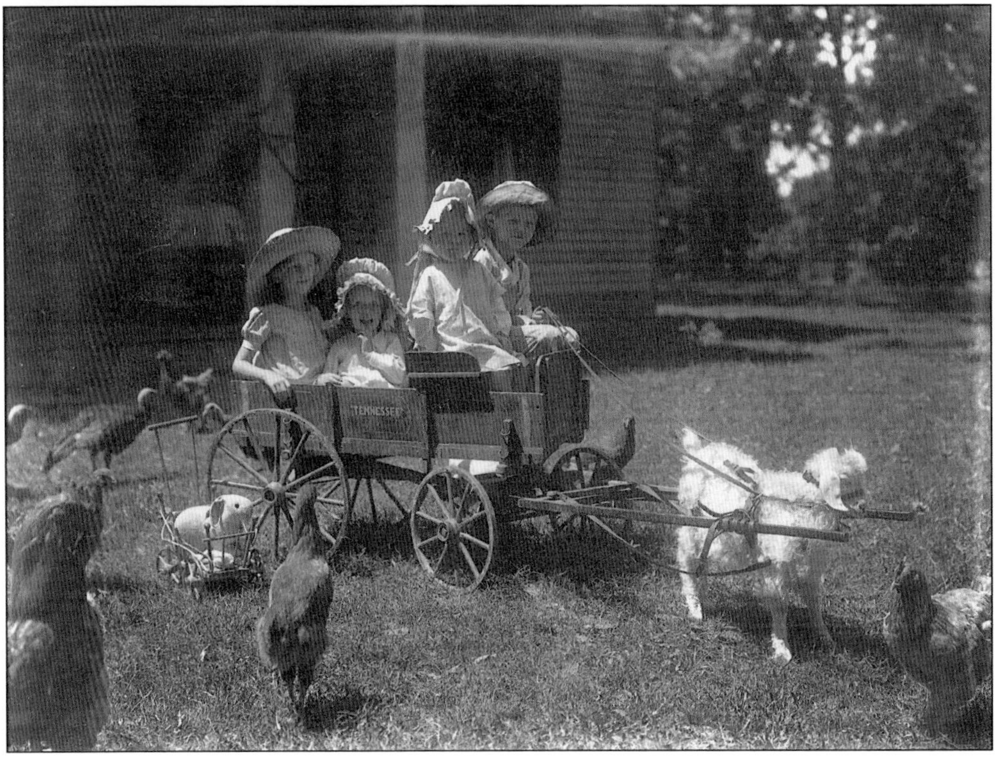

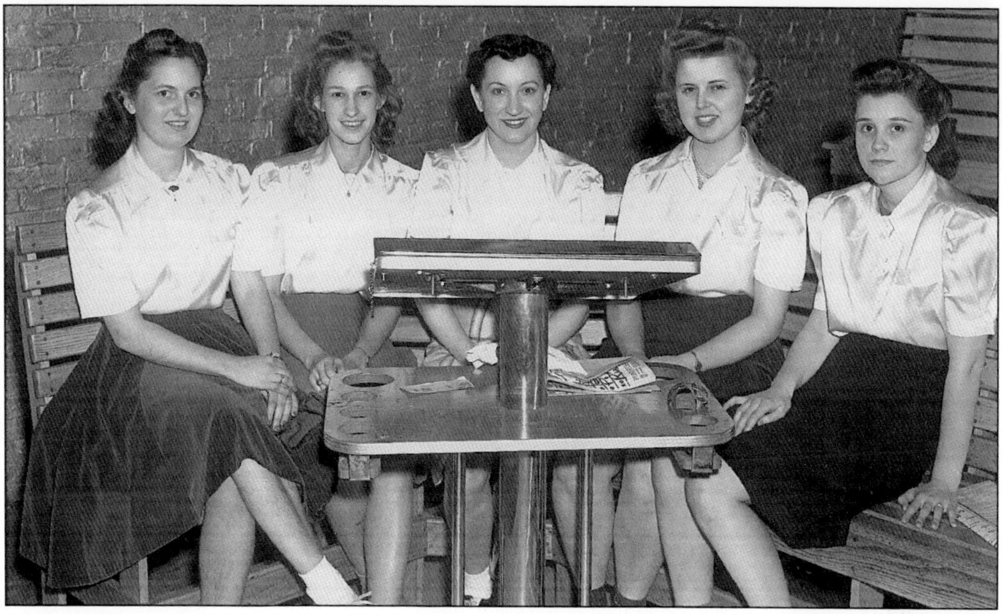

LADIES NIGHT OUT. This bevy of bowling beauties represented Union Underwear in one of the many leagues that met throughout the week at local bowling lanes. The introduction of the automatic pinsetter in 1952 revolutionized bowling. With machines replacing pin boys, air-conditioned lanes became available 24 hours a day in many locations. Ten-pin alleys were located in several older local buildings, including the old McCormack Building, the YMCA, and Potter College.

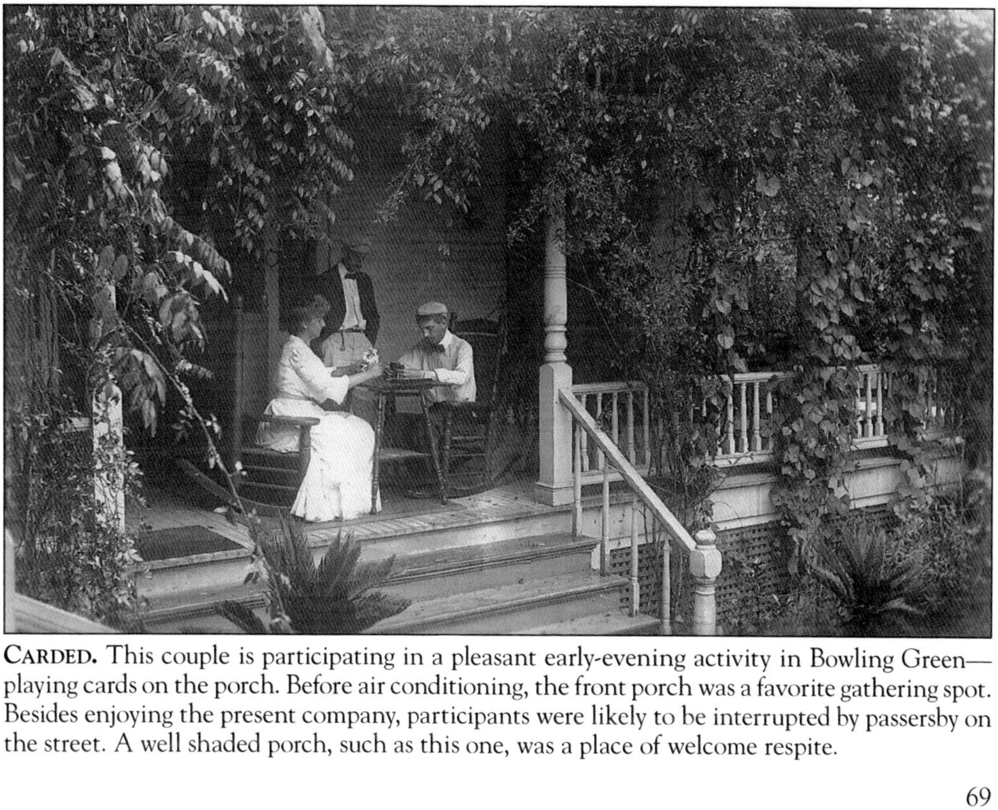

CARDED. This couple is participating in a pleasant early-evening activity in Bowling Green—playing cards on the porch. Before air conditioning, the front porch was a favorite gathering spot. Besides enjoying the present company, participants were likely to be interrupted by passersby on the street. A well shaded porch, such as this one, was a place of welcome respite.

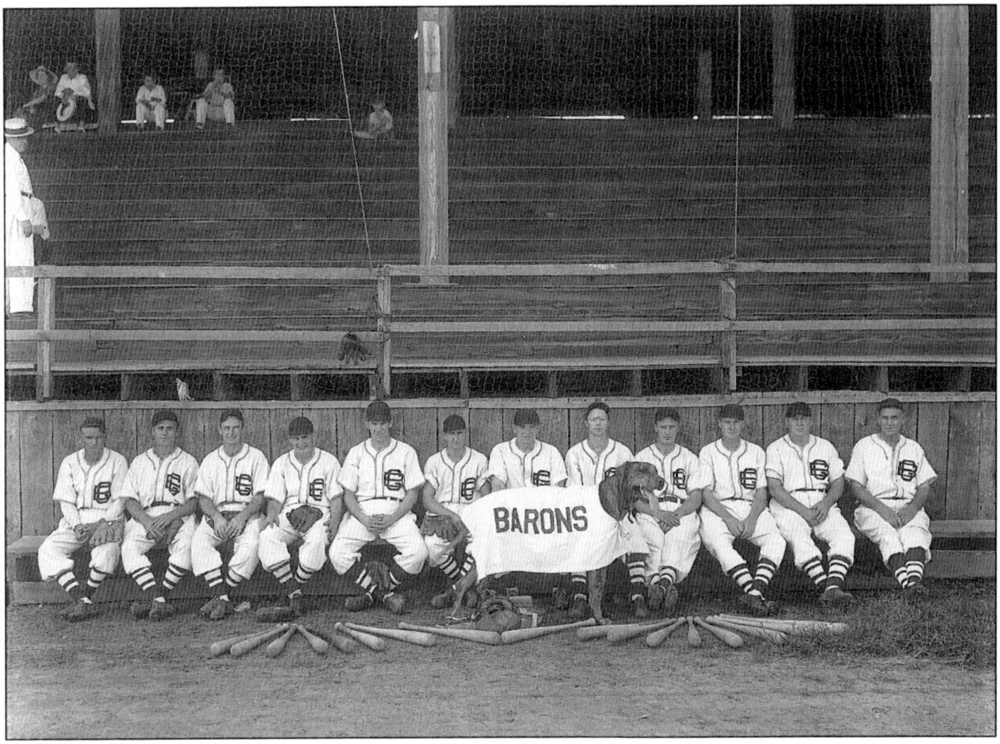

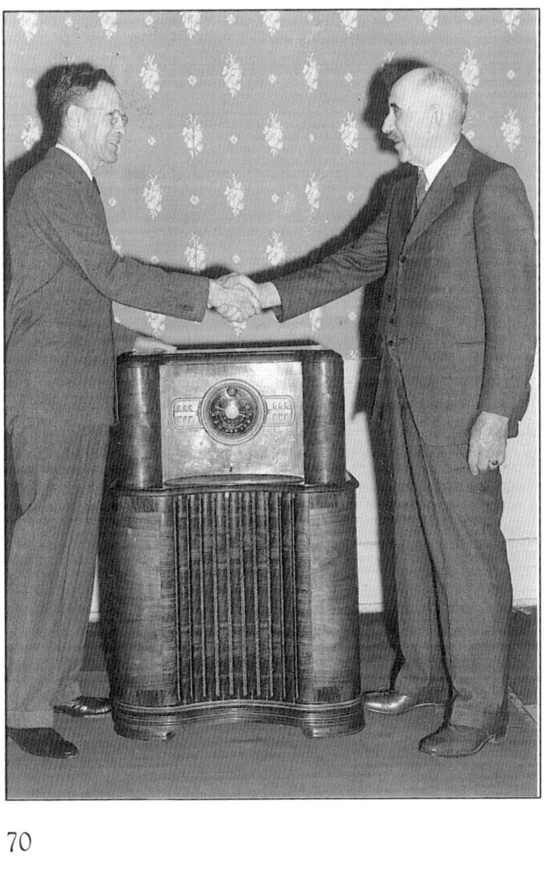

BOYS OF SUMMER. Bowling Green had organized baseball teams as early as 1887. The team seated here is the Bowling Green Barons, a mid-20th century team that played in the Class-D Kitty League. The men are posed with their mascot at the old fairground's grandstand. The Kitty League lasted from 1903 until 1955.

SELLING THE AIRWAYS. Radios were the absolute rage in the 1920s and 1930s. Many stores in Bowling Green sold radios and radio kits. During promotions a radio might be raffled or given away. Every fashionable home had a radio in their living room and if money would allow the family would own a large radio console, such as this one with improved sound quality.

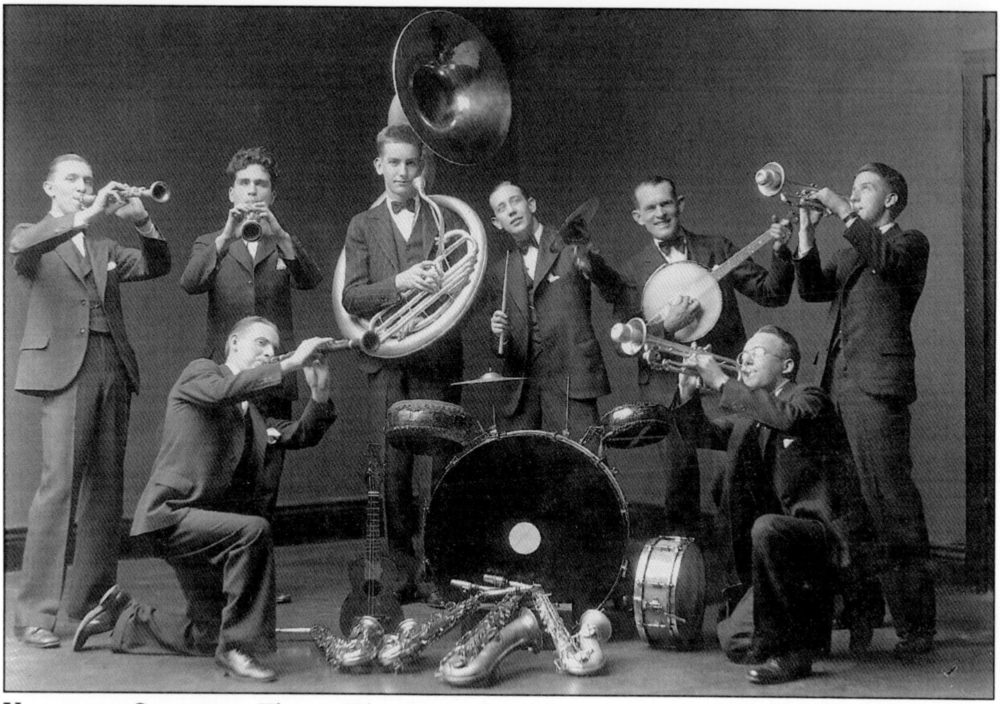

Kentucky Colonels. This is "The Original Southern Colonels" band from Bowling Green. The band played for dances in this city, Elkton, Elizabethtown, Bardstown, and Glasgow in the early 1930s. The members are, from left to right, (kneeling) Marvin Brown and Johnny Kight; (standing) Jimmy Jones, Bill Bushong, Tom Pollard, Leon Spillman, Sid Hendricks, and Chester Travelstead.

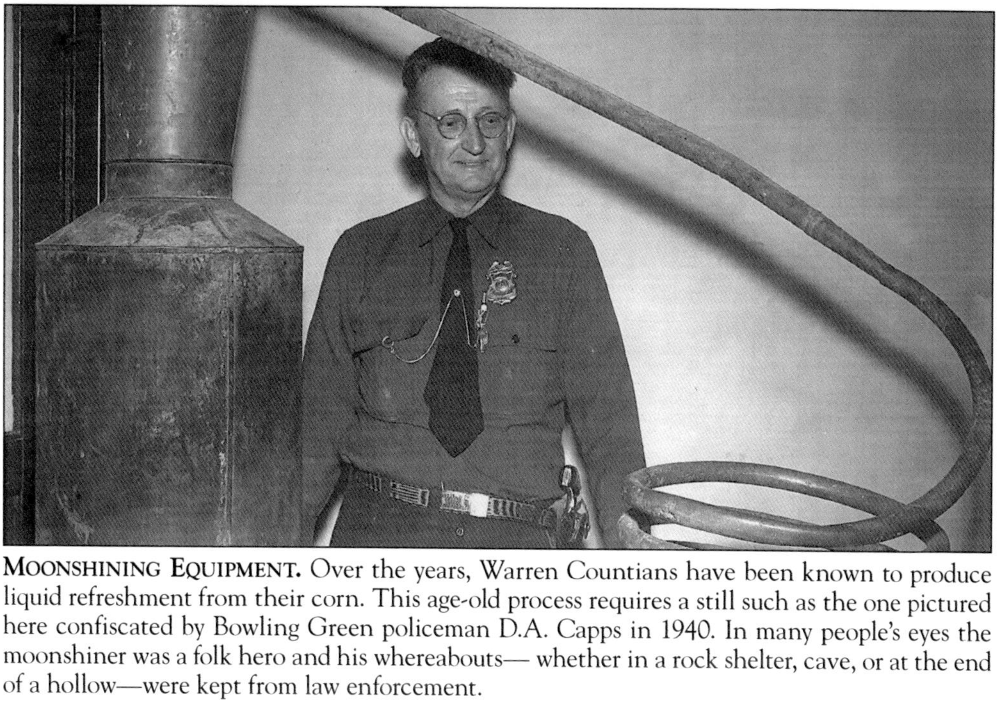

Moonshining Equipment. Over the years, Warren Countians have been known to produce liquid refreshment from their corn. This age-old process requires a still such as the one pictured here confiscated by Bowling Green policeman D.A. Capps in 1940. In many people's eyes the moonshiner was a folk hero and his whereabouts— whether in a rock shelter, cave, or at the end of a hollow—were kept from law enforcement.

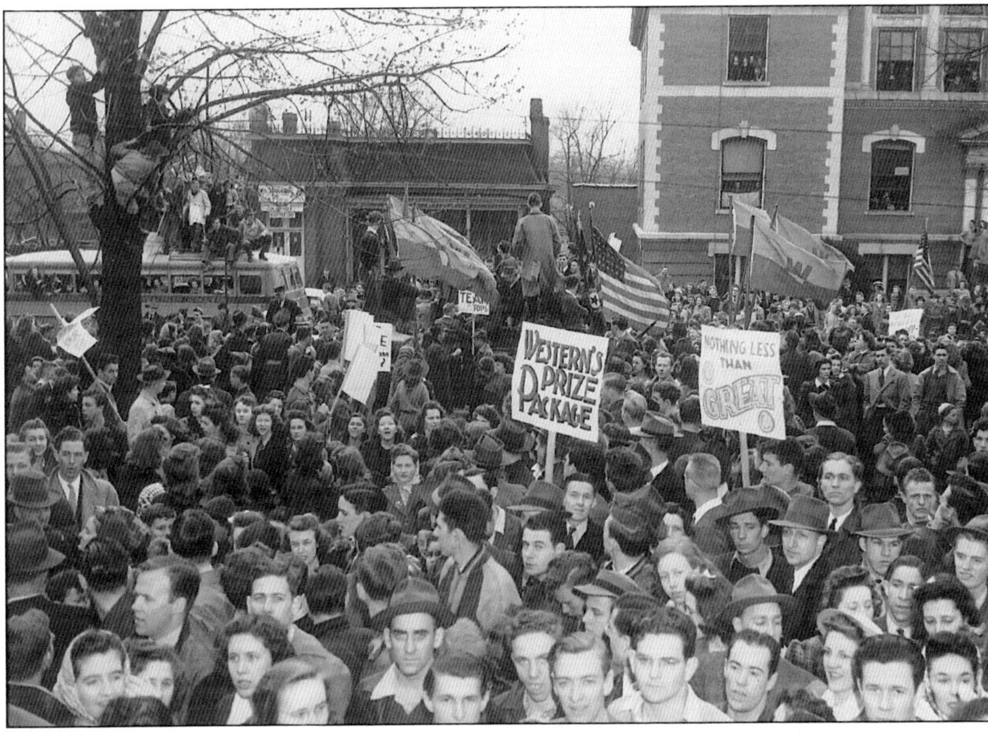

WHIPPED INTO A FRENZY. What appears to be a riot scene is actually Bowling Green turning out en masse to welcome back Western Kentucky University's basketball Hilltoppers after a big victory. The team is atop a fire engine that is literally swarmed with fans. Most of the crowd is in the courthouse lawn with City Hall in the background.

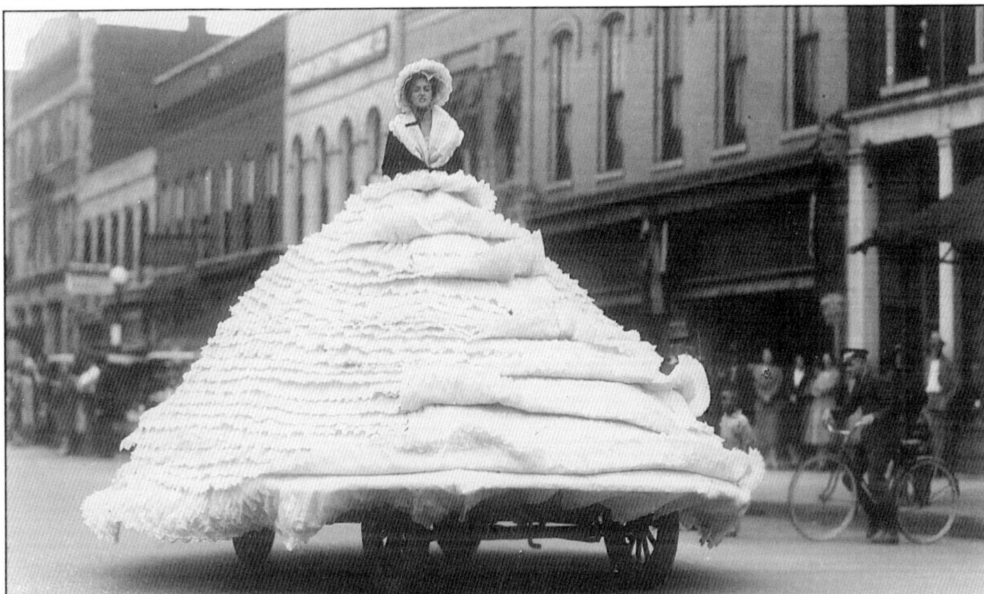

HOW DID SHE EVER WALK? This young lady with a titan-sized hoop skirt is participating in the 1936 Christmas parade. This fashion could have been created in honor of the popular book of that year, *Gone with the Wind*, which was made into a movie in 1939.

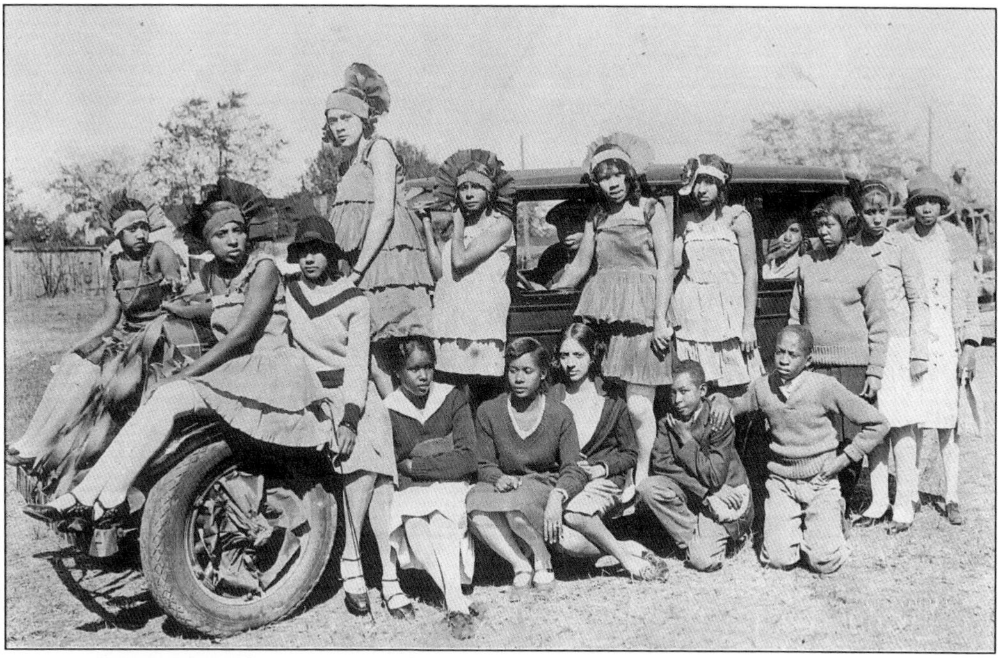

Young Scholars. These young African Americans represent approximately one-half of State Street School's class of 1929. Judging from the natty costumes, the adolescents are enjoying a class outing or parade. The bunting on the wheels and a portion of a decorated car behind the one featured suggest this is part of a parade.

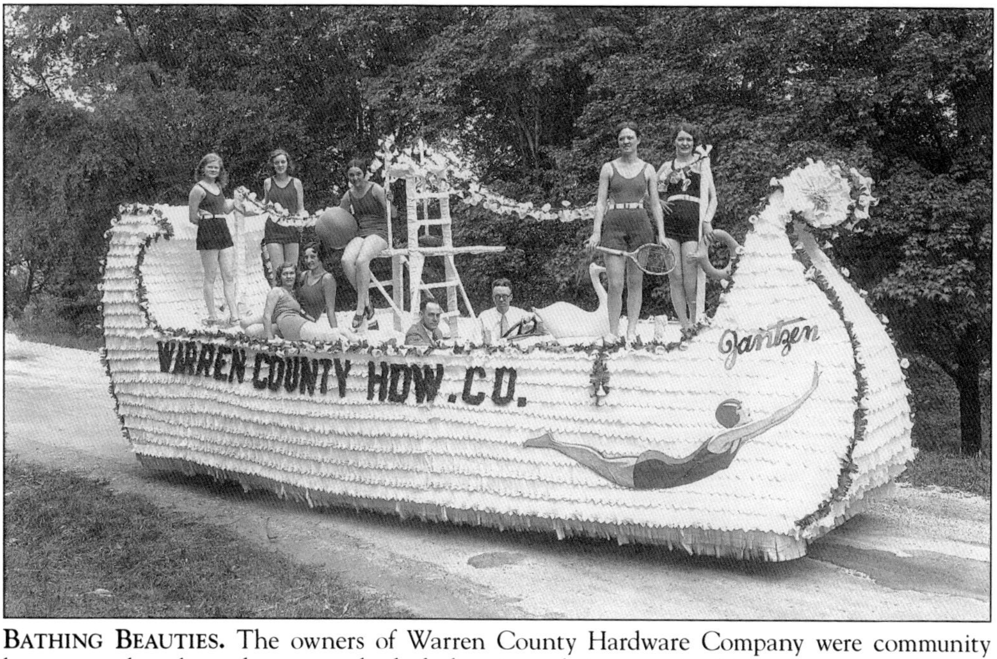

Bathing Beauties. The owners of Warren County Hardware Company were community boosters and used parades as a method of advertising their wares, in this case, sports equipment. The sponsors have employed only attractive young coeds from the Western Kentucky University physical education department as models. The driver of the float is Herman Lowe, a winsome personality and a favorite storyteller.

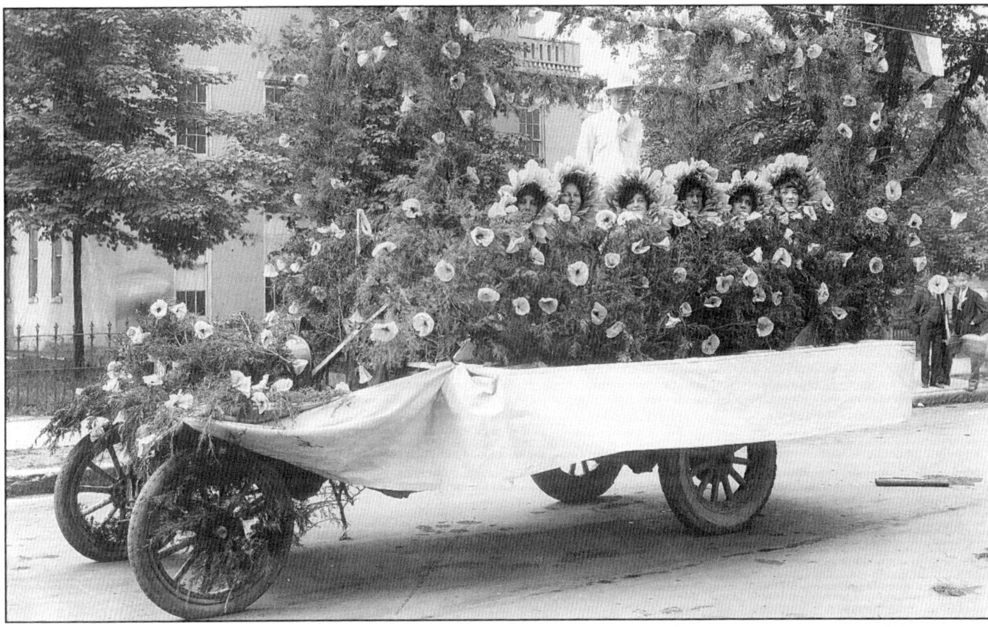

DEBATE FLOAT. A signal event during the academic year at Bowling Green Business University was the annual Big Four and Coreco Debates. These two societies vied each year to win the coveted debate trophy. The event was heralded with a parade. This basket of beauties is from a 1920s parade.

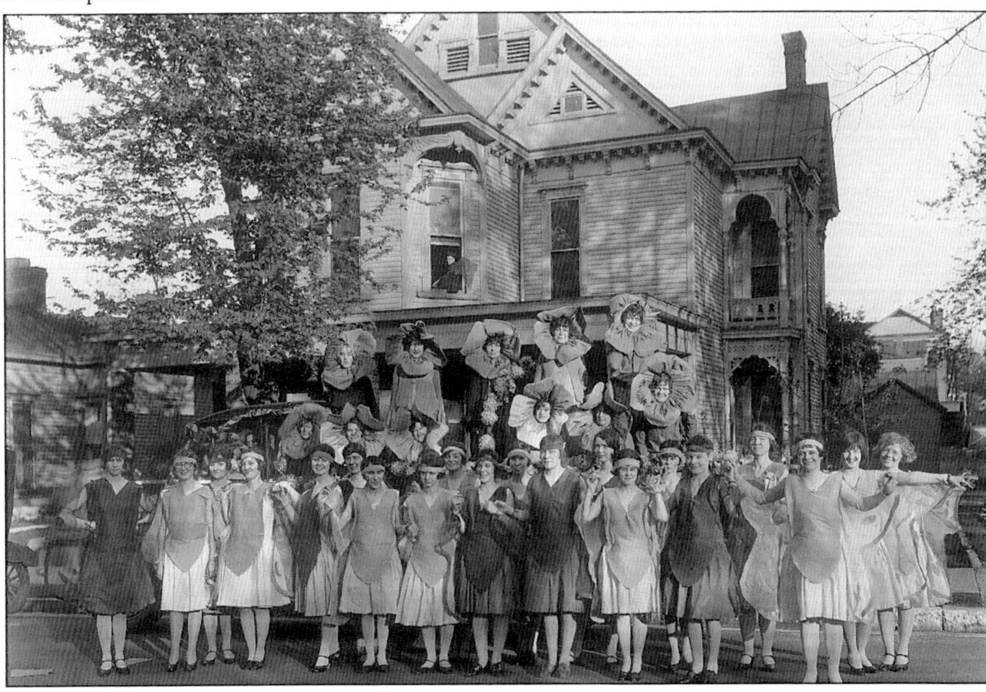

A BEAUTIFUL BOUQUET. These ladies are dressed in their spring finery to support the Coreco Debating Society at the Business University in the mid-1920s. The girls atop the float are dressed as flowers and the girls at street level depict butterflies. Because the debate took place in the spring, it is no wonder that many floats had an emphasis on nature.

Four

Bowling Green at Work

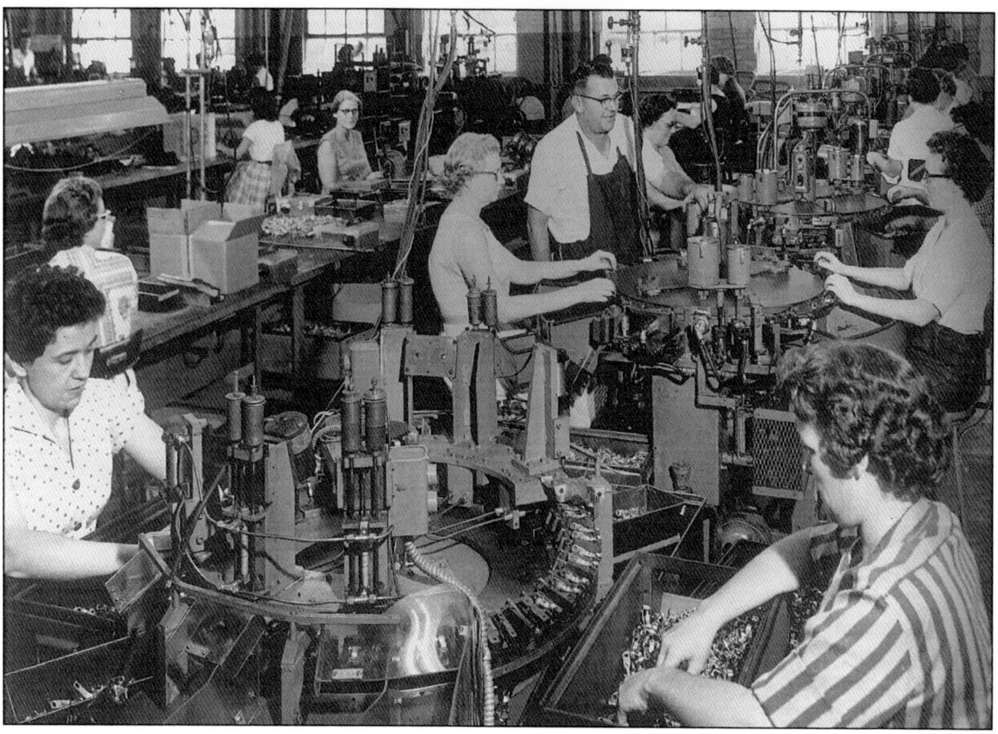

VRMMMMM! In 2002, Holley Carburetor celebrated 50 years of operation in Bowling Green. At one time the company operated two plants in the city and was for a time Bowling Green's largest employer. The company builds automobile carburetors and distributors. In 1960, when this photograph was taken, a company spokesman stated that about 35 to 40 percent of Holley's employees were women. (Photo by Tommy Hughes.)

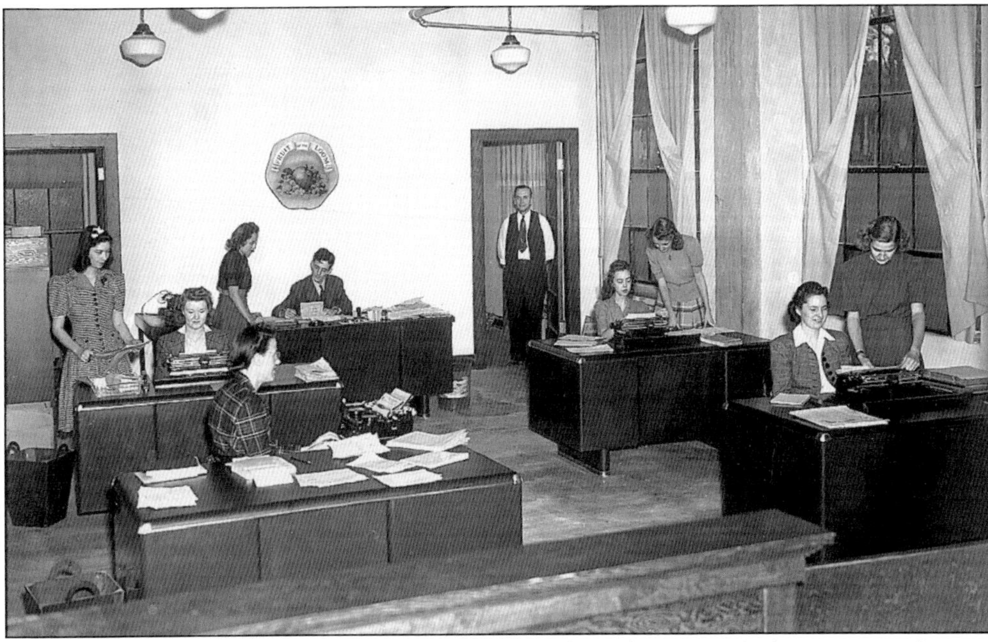

UNION UNDERWEAR. Union Underwear was one of Bowling Green's first major industries. A plant designed by James Maurice Ingram opened on lower Church Street in 1940. Soon thereafter the company received war contracts to provide underwear for American servicemen. Houchens Industries purchased the Church Street plant in the late 1990s. This photo shows the office staff in 1941. Everett Moore, long time administrator for Union Underwear, is shown in the doorway.

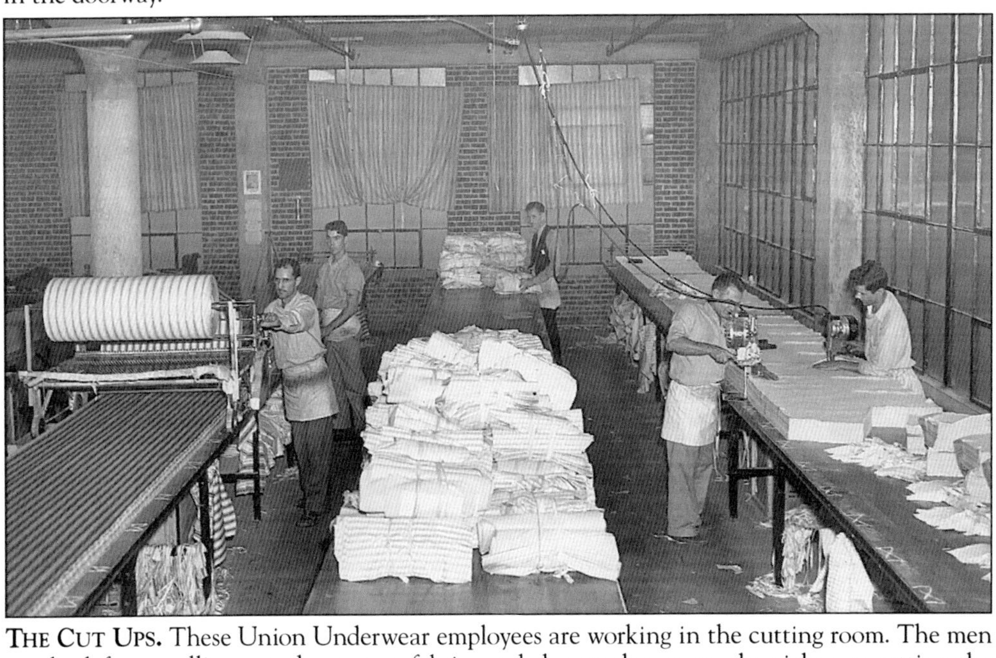

THE CUT UPS. These Union Underwear employees are working in the cutting room. The men on the left are rolling out the cotton fabric, and the employees on the right are cutting the patterns. The fabric could be rolled out as long as 270 feet and the electrical knives were capable of cutting through 504 layers of cloth.

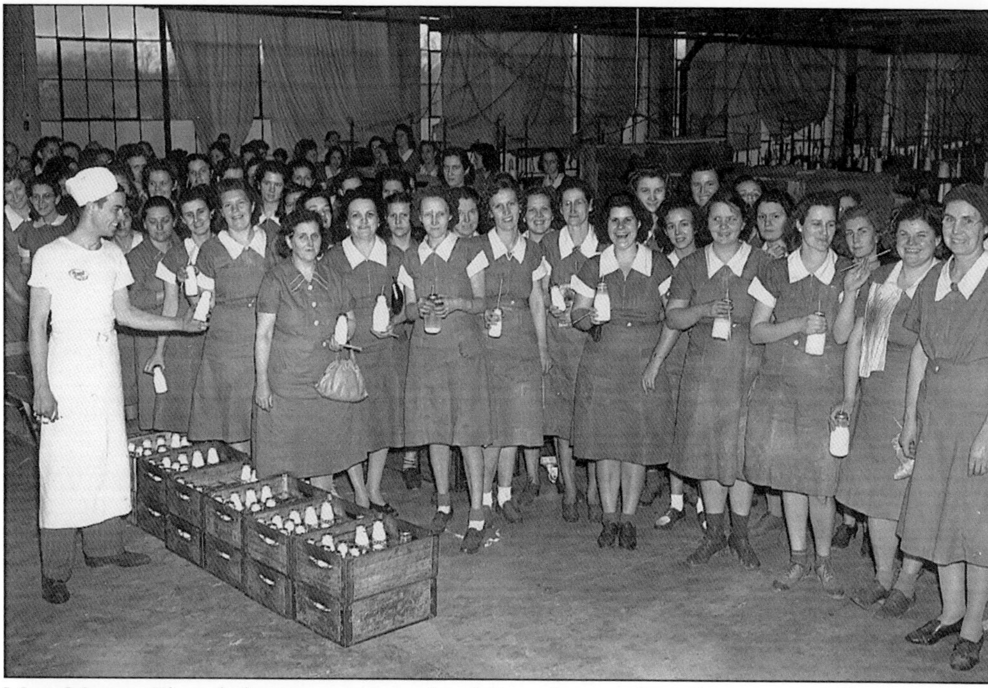

MILK MAIDS. These ladies are enjoying a break from their work on the sewing machines at Union Underwear in the early 1940s. Over 600 sewing machines were employed at the Church Street location and they were chiefly operated by women. The company provided secure jobs at decent wages and some benefits, which were greatly appreciated by its employees.

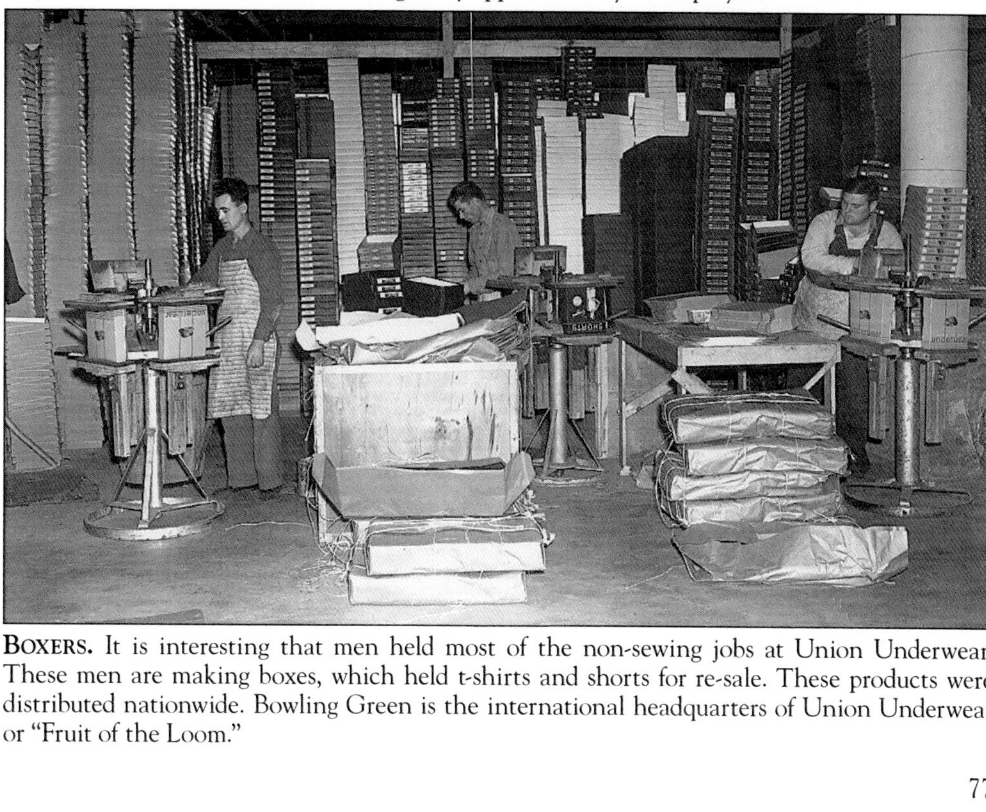

BOXERS. It is interesting that men held most of the non-sewing jobs at Union Underwear. These men are making boxes, which held t-shirts and shorts for re-sale. These products were distributed nationwide. Bowling Green is the international headquarters of Union Underwear or "Fruit of the Loom."

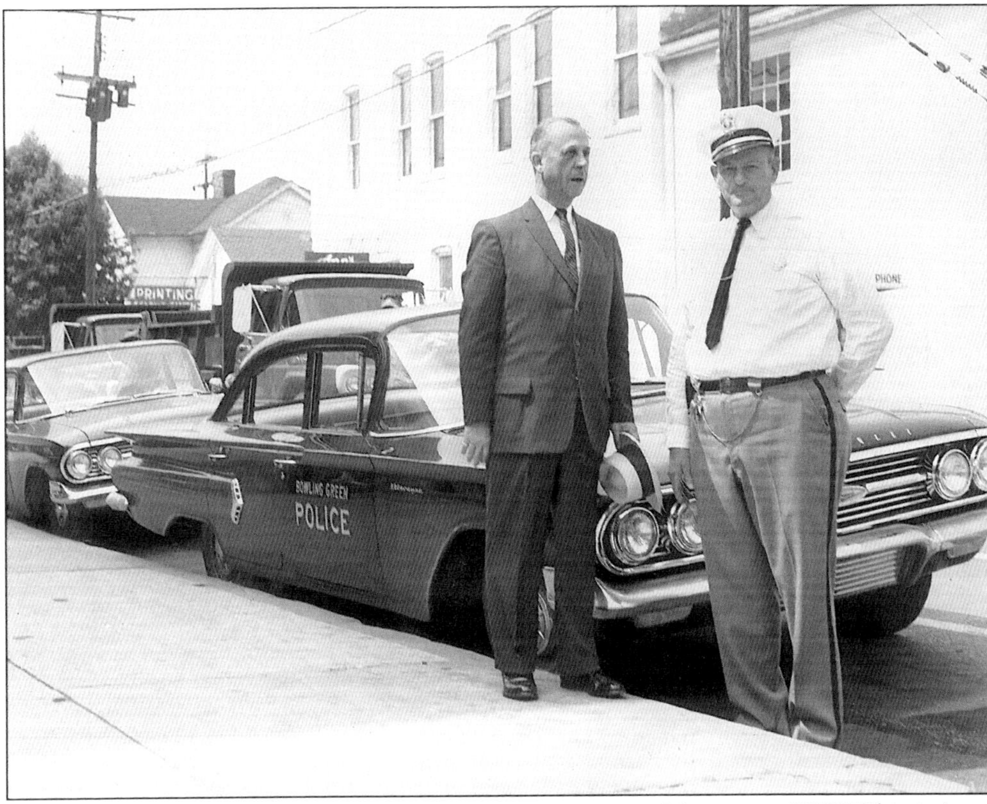

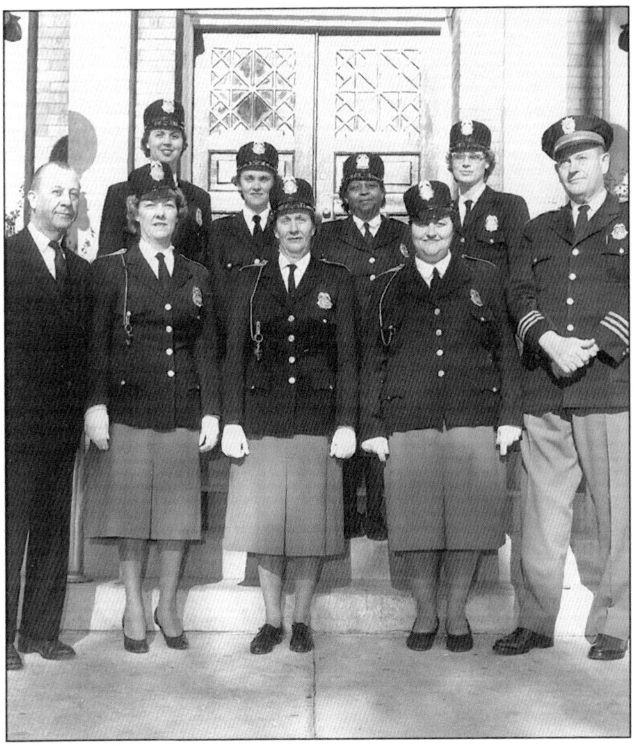

MAYBERRY RFD? This isn't sheriff Andy Taylor. Rather, it is Bowling Green city police chief Horace Snell and mayor Robert Graham checking out the city's new squad cars in June 1960. Two new street department trucks were also on hand for inspection. They are parked along 10th Street with the Gerard Funeral Home in the background. (Photo by Ches Johnson.)

STEEL MAGNOLIAS. These ladies are Bowling Green's meter maids in 1960. The two gentlemen are mayor Robert Graham (left) and police chief Horace Snell. The ladies are posed on the steps of City Hall.

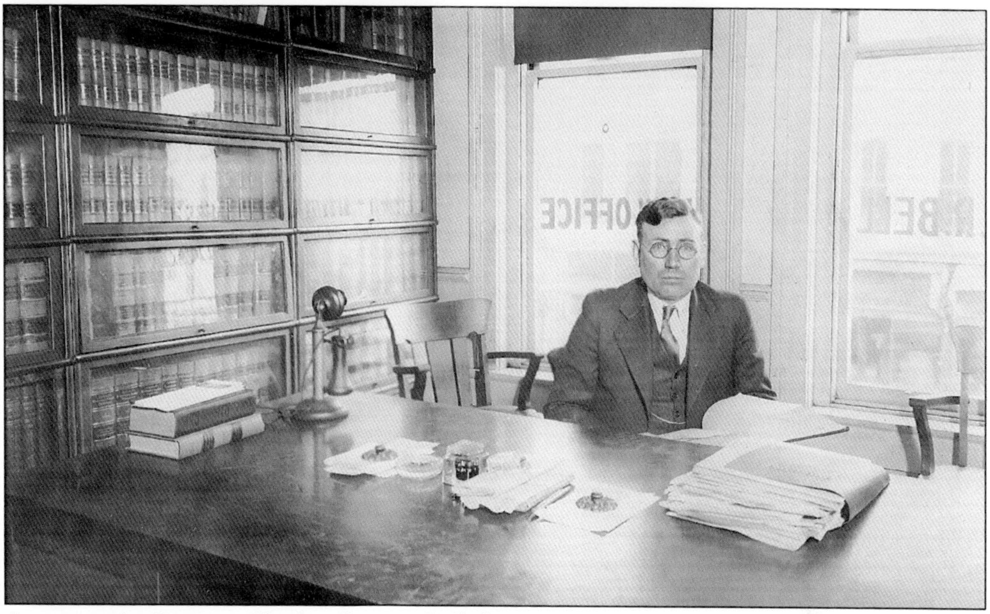

ATTORNEY'S OFFICE. Charles Rowan Bell (1891–1976) was one of Bowling Green's most accomplished attorneys. An Ohio County native, Bell attended Western Kentucky University and became principal of the Oakland School for three years. In this photo, Bell is sitting behind a rather clean desk surrounded by his law books. Bell served as county attorney (1930–1937) and city attorney (1940–1941). He was a founding partner of the prestigious Bell, Orr, Ayers, and Moore law firm.

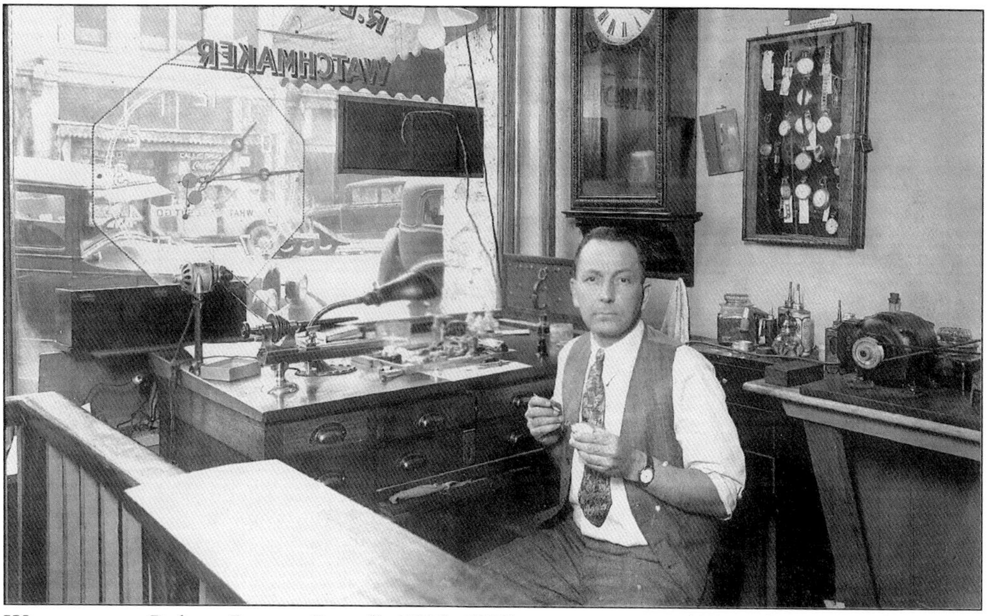

WATCHMAN. Robert Burton Russell (1895–1983) was a native of Hart County and came to Bowling Green as an employee of the L&N railroad. He was a jeweler by trade and specifically a watchmaker. After retiring from the L&N, he opened up a small clock and watch repair shop on State Street, where this photo was taken. He eventually moved the shop to his home at 1126 College Street.

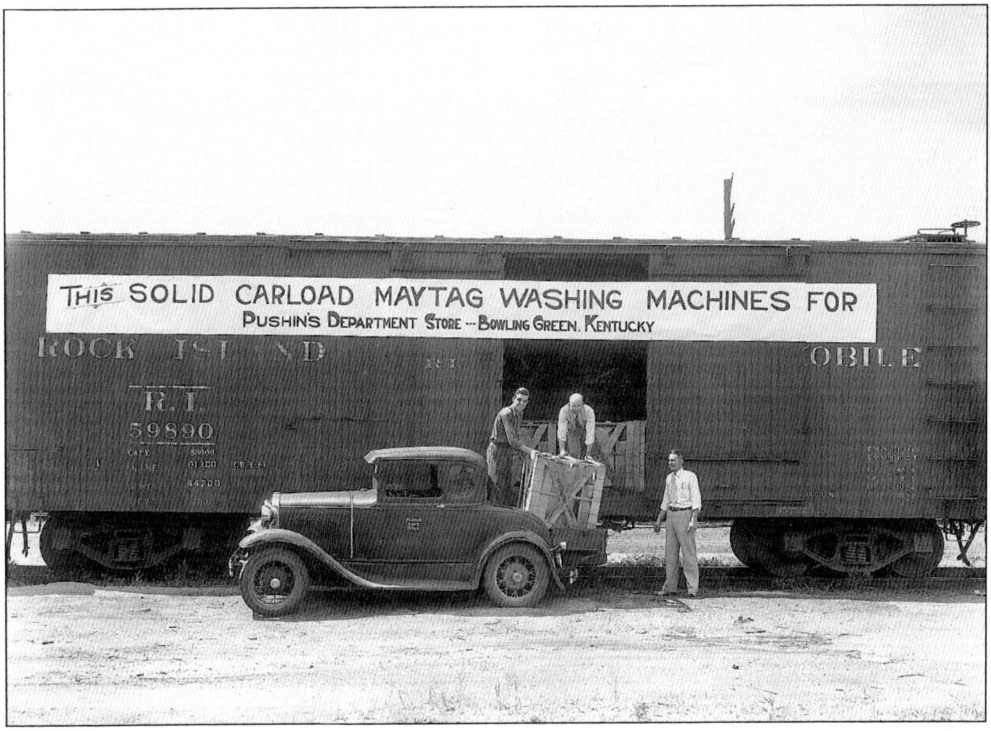

LOADING LAUNDRY. These men from Pushin's Department Store are unloading Maytag washers at the old Main Street depot, three blocks from the downtown store. The man on the right is Louie Pushin, the son of store owner Sam Pushin.

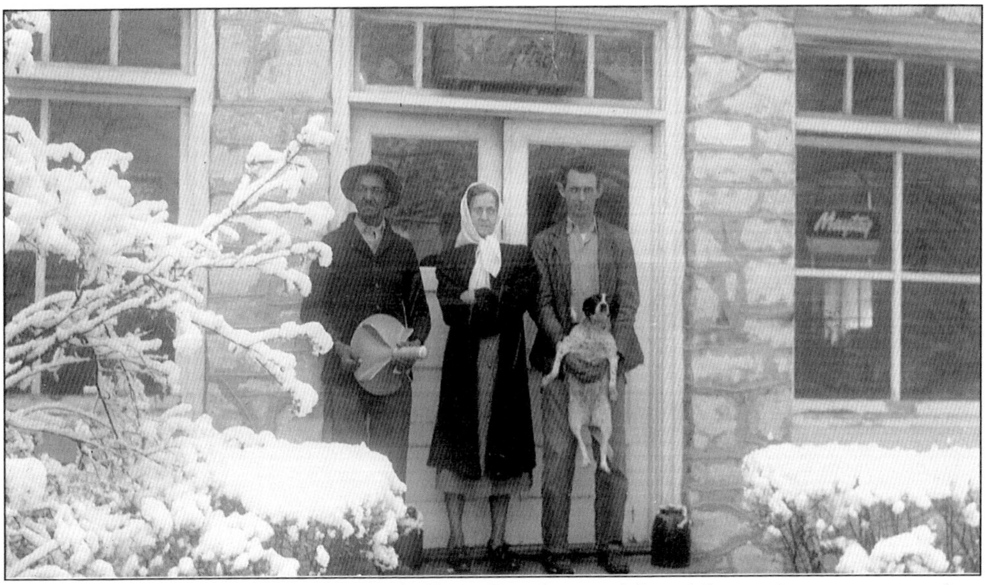

THE LONELIEST REPAIR MAN. Mitchell C. Boucher and his African-American coworker, Gatewood, handled repairs for May Igleheart's Washing Machine Shop at 1170 Kentucky Street. The firm chiefly sold and repaired the popular Maytag brand as seen in the window sign, but their advertising noted: "We repair all makes of washing machine." The employees are posing in front of the store after a big snow in February 1951.

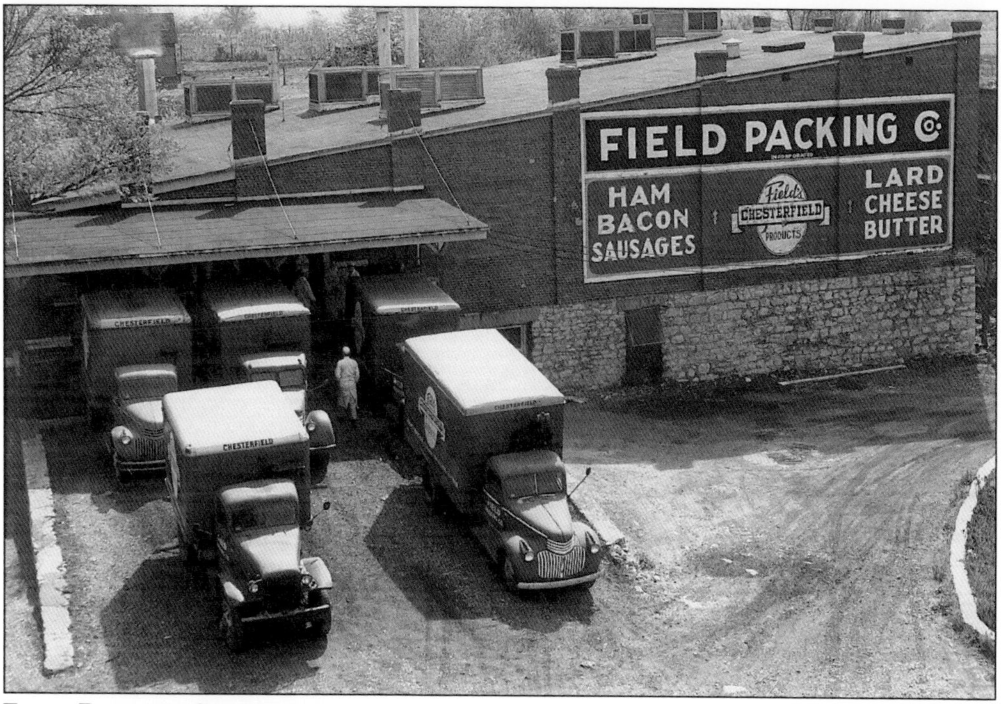

FIELD PACKING COMPANY. Bowling Green has long been a center for meat production, particularly pork. Field Packing Company, headquartered in Owensboro, built a meat packing house on Richardsville Road in 1930 (above.) Field continues to be a name associated with quality meat products, though it no longer operates in Bowling Green. Below, one of Field's meat inspectors checks the hanging meat.

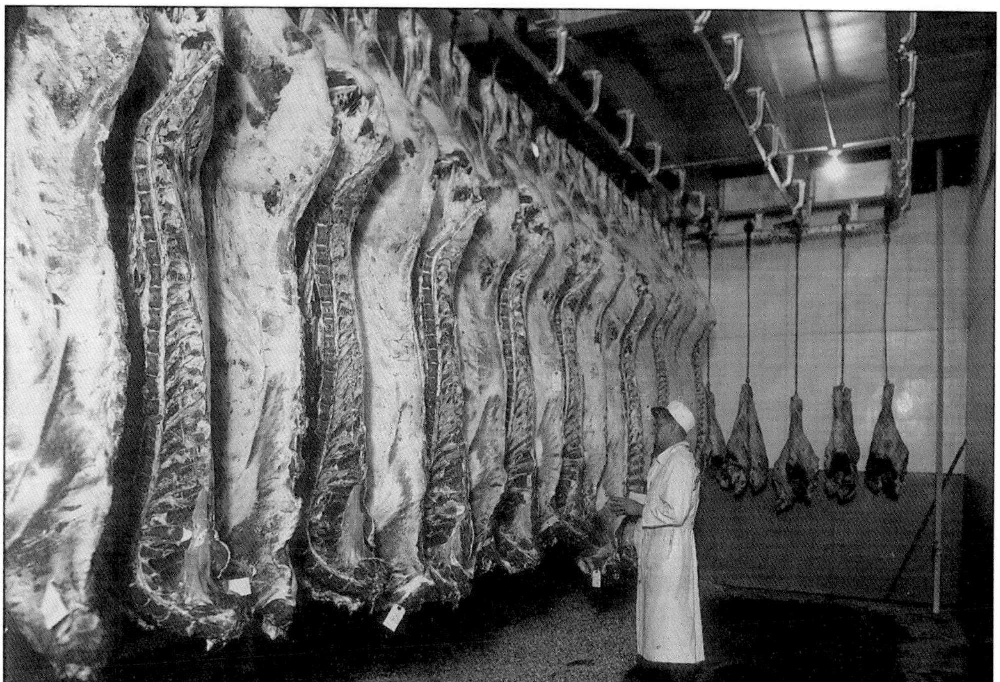

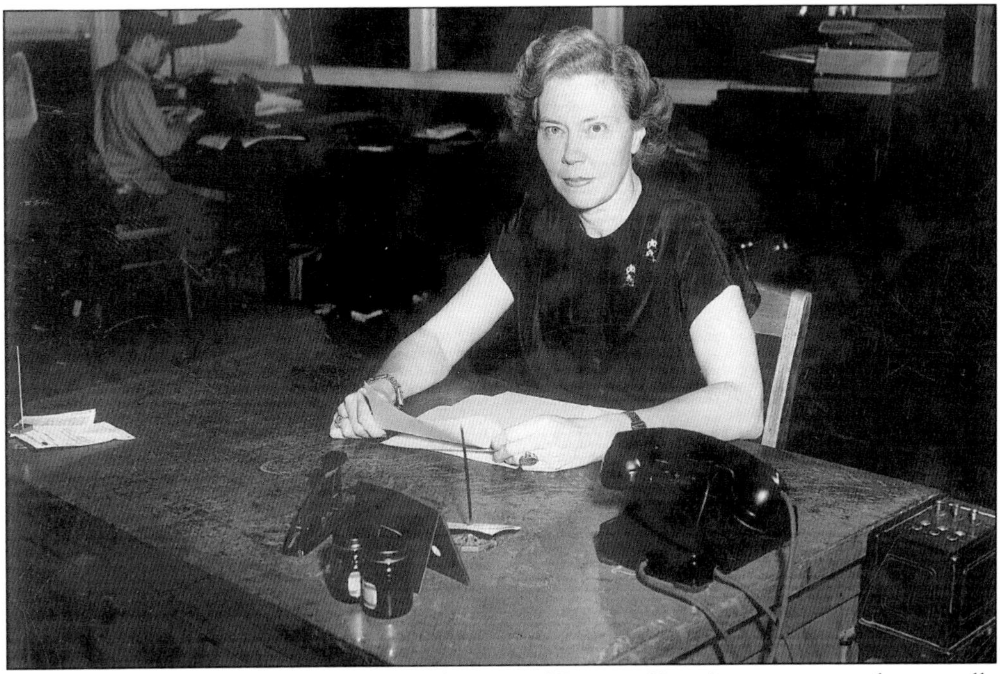

MAKE A NOTE OF IT. Edith Wilson served as one of Duncan Hines's secretaries and eventually was made office manager at the publisher's Bowling Green office. Hines's office was a busy place, often receiving up to 600 letters a day from people ordering copies of his book, providing or requesting information about listed eateries, sending recipes for local specialties, or inquiring about his "Recommended by Duncan Hines" signs.

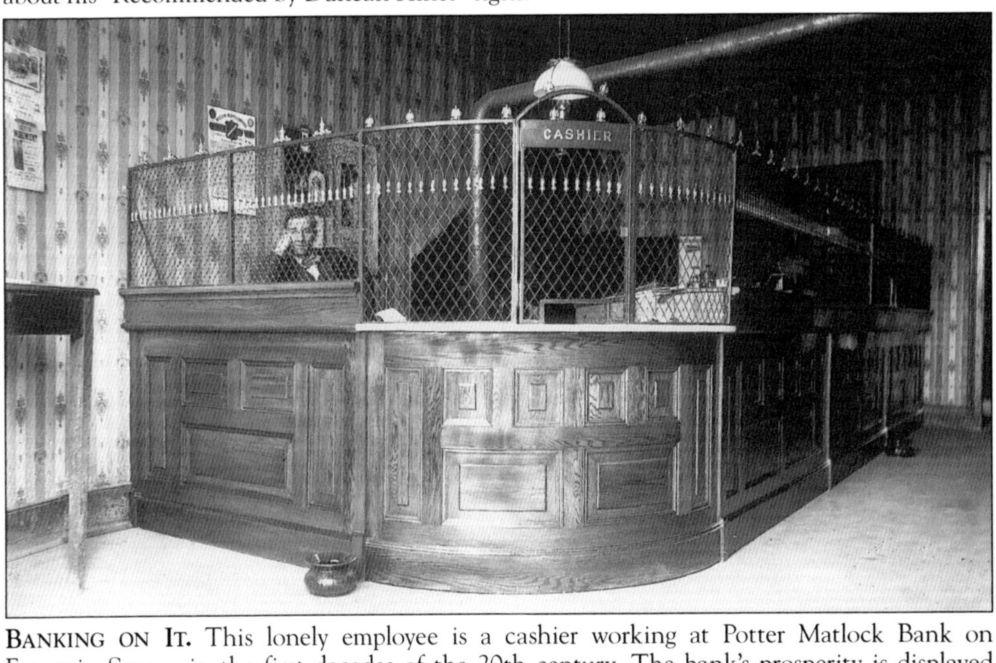

BANKING ON IT. This lonely employee is a cashier working at Potter Matlock Bank on Fountain Square in the first decades of the 20th century. The bank's prosperity is displayed in the beautiful wood counter with raised panels and decorative wire mesh wicket. Notice the necessary spittoons on the floor and the stylish wallpaper. (Photo by George Dabbs.)

BLACK GOLD. During the early 1920s, Bowling Green and Warren County experienced an oil boom. The discovery of the Davenport and Moulder pools produced a frenzy of activity as local soil was punctured unmercilessly in search of petroleum. The abandoned First Baptist Church on Main Street was quickly converted to the Bowling Green Oil Exchange. Oil is still pumped from some of these wells. The boom ended by the mid-1920s.

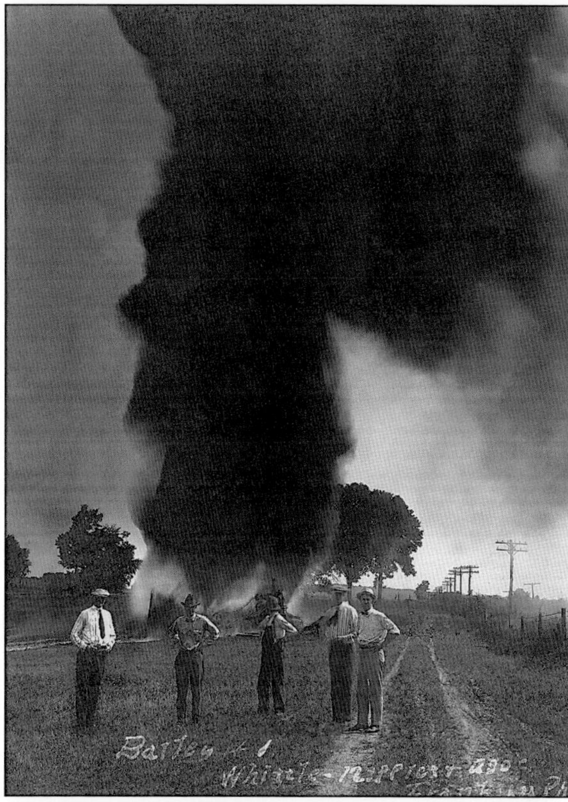

THE GREAT ARCH OIL COMPANY. Speculation in oil drilling reached a frenetic level in the early 1920s. Dozens of local companies were established to purchase land options and finance drilling. The Great Arch Oil Company was established in 1920 to explore for oil on Western Kentucky University's 91-acre farm. Stock was sold to faculty and staff as well as local citizens. The company was never financially successful.

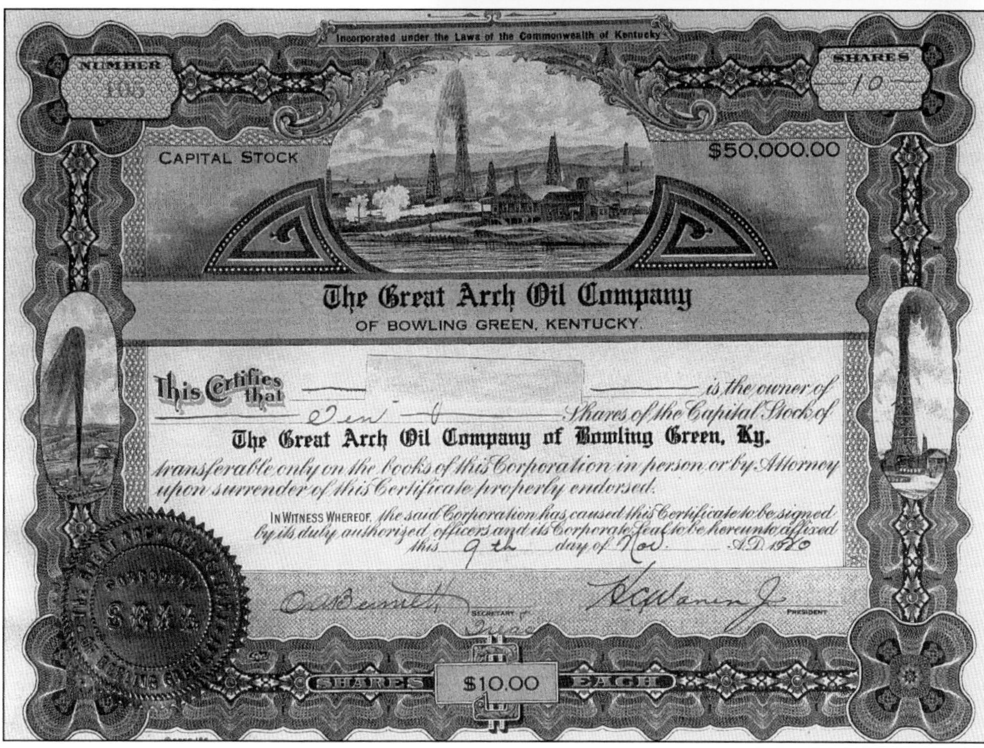

Incorporated under the Laws of the Commonwealth of Kentucky

NUMBER 105

SHARES 10

CAPITAL STOCK $50,000.00

The Great Arch Oil Company
OF BOWLING GREEN, KENTUCKY

This Certifies that ______ is the owner of Ten Shares of the Capital Stock of
The Great Arch Oil Company of Bowling Green, Ky.
transferable only on the books of this Corporation in person or by Attorney upon surrender of this Certificate properly endorsed.

In Witness Whereof, the said Corporation has caused this Certificate to be signed by its duly authorized officers and its Corporate Seal to be hereunto affixed this 9th day of Nov. A.D. 1920

SECRETARY

PRESIDENT

SHARES $10.00 EACH

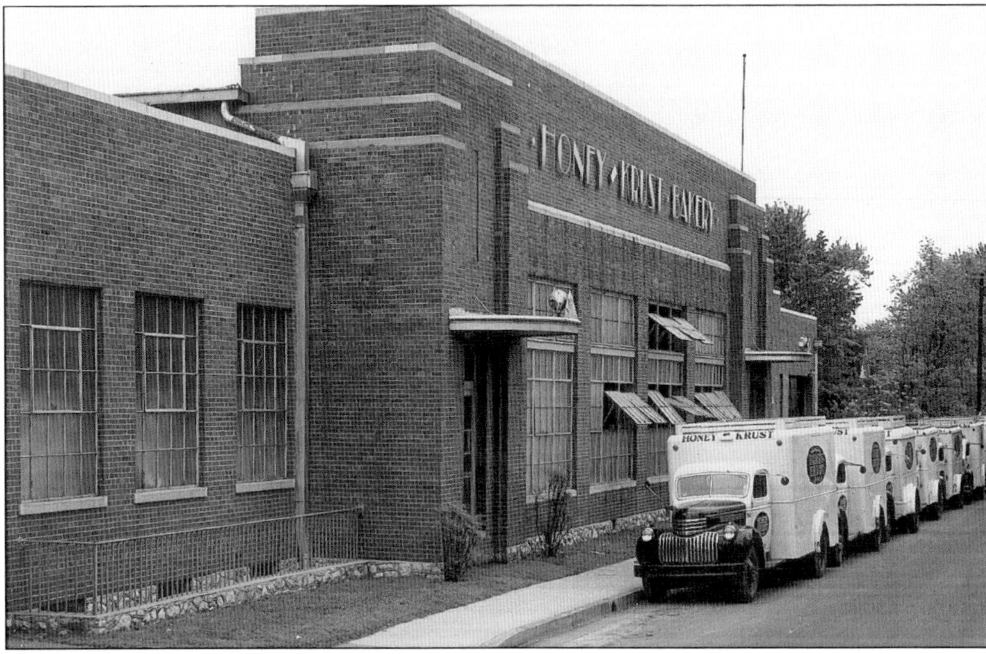

ROLLING IN THE DOUGH. The Honey Krust Bakery operated at this 1349 Adams Street facility for nearly 50 years. Local architect, James M. Ingram, designed this Streamline Moderne building in 1936. This was one of Ingram's first major commissions and he won an industrial design award for this important Bowling Green landmark. The bakery was later called Colonial Krust Bakery.

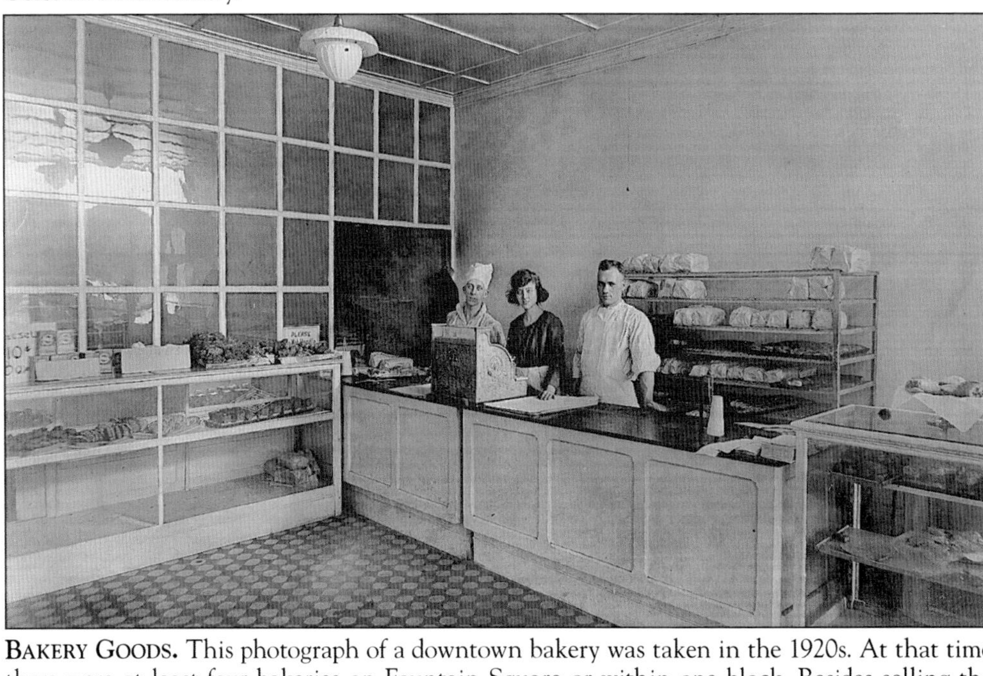

BAKERY GOODS. This photograph of a downtown bakery was taken in the 1920s. At that time there were at least four bakeries on Fountain Square or within one block. Besides selling the ubiquitous white bread, local bakeries also sold baked sweets, rolls, cakes, pies, and even pretzels. In this photo a small sign to the left advertises a box of pretzels for a dime.

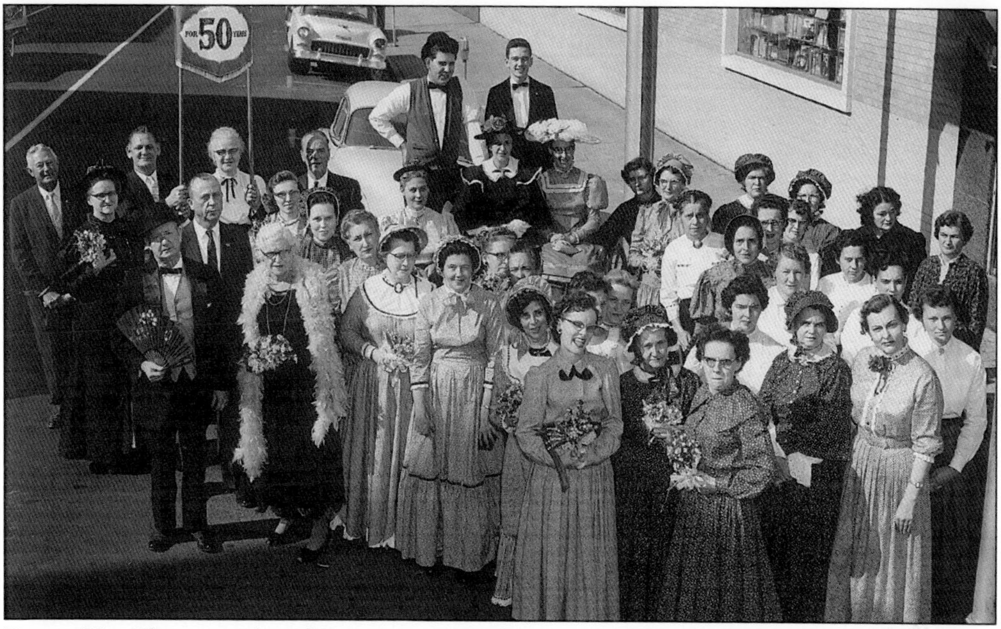

DRESS UP. These people, who appear to at play, are actually the employees of Woolworth's celebrating the store's 50th anniversary in Bowling Green on September 24, 1959. The store was located at the corner of Park Row and State Street. It was razed in June 1992.

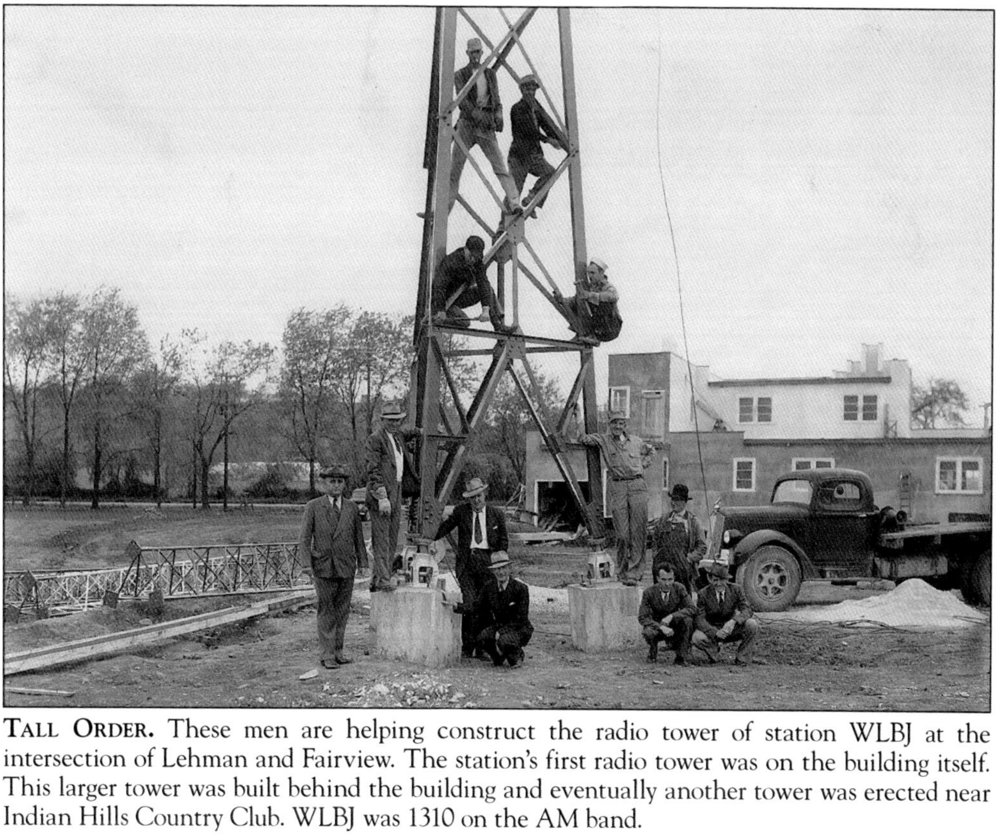

TALL ORDER. These men are helping construct the radio tower of station WLBJ at the intersection of Lehman and Fairview. The station's first radio tower was on the building itself. This larger tower was built behind the building and eventually another tower was erected near Indian Hills Country Club. WLBJ was 1310 on the AM band.

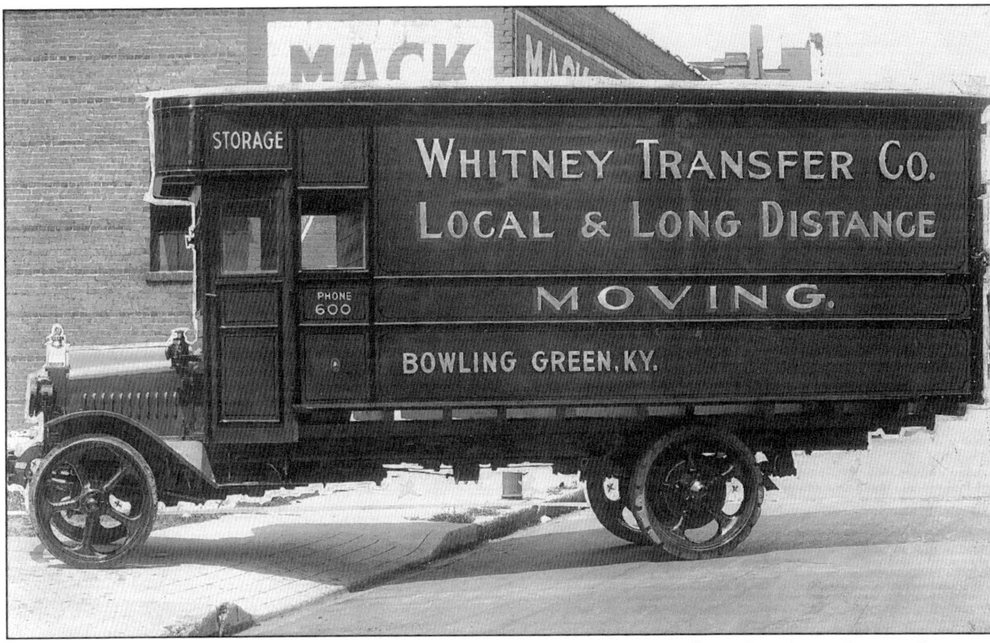

KEEP ON TRUCKING. The Whitney Transfer Company operated in Bowling Green for over 50 years and, for many of those years, had its headquarters at the corner of 10th and Clay Streets. Andrew Whitney began the business in 1923, engaging exclusively in local moving and freight deliveries before branching out into long distance moving and storage.

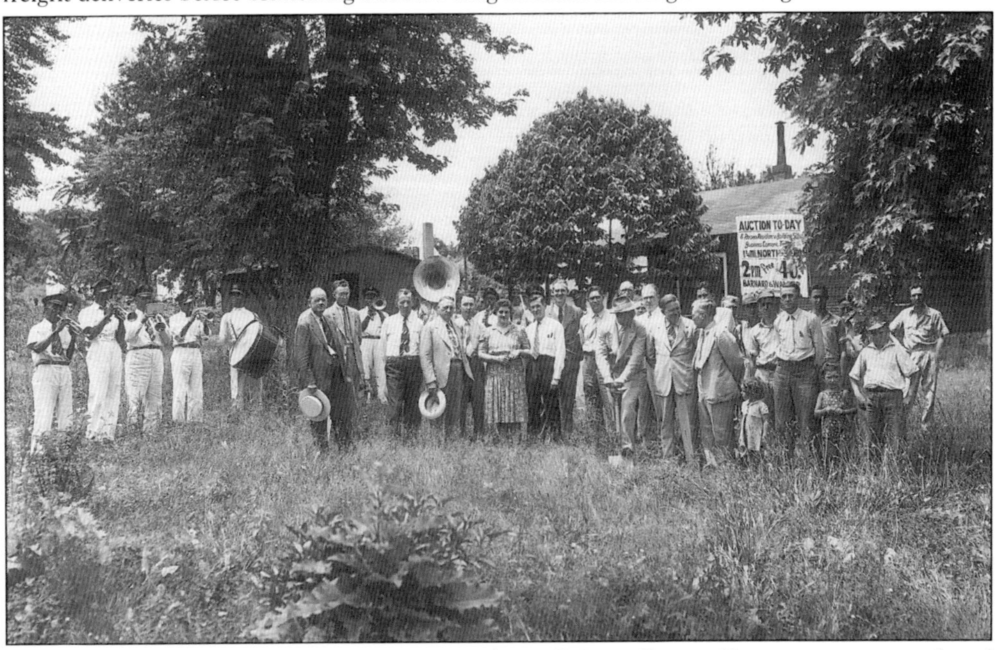

WORK WHILE YOU PLAY. Auctions were often all-day affairs; effective auctioneers hired musicians for the day and sometimes provided meals for free or at low cost. Here a group of potential buyers enjoys the tunes of a local African American band. Barnard & Walker held this *c.* 1940s auction. The auctioneers were Edgar C. Walker and Jacob H. "Jake" Barnard, whose offices for many years were in the Helm Hotel.

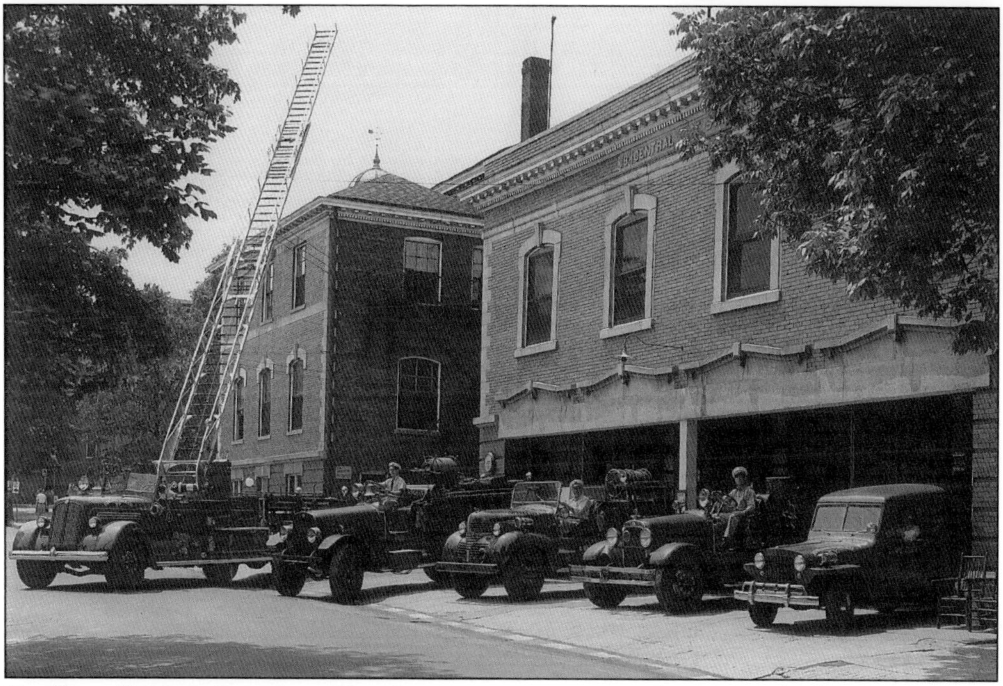

ON CALL. Bowling Green's paid fire department was organized in 1898. It had several locations before the completion of the Central Fire Station behind City Hall in 1908. Because Brinton B. Davis designed both buildings, they had a degree of architectural integrity rarely enjoyed in municipal structures. Here the department's equipment is carefully displayed for a photograph.

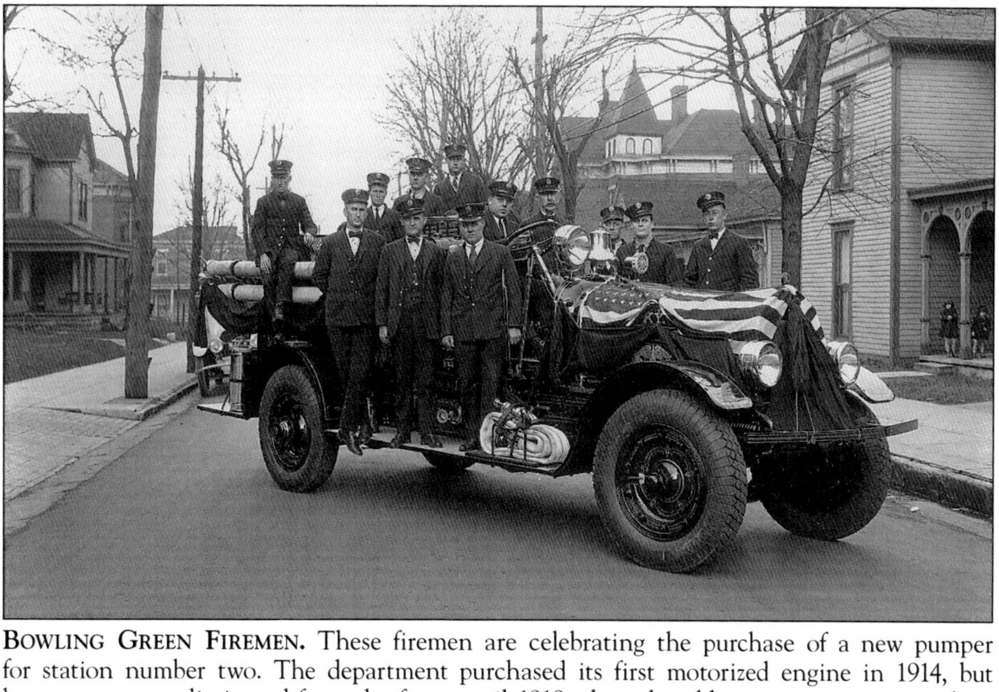

BOWLING GREEN FIREMEN. These firemen are celebrating the purchase of a new pumper for station number two. The department purchased its first motorized engine in 1914, but horses were not eliminated from the force until 1918 when the old wagons were mounted on commercial truck bodies.

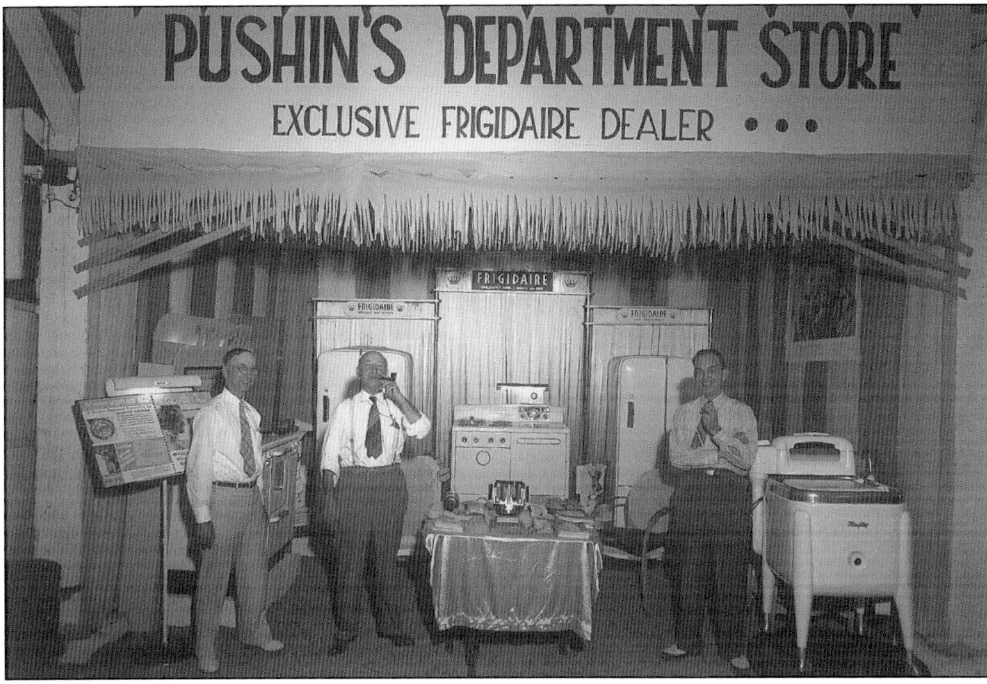

AN EXCLUSIVE. This photograph was taken during Frigidaire Value Week at Pushin's Department Store. The center table contains product information about the various Frigidaire products sold in the store. One of the highlighted features of the range was a lighted oven. The man in the center is Sam Pushin, who typically carried a pipe, and the salesman on the right is Joe Spugnardi.

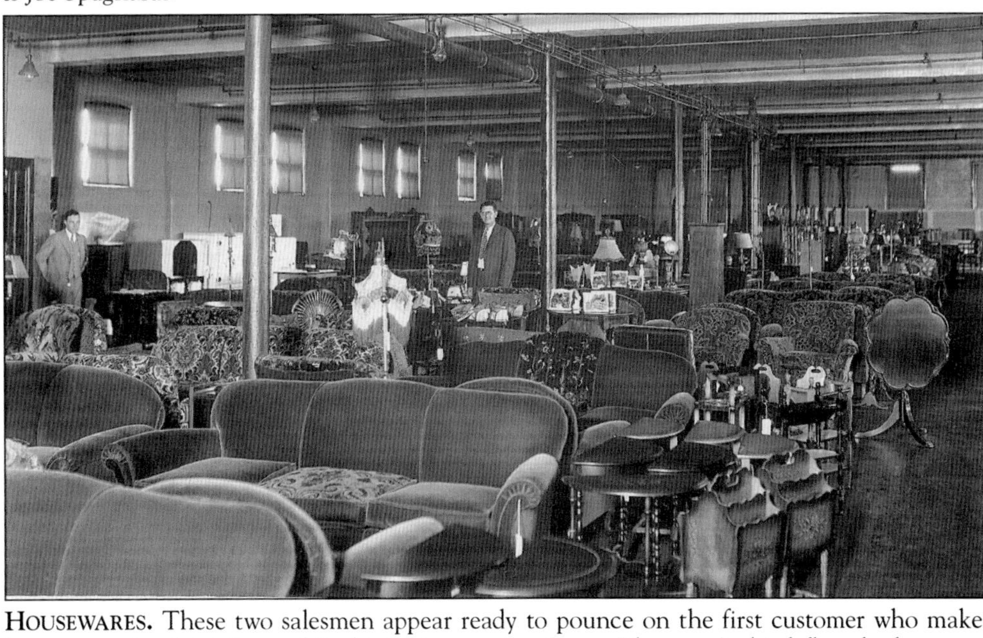

HOUSEWARES. These two salesmen appear ready to pounce on the first customer who makes his way to the third floor of Pushin's Department Store. The store's third floor had more of a Spartan warehouse appearance, but it was a favorite place to find furniture, lamps, and decorative accessories at reasonable prices.

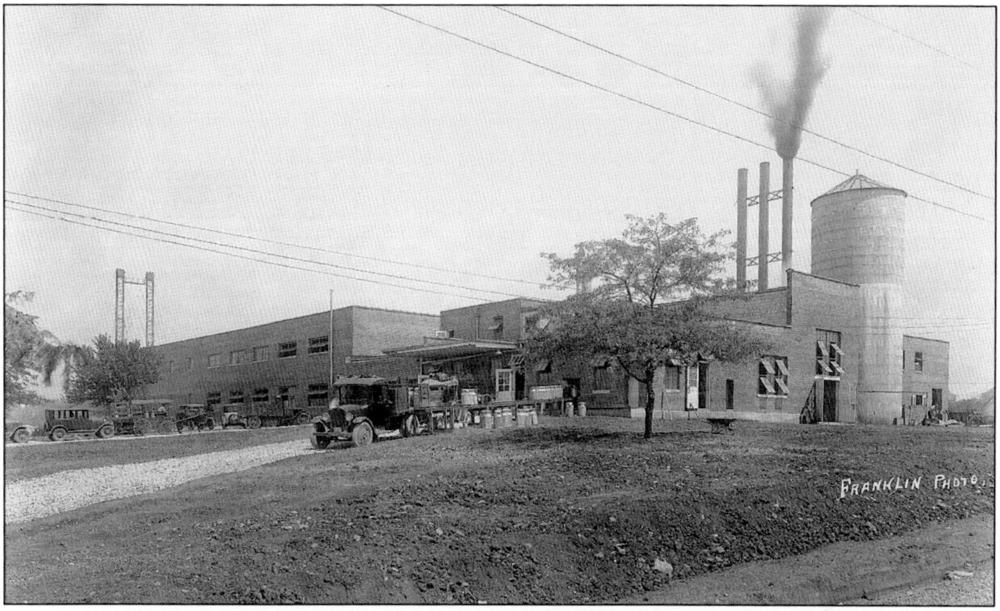

GOT MILK? Pet Milk operated this Church Street plant from 1927 to 1975 to process condensed milk. This plant's milk demand helped Warren County become a top ten milk producing county for several decades. In this 1927 photo, farmers are delivering—via cars and trucks (and if you look carefully one wagon)—cans of fresh milk. The cans were unloaded onto a conveyor that took them into the building.

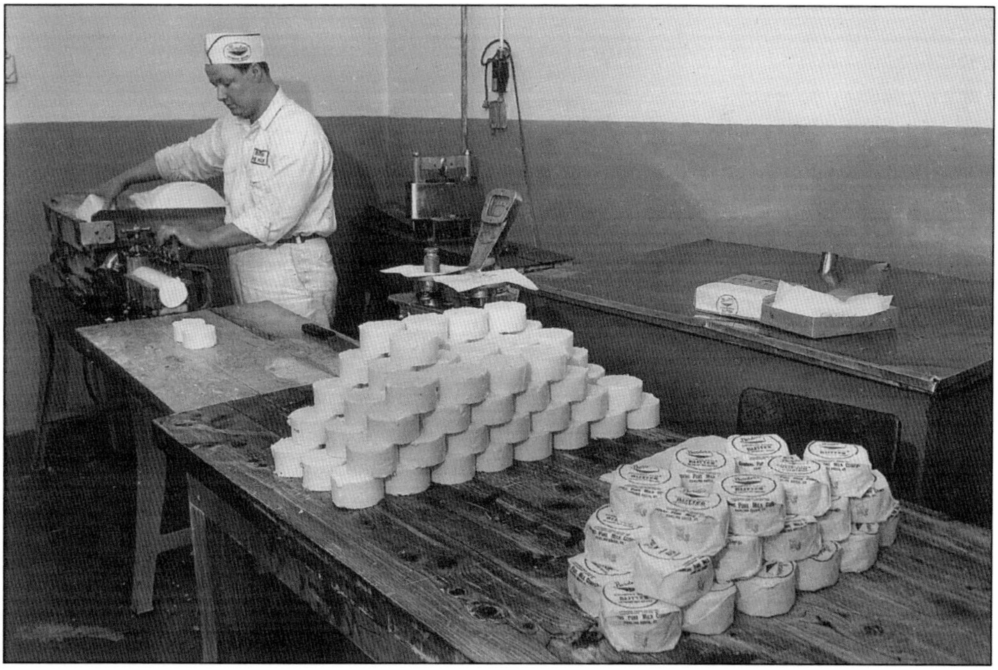

BUTTER HIM UP. This gentleman is cutting butter in rounds for the Border Pure Milk Company. This firm processed all types of dairy products, including milk, sour cream buttermilk, cottage cheese, butter, and ice cream. The Borders processing plant was located at 213 East 10th Street.

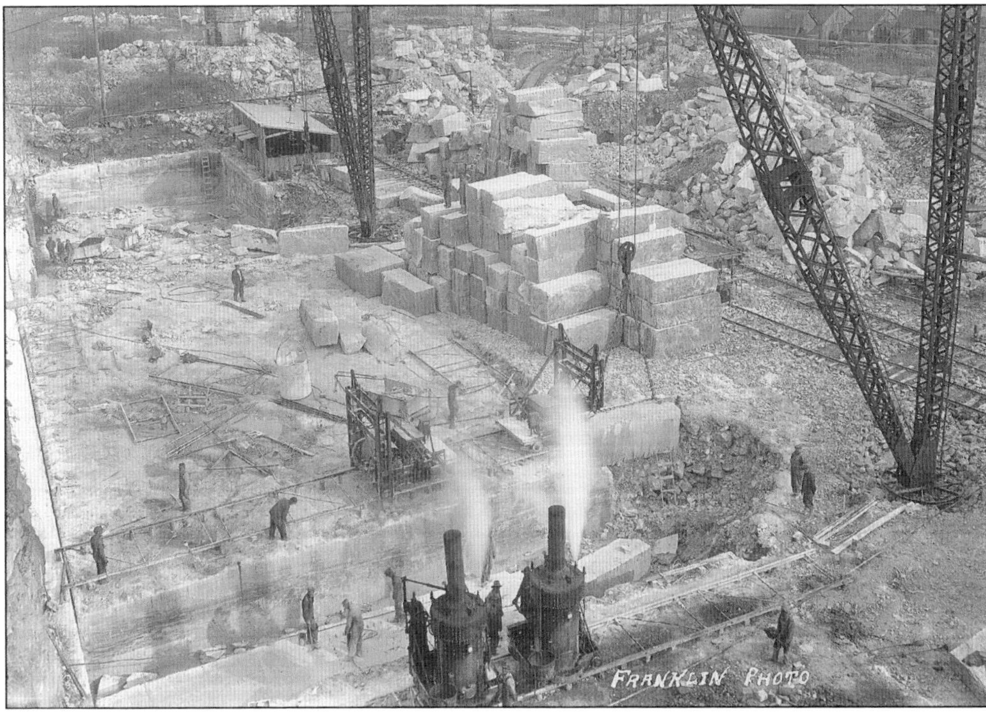

WHITE STONE QUARRY. White oolitic limestone was removed from this quarry, located approximately four miles west of Bowling Green, as early as the 1840s. In 1872, a spur line from the L&N made exploitation of the quarry possible. The stone boasts superior strength and bleaches white when exposed to the sun. Notice the steam-powered machinery used to extricate the stone.

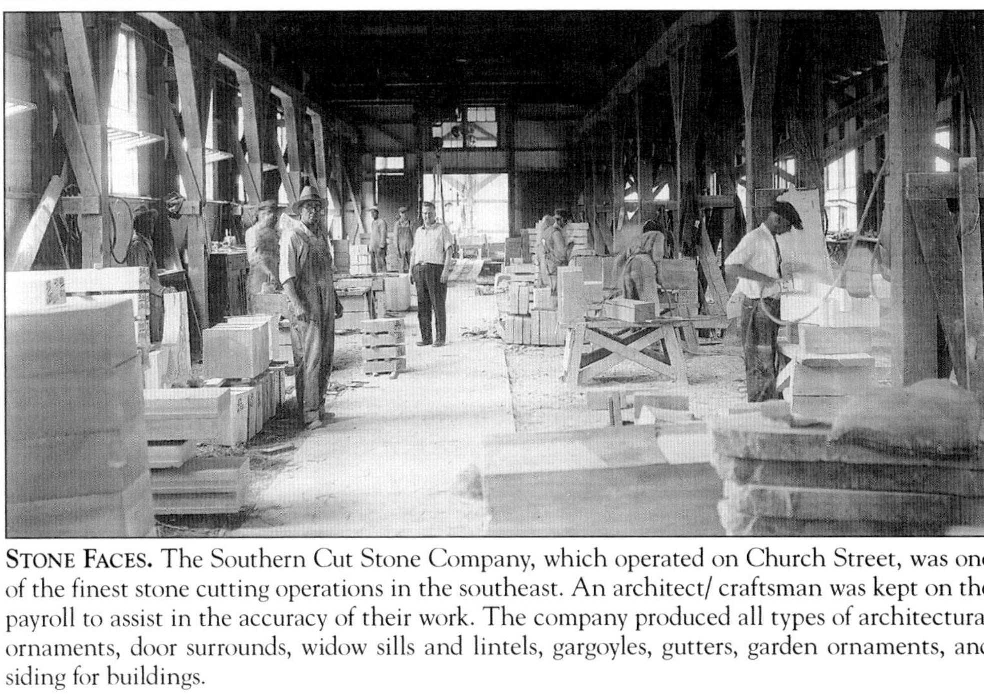

STONE FACES. The Southern Cut Stone Company, which operated on Church Street, was one of the finest stone cutting operations in the southeast. An architect/ craftsman was kept on the payroll to assist in the accuracy of their work. The company produced all types of architectural ornaments, door surrounds, widow sills and lintels, gargoyles, gutters, garden ornaments, and siding for buildings.

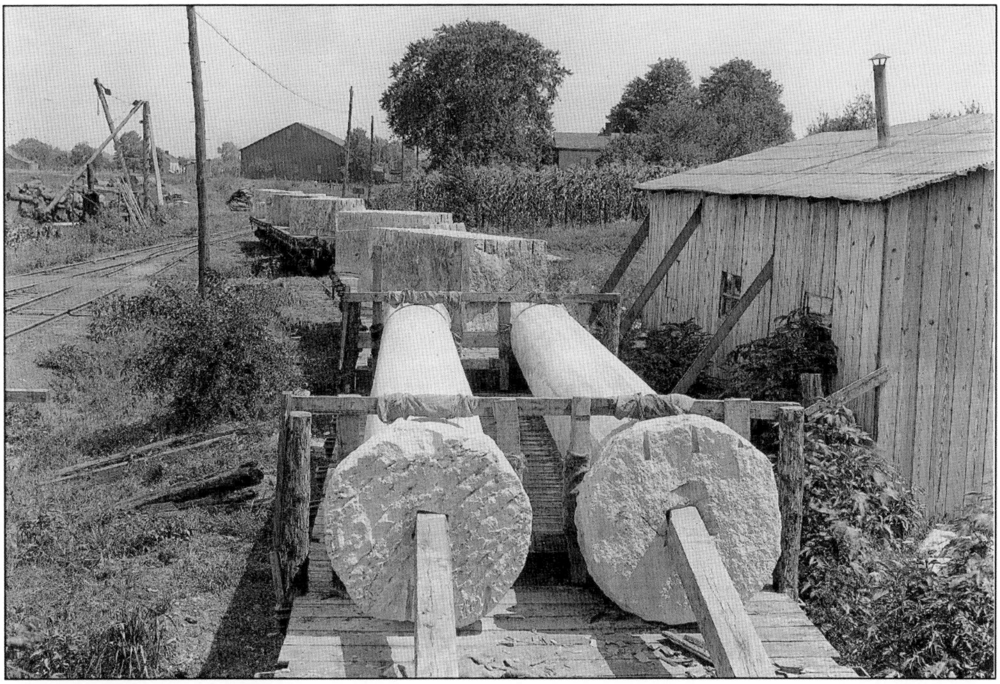

GETTING SHAFTED. The Southern Cut Stone Company turned columns and cut numerous other types of architectural ornaments for builders. Here two columns are loaded on a rail car for shipping.

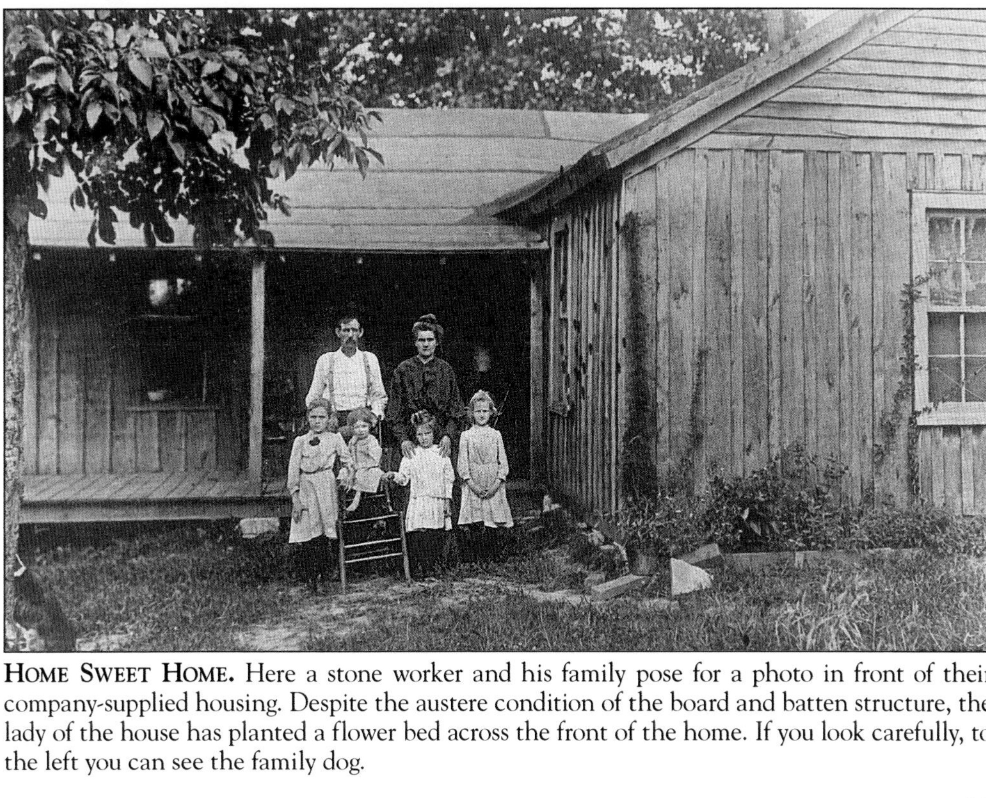

HOME SWEET HOME. Here a stone worker and his family pose for a photo in front of their company-supplied housing. Despite the austere condition of the board and batten structure, the lady of the house has planted a flower bed across the front of the home. If you look carefully, to the left you can see the family dog.

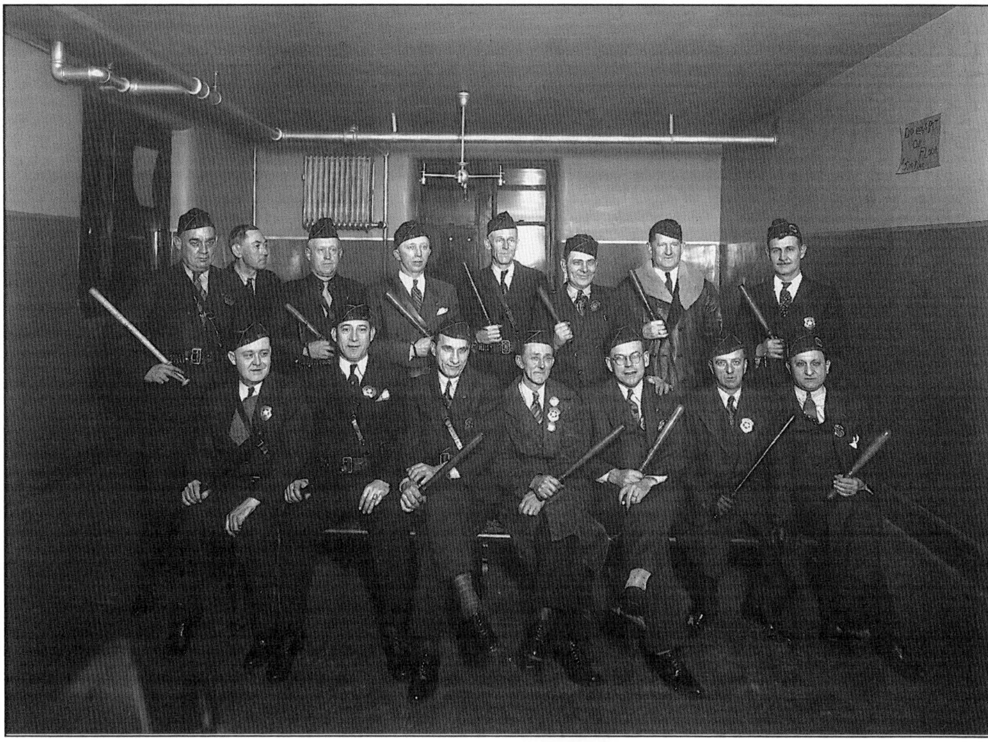

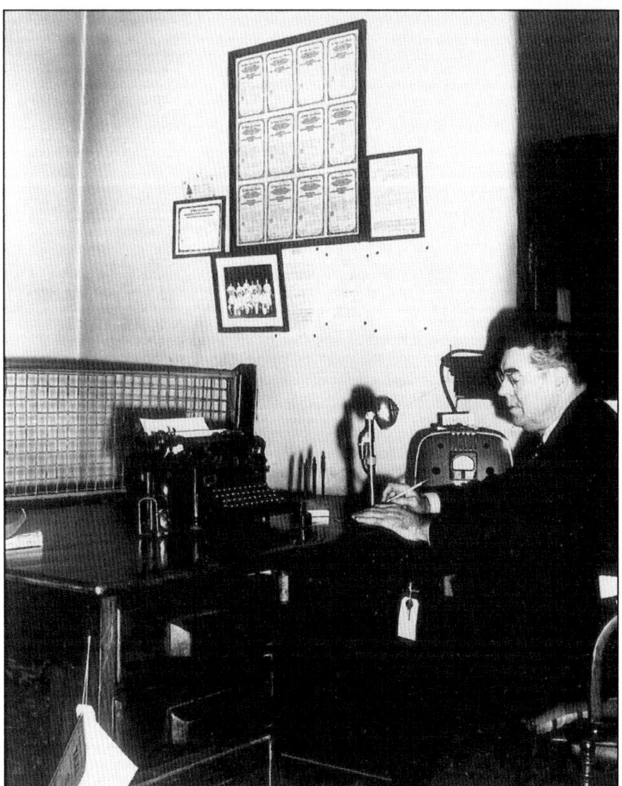

WATCH IT! This group of men from local American Legion Post 23 is taking charge of police duties on March 17, 1938 as a public service activity.

CHIEF OF POLICE. Robert Edward "Ed" Monohan (1886–1949) served as Bowling Green's Chief of Police from 1939 to 1946. He is seen here in his City Hall office. He introduced a two-way radio system and was responsible for implementing fingerprinting technology for the force. Monohan began service with the local police in 1929.

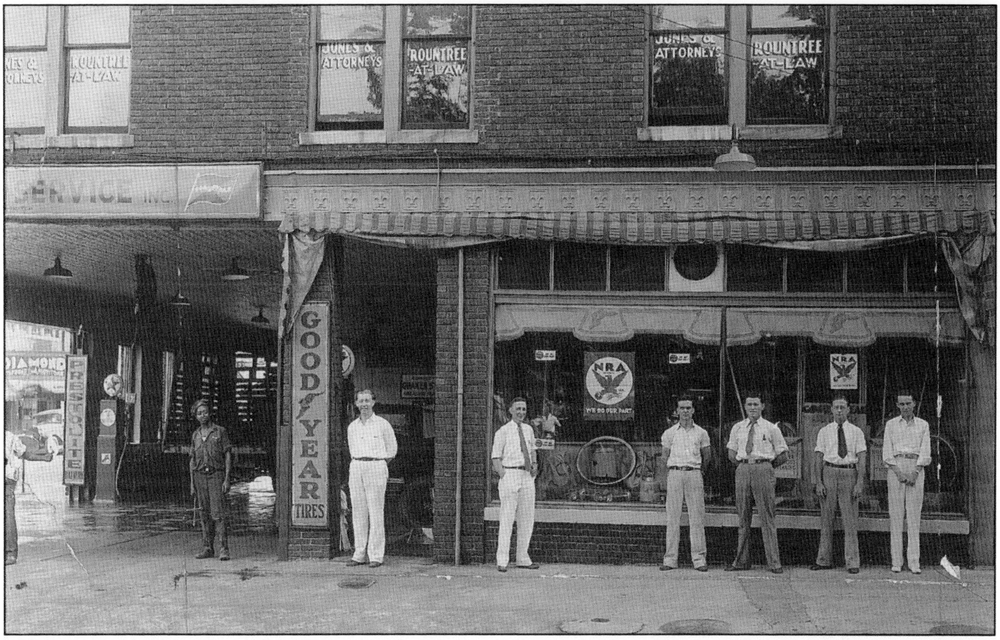

Tire Store. This Goodyear Service Center occupied an enviable location at the corner of 10th and College Streets, directly across from the Warren County Courthouse. The NRA poster in the window indicates the company's participation in the New Deal–era National Recovery Administration, which set wages and product prices. If you look carefully to the left, you can see the Diamond Theater's marquee.

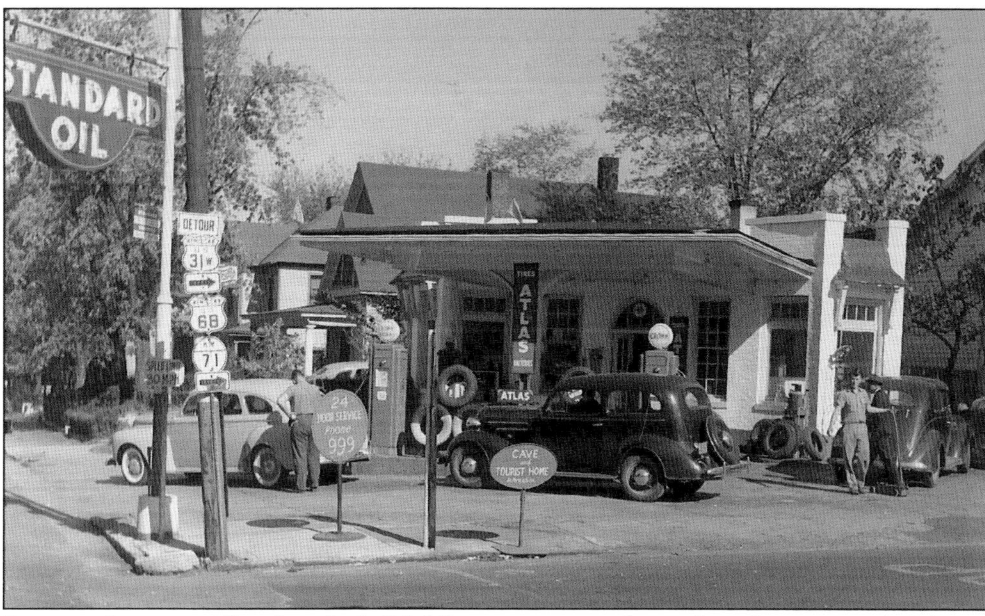

Service Station. This Standard Oil filling station was located at the corner of 13th and Center Streets. Before self-service pumps, service was a key word at a filling station. This station offers "24 hour service" and "cave and tourist home information" to patrons. This is a good example of an early station; garages were attached to such stations in the 1940s to offer more service and consequently more business.

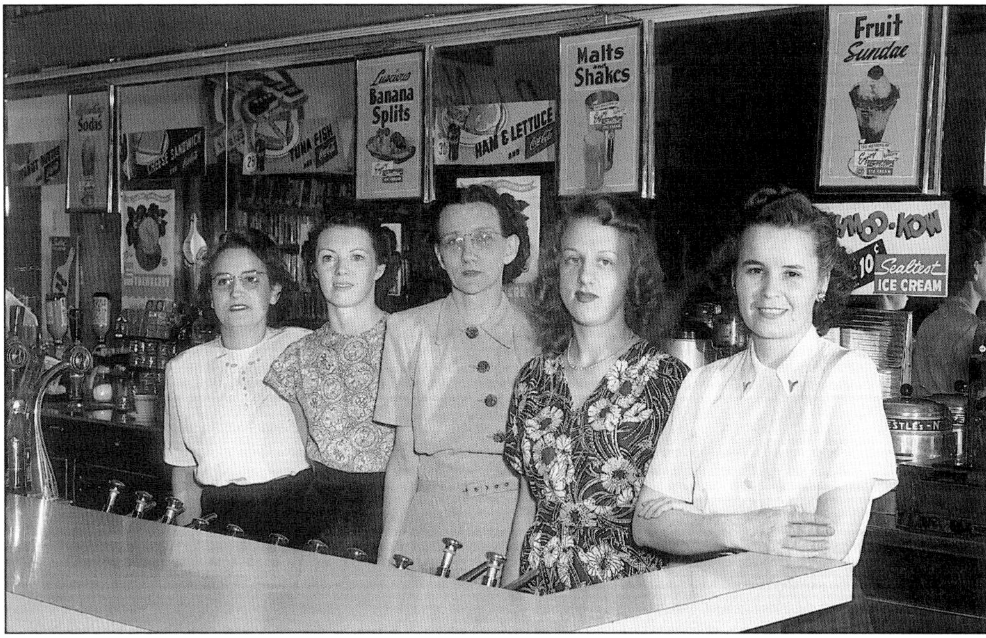

Fountain Fairies. CDS #4, a drugstore located at 1002 State Street in the Price Building, employed these ladies at its soda fountain. The popular downtown eateries usually featured sandwiches, but some stores, such as Woolworth's, boasted a good lunch plate special every day. In this 1940s photograph, a cheese or tuna fish sandwich was served for a quarter and a chocolate shake for a dime.

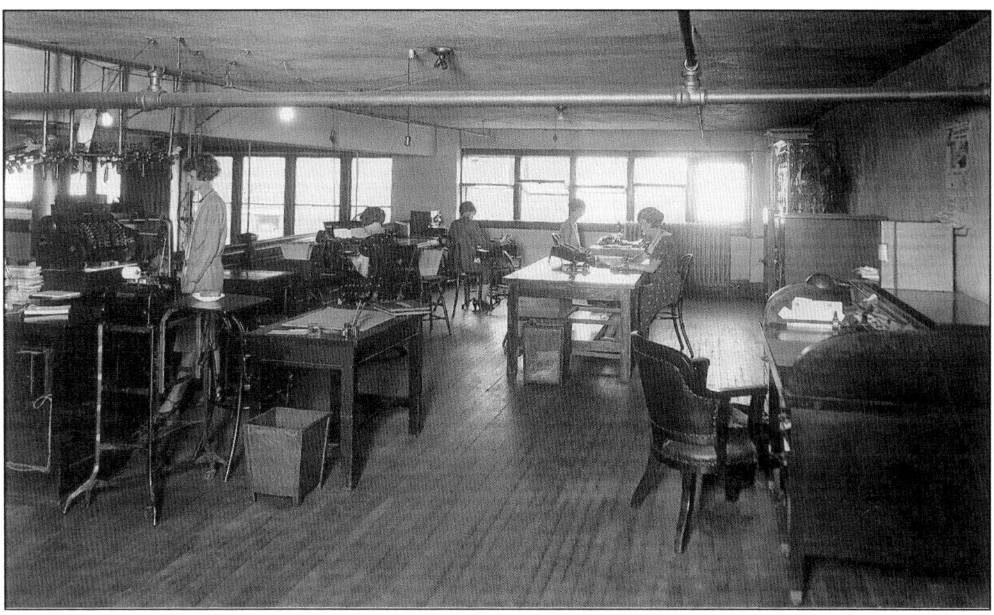

Money Changers. Clerking in a store was one of the few jobs open to women in the first half of the 20th century. These women were employed by Sam Pushin at his downtown department store. Clerks throughout the store totaled merchandise on tickets, which were sent with cash to the office on the mezzanine level via pneumatic tubes. The cashier, on the left, rang up sales and returned any change and the receipt.

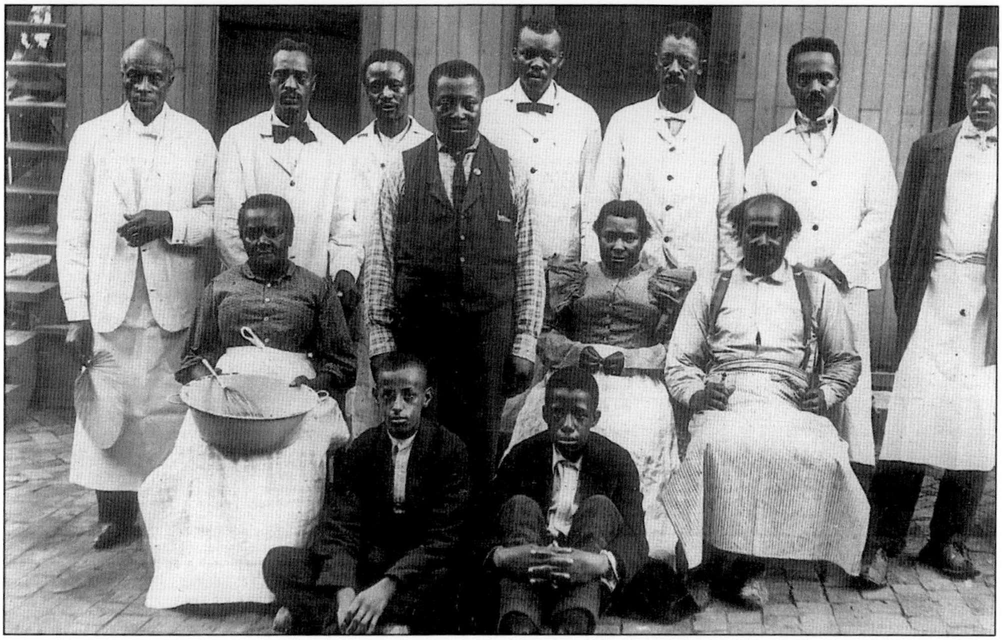

Morehead House Crew. These African Americans represent the kitchen and wait staff of the old Morehead House hotel near the turn of the century. The Morehead House, at the corner of Main and State Streets, was known for superior food and service. It was razed in the early 1920s to make room for the Helm Hotel.

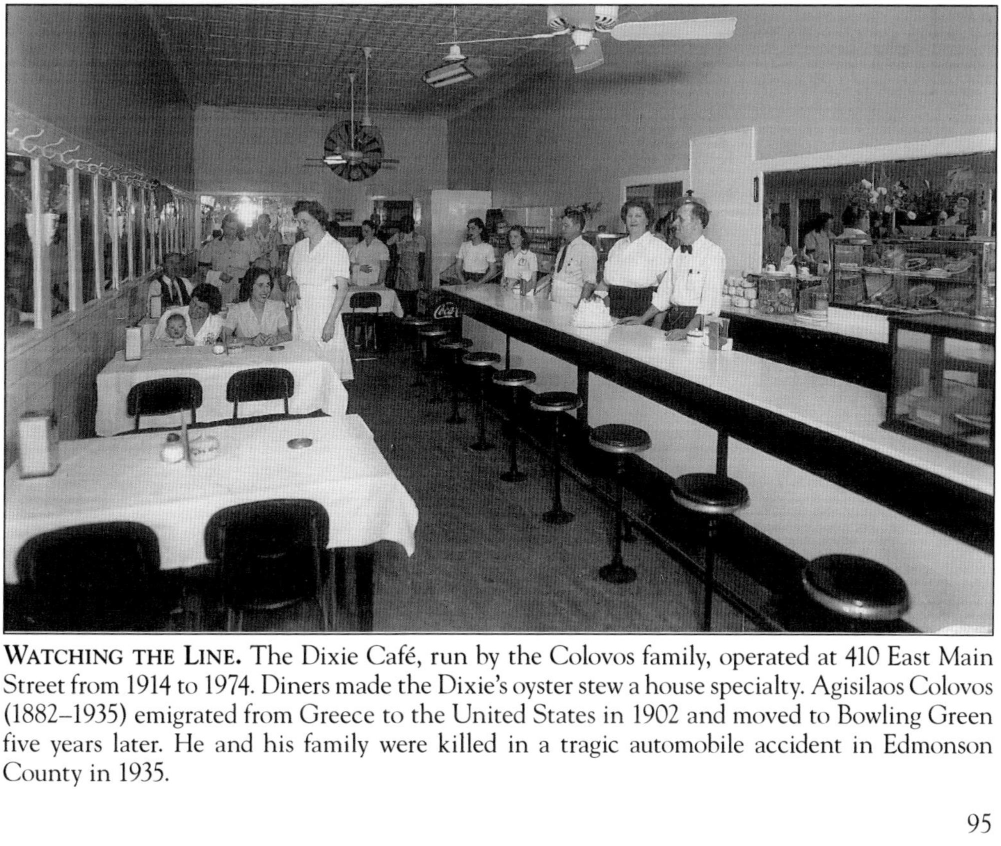

Watching the Line. The Dixie Café, run by the Colovos family, operated at 410 East Main Street from 1914 to 1974. Diners made the Dixie's oyster stew a house specialty. Agisilaos Colovos (1882–1935) emigrated from Greece to the United States in 1902 and moved to Bowling Green five years later. He and his family were killed in a tragic automobile accident in Edmonson County in 1935.

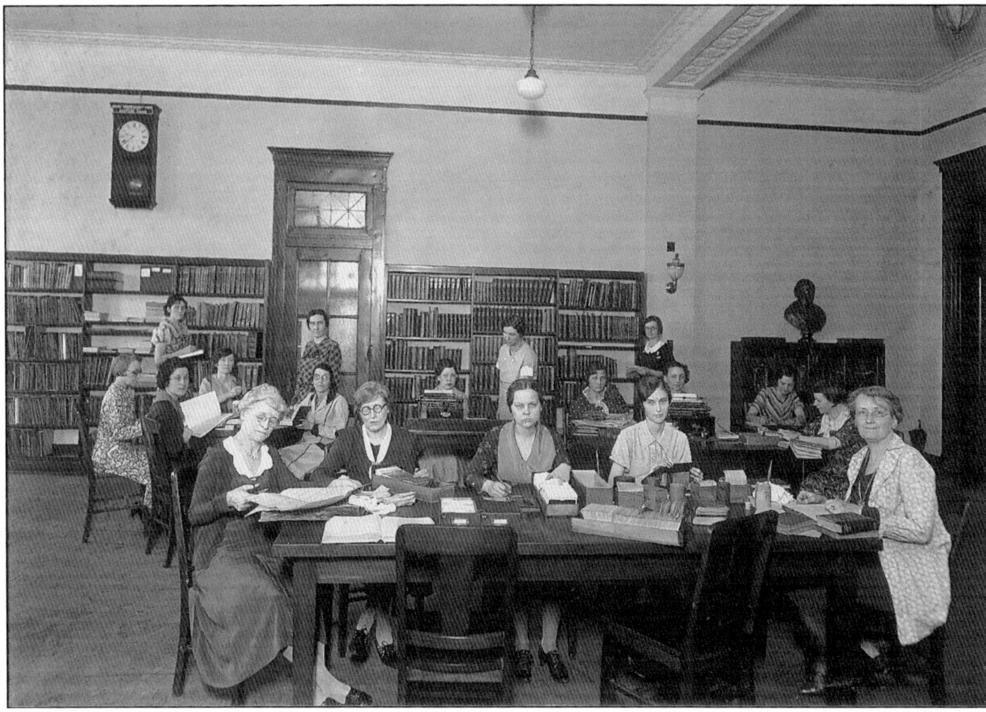

LIBRARY WORKERS. These ladies are participating in a work program sponsored by the Federal Emergency Relief Administration during the Great Depression. They are clipping newspapers, cataloging and repairing books, and typescripting old records for the Kentucky Library at Western Kentucky University.

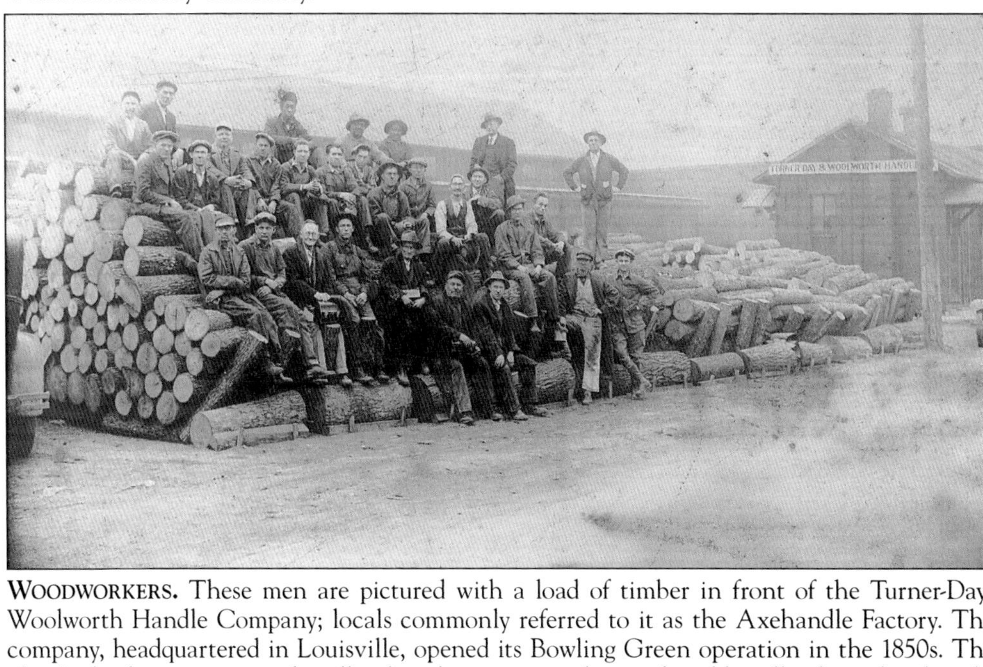

WOODWORKERS. These men are pictured with a load of timber in front of the Turner-Day-Woolworth Handle Company; locals commonly referred to it as the Axehandle Factory. The company, headquartered in Louisville, opened its Bowling Green operation in the 1850s. The plant's chief output was axehandles, but the company also produced handles for picks, shovels, and other handtools. The company once boasted that it made 2,400 different types of handles.

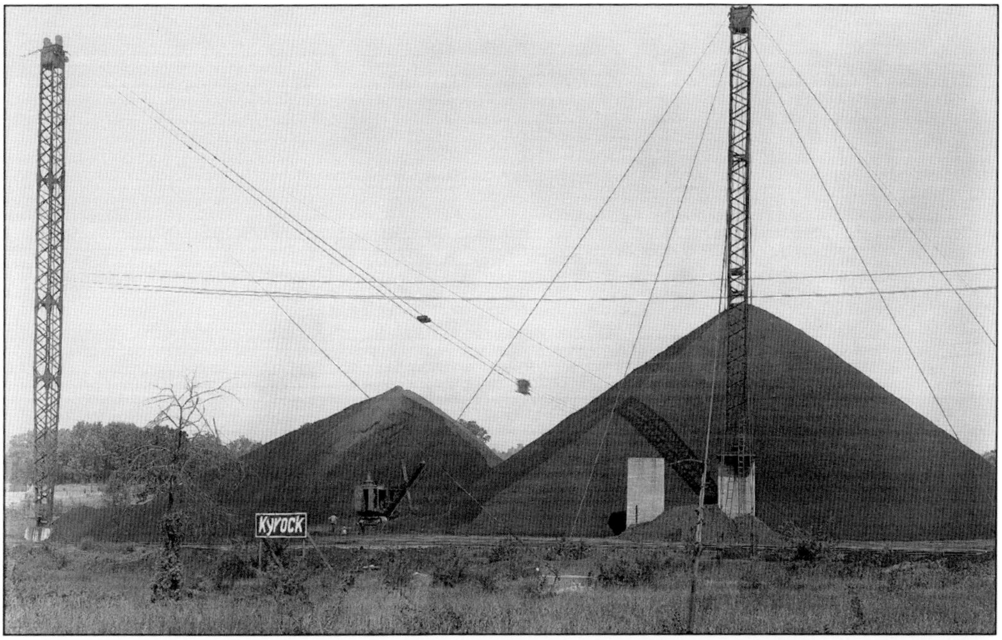

PAVING THE WAY. Natural rock asphalt was mined in abundance near Kyrock in Edmonson County, but most of it was shipped from Bowling Green via barges or railroad to over 35 states. Chicago's State Street was once paved with high-grade asphalt from this region. This shipping yard was located at the boatlanding, near the end of Church Street.

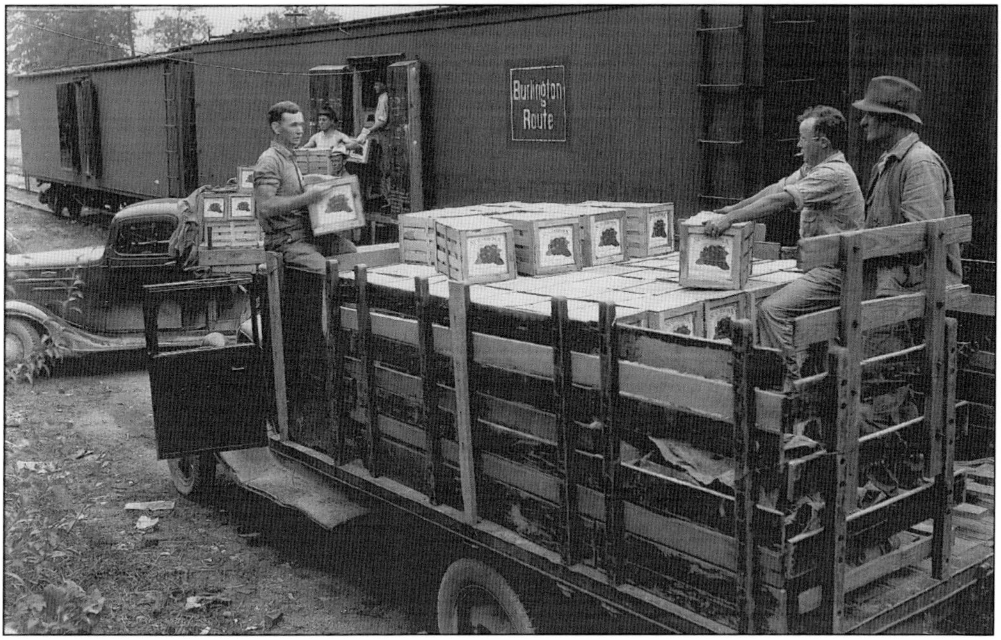

STRAWBERRIES. Local promoters once referred to Warren County as the "Strawberry Capital of the World." Strawberry growers' associations helped purchase supplies and plants, and more importantly, they helped recruit labor and market the fruit. In 1916, the associations banded together to build strawberry loading sheds on a spur off the L&N railroad downtown. The boxes being loaded are filled with Aroma berries, the most popular in the region.

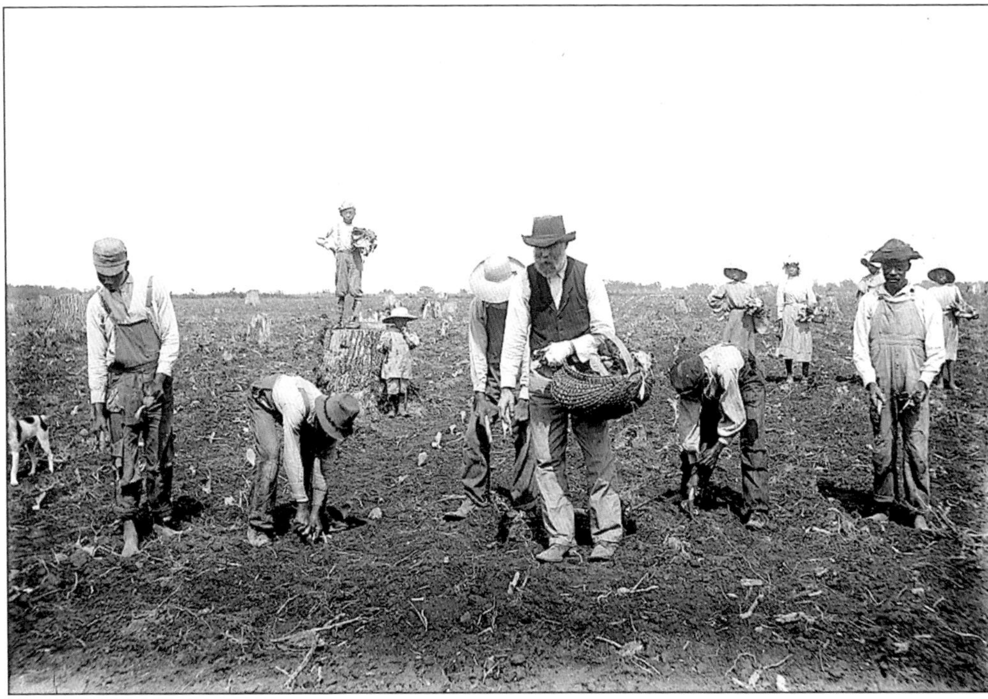

SETTING. Tobacco remains Kentucky's chief cash crop. Planters usually worked in crews when "setting plants." The older gentleman in the center and the crew in the background are carrying baskets of seedlings which were laid out in rows at regular intervals. Another group followed inserting the plants into the ground with a little tool, which was sometimes just a curved stick. After planting the farmer prayed for a good growing season.

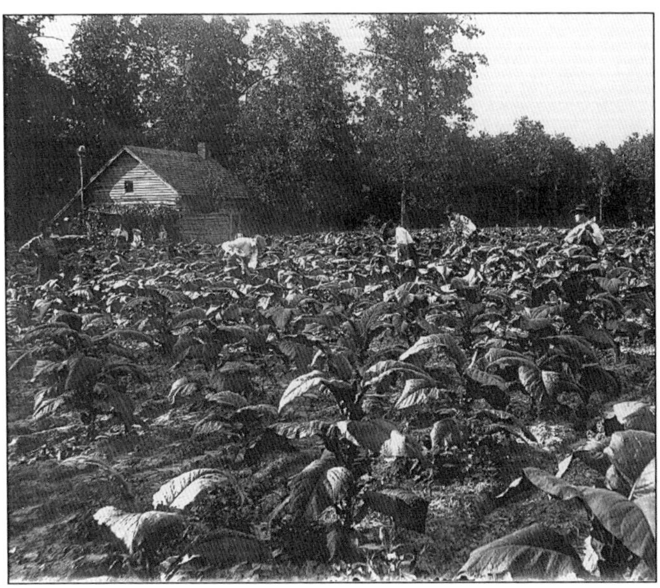

INSPECTING. These men and boys are out inspecting the tobacco for tobacco worms and disease. Tobacco worms are large green caterpillars that were extracted from the plants by hand and manually executed or placed in buckets of kerosene or water. Here we actually have a man with guitar in hand either crooning the workers or just goofing off. An outdoor summer kitchen can be seen in the background.

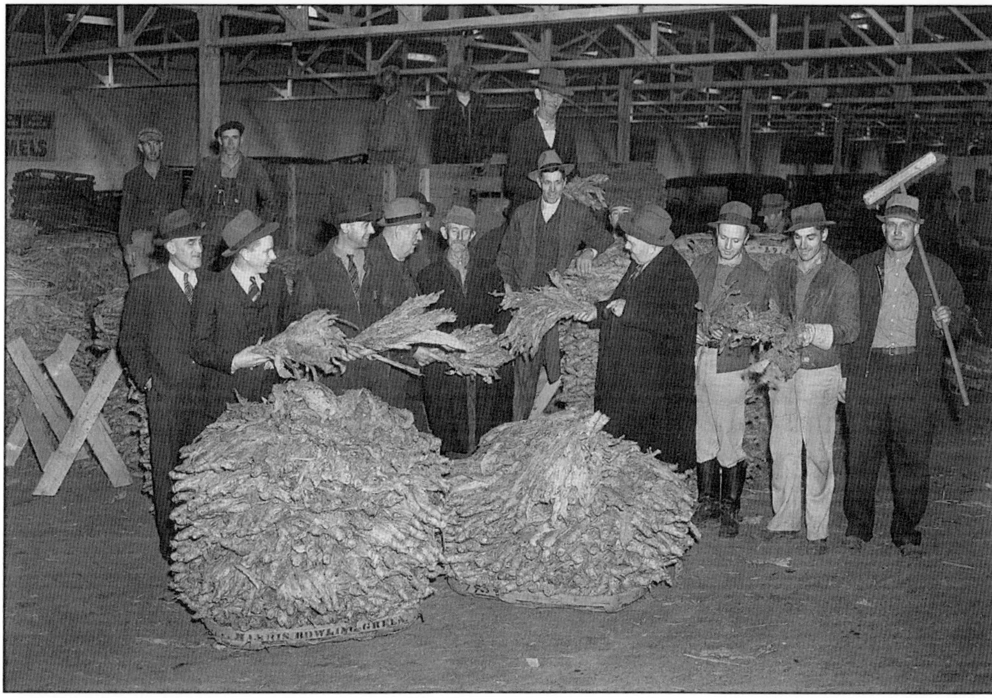

BUYERS AND SELLERS. Buyers and sellers are gathered in early December 1941 at Bowling Green's Farmers Tobacco Warehouse to inspect and grade the crop. E.P. Harris served as the manager of this large facility located at 730 East 5th Street.

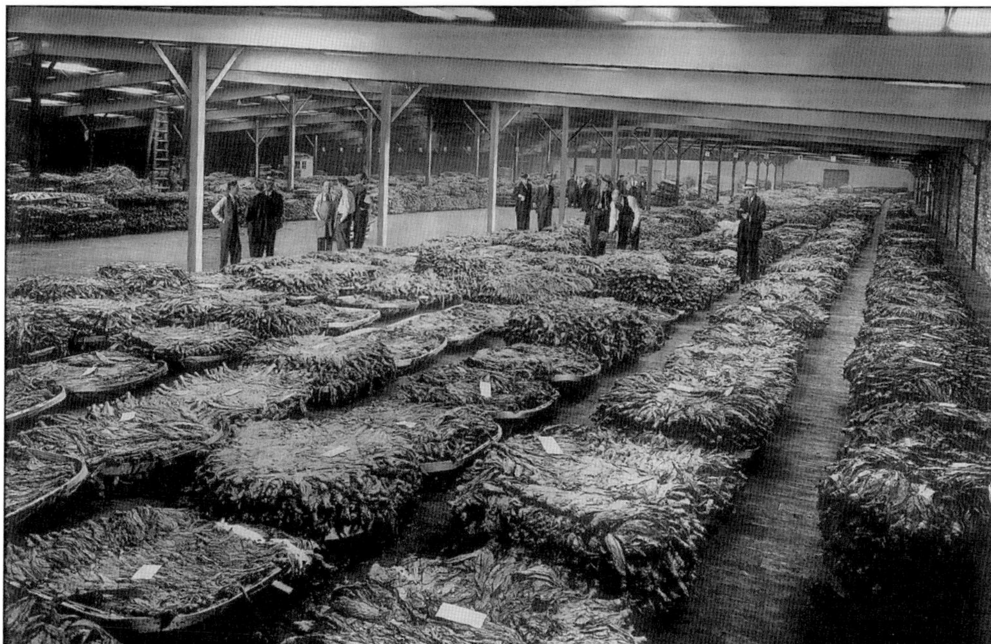

STACKED UP. This warehouse photo from 1941 shows the tobacco tied in hands and stacked ready for the auctioneer to move up and down the aisles for sale. The tobacco baskets, which were usually marked with the warehouse name, are now collectors' items.

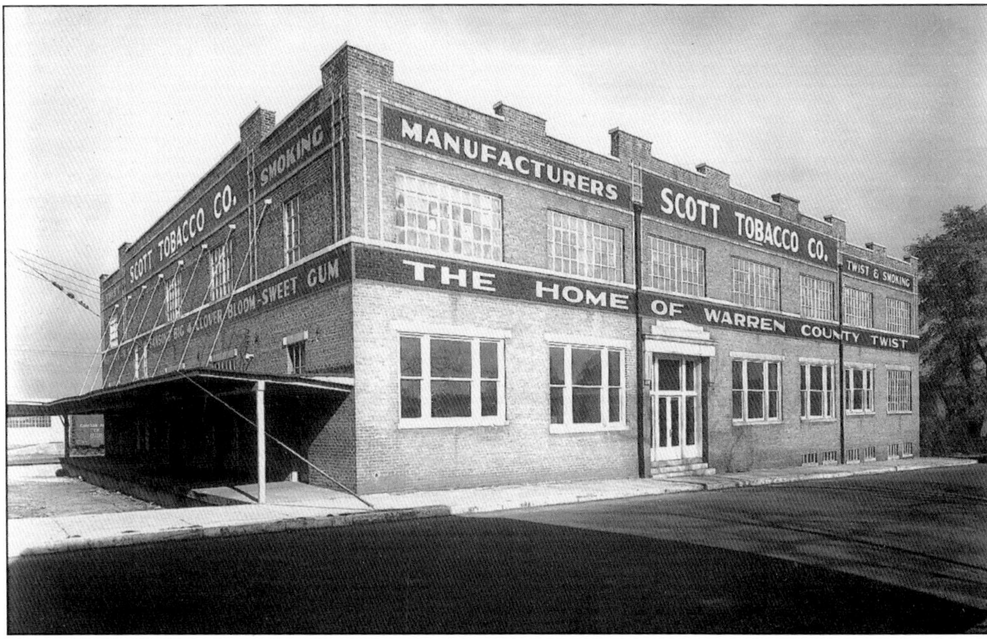

SCOTT TOBACCO. Local tobacco was sold chiefly as filler for cigarettes, but some was processed locally into loose smoking tobacco and chewing tobacco. The Scott Tobacco Company was founded in 1900 by H. Brown Scott and moved to this building in 1939. At one time, this facility, which is still in existence at the corner of 10th and Adams Streets, produced 19 different brands of tobacco products.

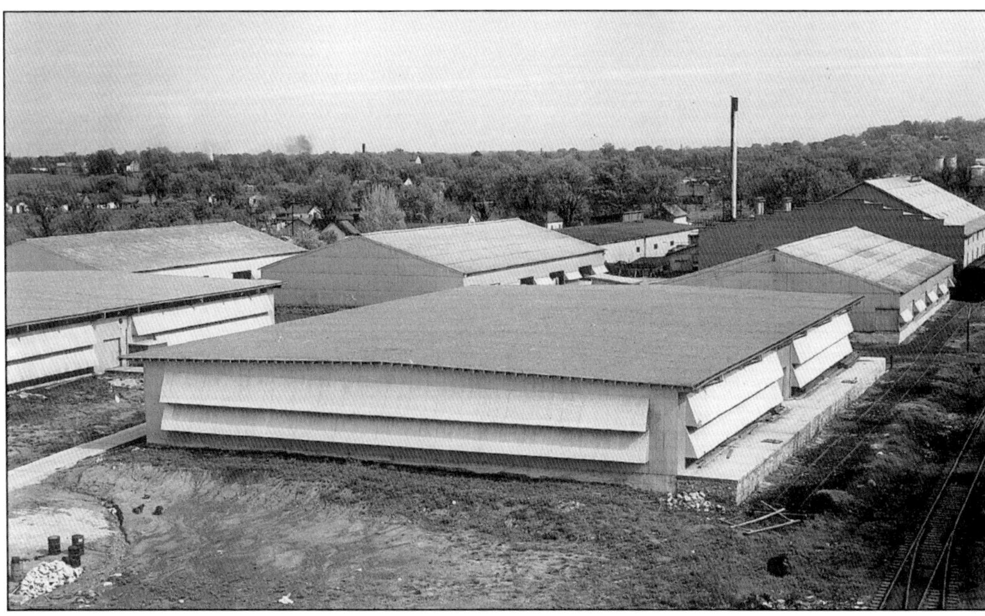

BURFORD TOBACCO. The Burford Tobacco Company was founded by William L. Burford in 1914. The company served as a buyer for Brown & Williamson Tobacco Company. Its warehouses and redryer were located on Hope Street. Mr. Burford was a director of the United States Tobacco Association and was one of the founders of the Burley Tobacco Leaf Association.

Five

BOWLING GREEN AT SCHOOL AND CHURCH

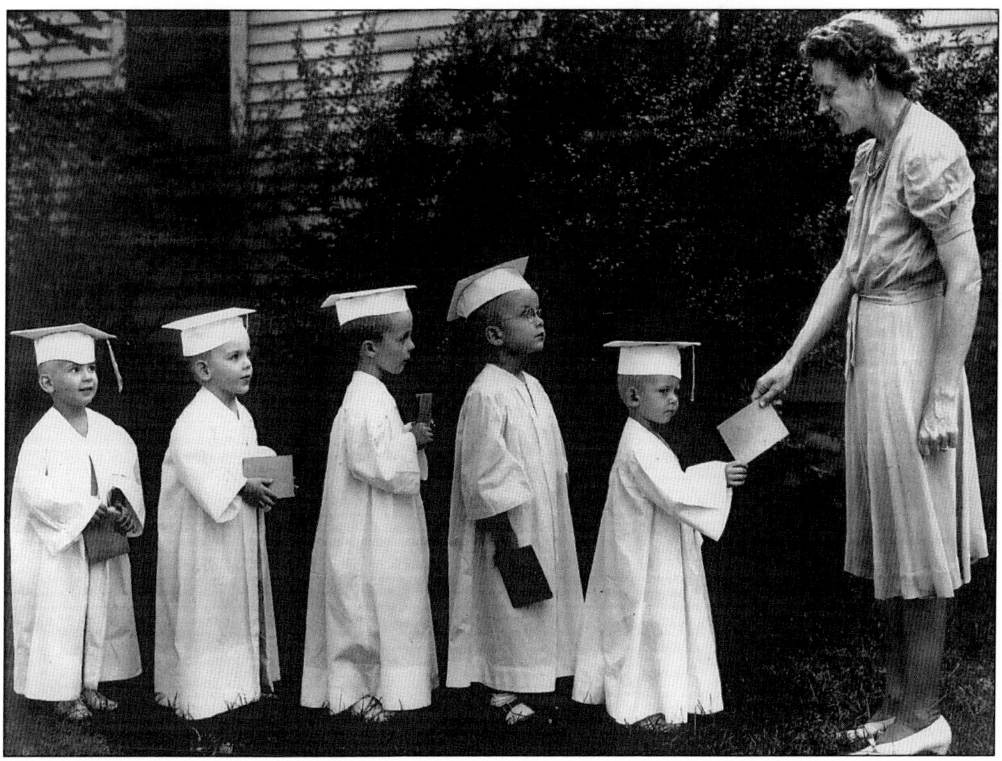

TOT SCHOLARS. These children are receiving diplomas from Cornelia H. McGeehee, who operated Bowling Green's first "play school" or kindergarten back in the 1940s at 513 East 17th Street. Those receiving diplomas, from left to right, are Thomas Urban, James Gilbert, Samuel Woosley, Joseph Givens, and James Cowgill.

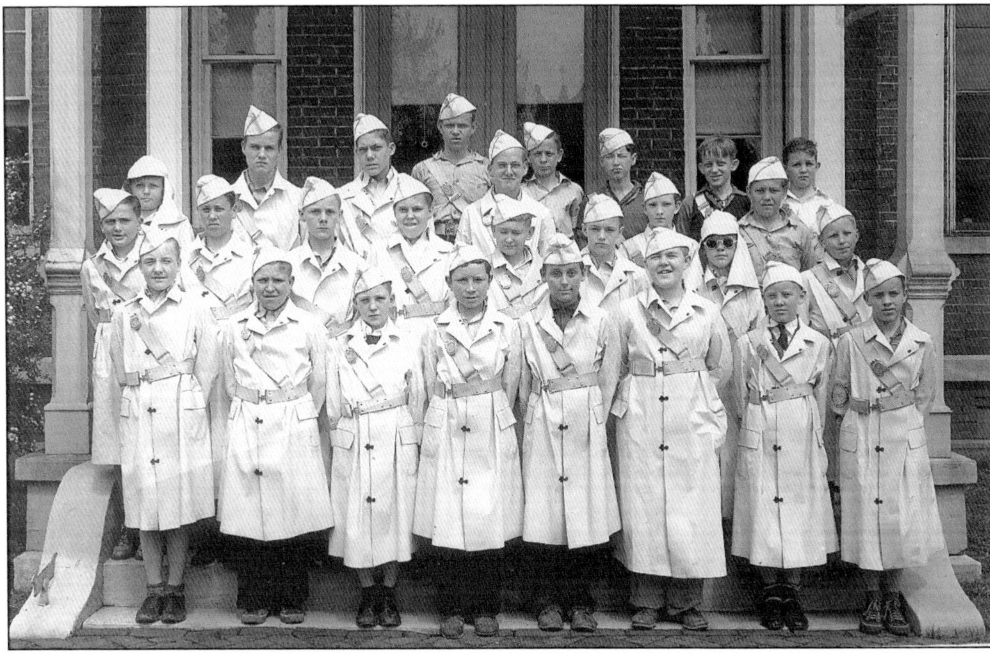

Don't Cross Them. This fine looking group of boys represents the crossing guards for College Street Elementary School. They served an important role for a school located in a very busy downtown neighborhood. Notice the cool cat in the second row with his sunglasses. The boys are posed on the school's College Street entrance.

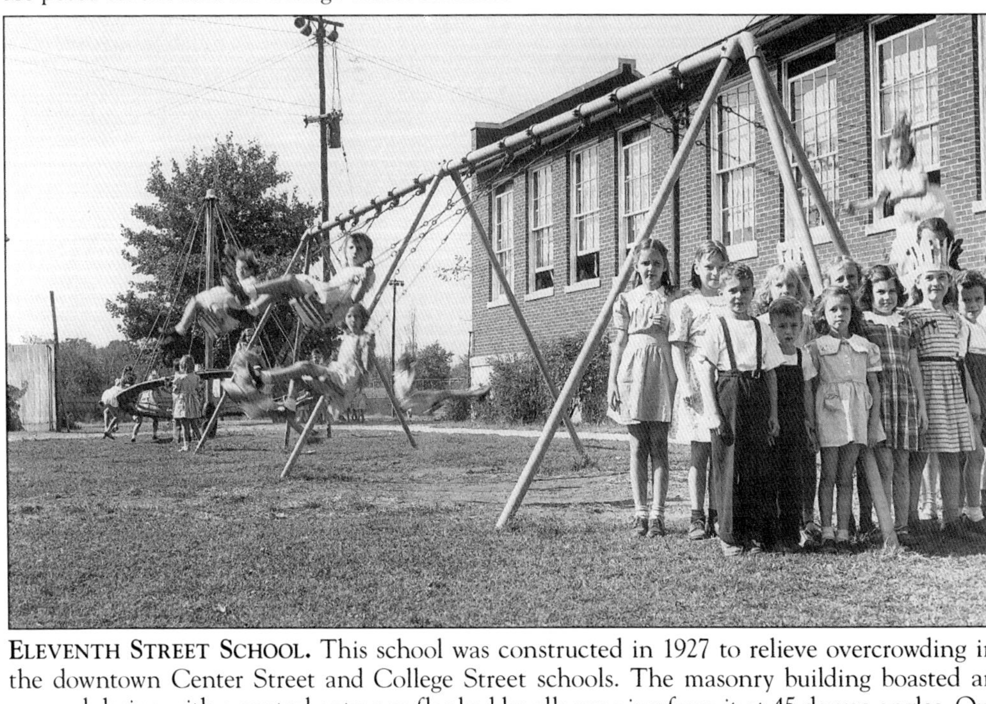

Eleventh Street School. This school was constructed in 1927 to relieve overcrowding in the downtown Center Street and College Street schools. The masonry building boasted an unusual design with a central entrance flanked by ells running from it at 45 degree angles. Out on the playground, those not posing for the camera are busy on the swings or on the unusual merry-go-round.

SMALL TIME VIRTUOSO. Little Sarah Josephine Porter, at only 3 years of age, learns how to properly handle the bow in 1927.

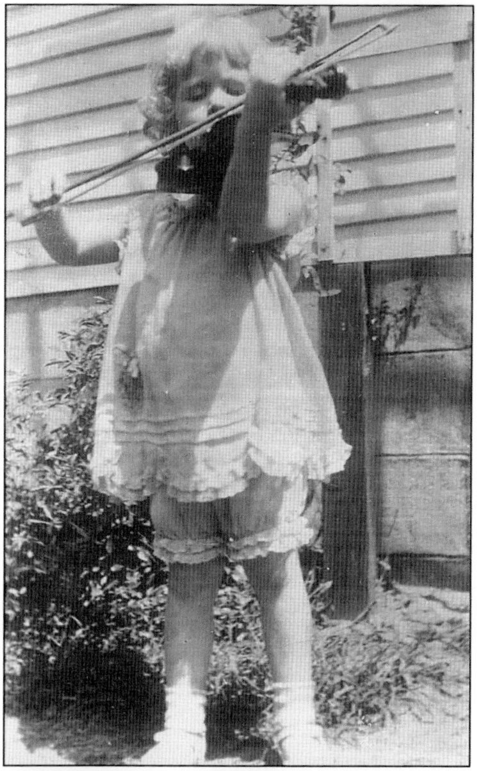

GIRL SCOUTS. Mrs. W.A. Hampton organized the first Girl Scout troop in Bowling Green in 1920. The movement was strengthened in the early 1930s through the work of Frances Gregory. This group is meeting at the Westminster Presbyterian Church with Rev. Dewey Kimbell. The exquisite stained glass windows were memorial gifts from parishioners.

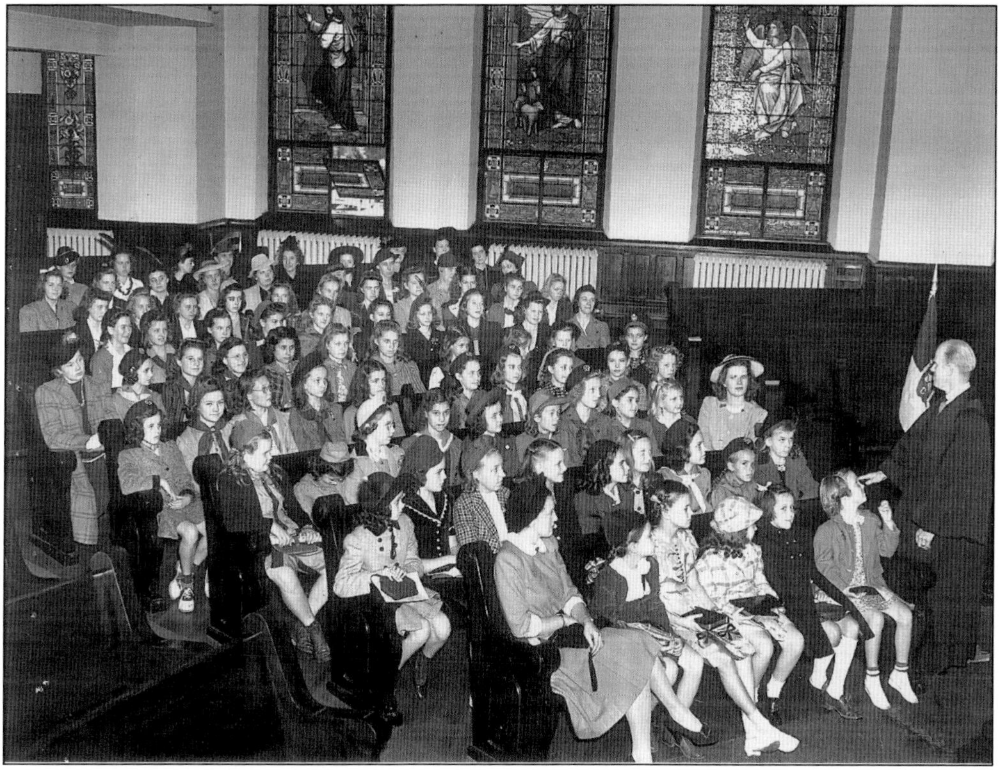

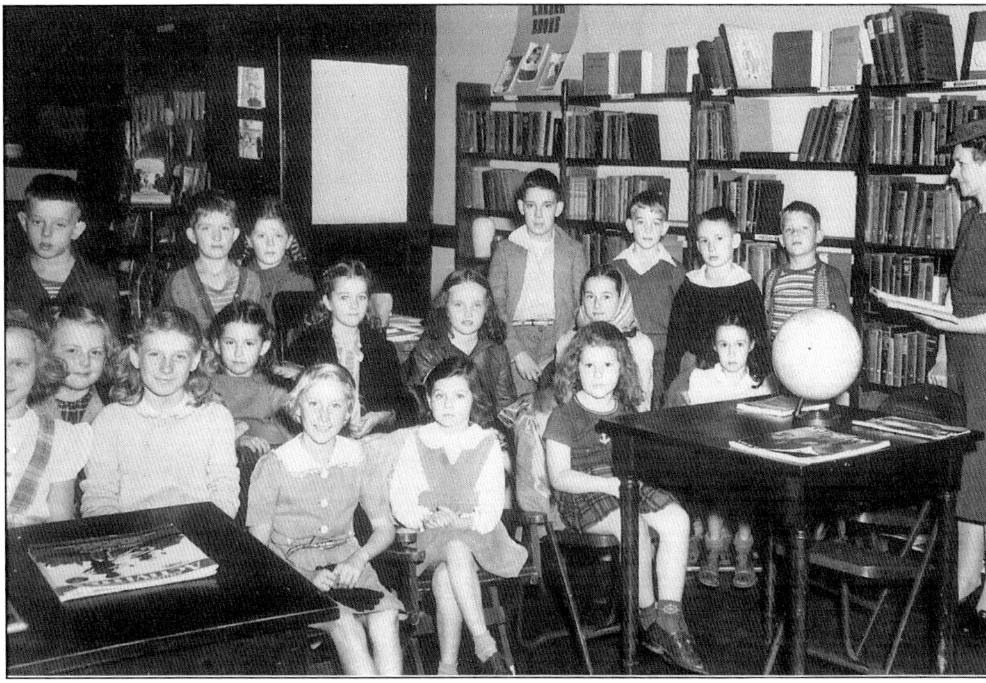

READING LESSONS. The Bowling Green Public Library started out as a Works Progress Administration project in the Helm Hotel. It moved to the Denhardt Armory on 10th Street in the early 1940s and was located there when it burned in December 1946, destroying the book collection. In this 1944 photo, Mrs. Emmett Daniel conducts a story hour in the Boys and Girls Room.

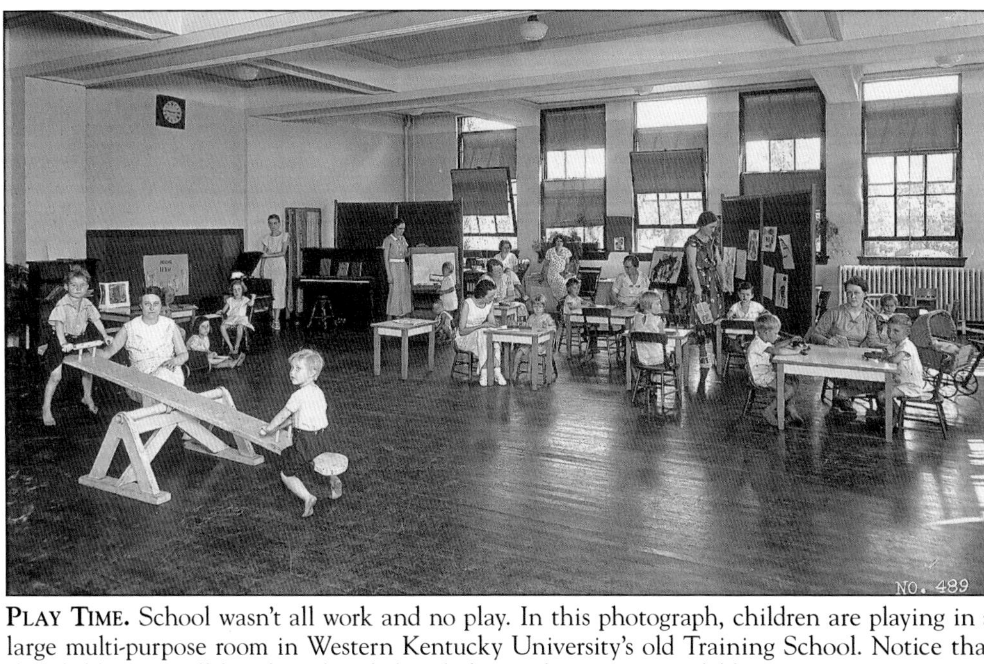

PLAY TIME. School wasn't all work and no play. In this photograph, children are playing in a large multi-purpose room in Western Kentucky University's old Training School. Notice that the children are all barefooted and the plethora of activities available: seesawing, art, music, and creative play.

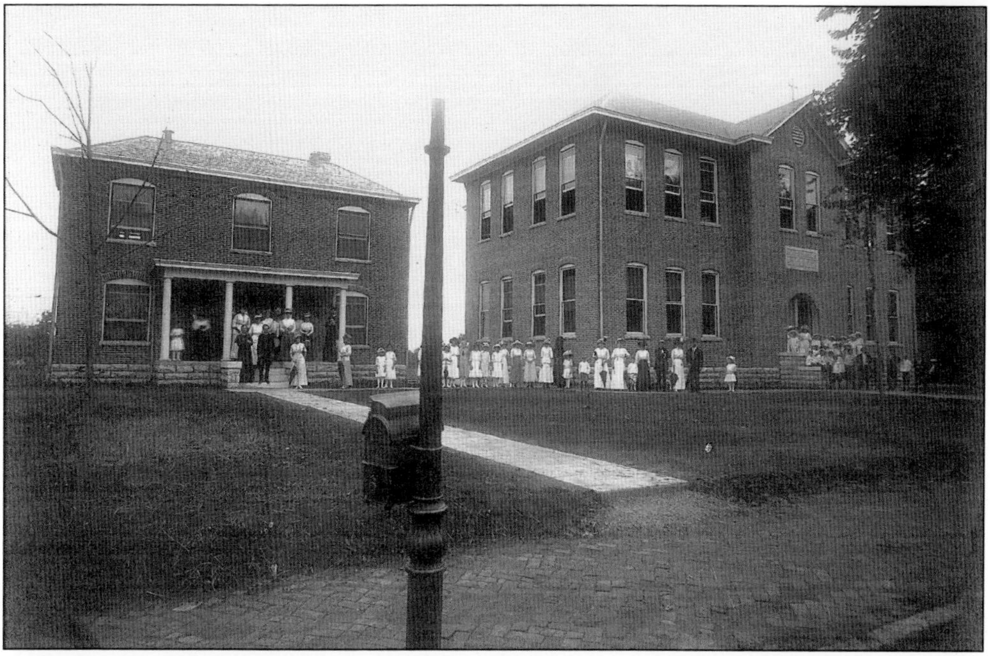

ST. JOSEPH CATHOLIC SCHOOL. Parents have gathered along with their children for a photo at St. Joseph's. The school, which opened in 1912, was located in the larger building on the right. The nuns who operated the school lived in the house on the left. The buildings, appropriately located on Church Street, are still standing.

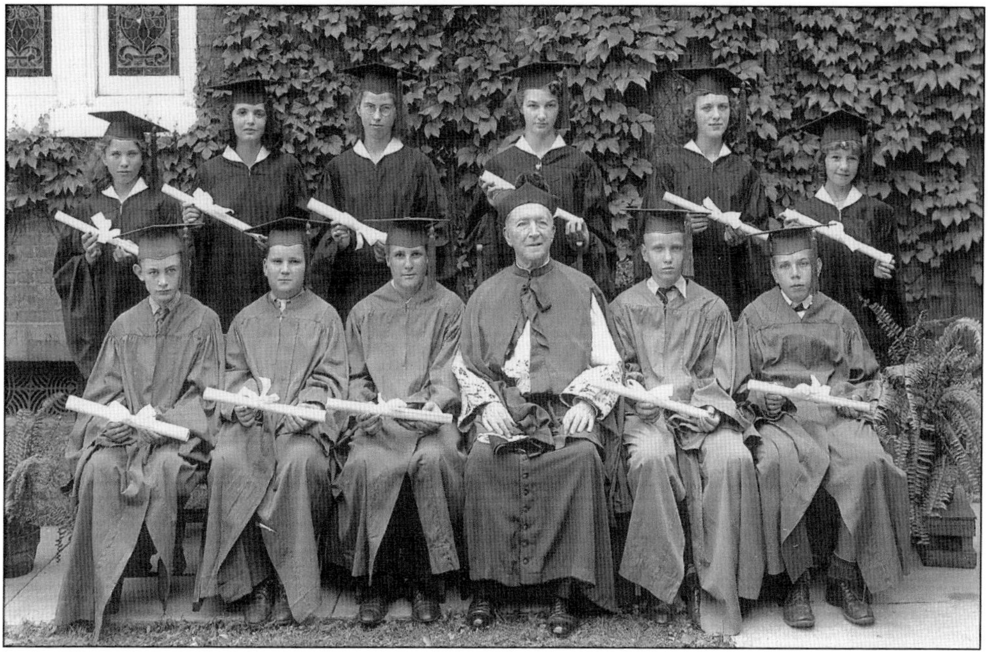

SCHOLARS. This group constitutes the St. Joseph Catholic School Class of 1940. The priest in the middle is Thomas Jefferson Hayes (1858–1946), who served at St. Joseph for 54 years. He died only three years after his resignation at the age of 85 and was buried in St. Joseph Catholic Cemetery.

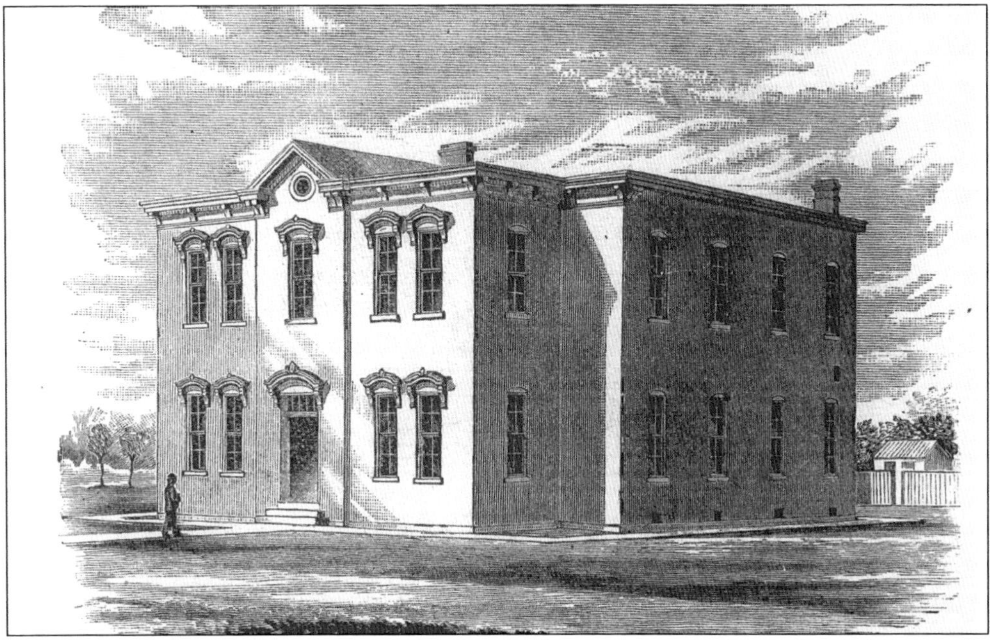

AFRICAN AMERICAN SCHOOL. Bowling Green offered primary and secondary education for African Americans in the segregated State Street School. This building was opened in the mid-1880s and was closed when High Street School was built in 1954. The school's gymnasium still stands on the old schoolyard at 200 State Street.

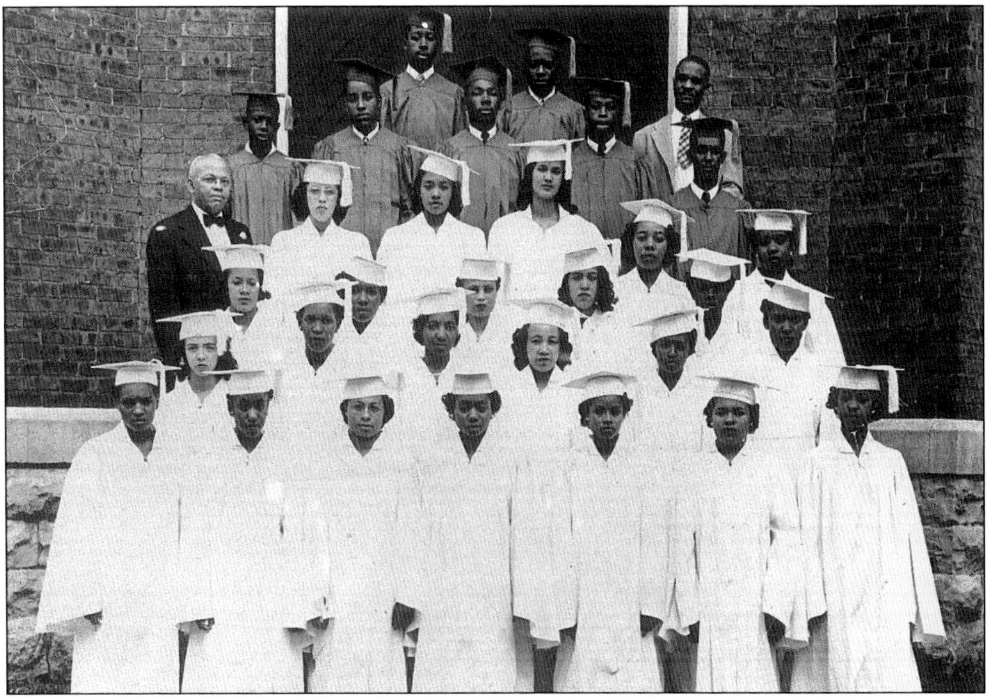

STATE STREET GRADUATES. These 7 men and 23 young ladies compose the graduating class of 1946. The group is posed on the front steps of State Street Baptist Church where graduation exercises were held.

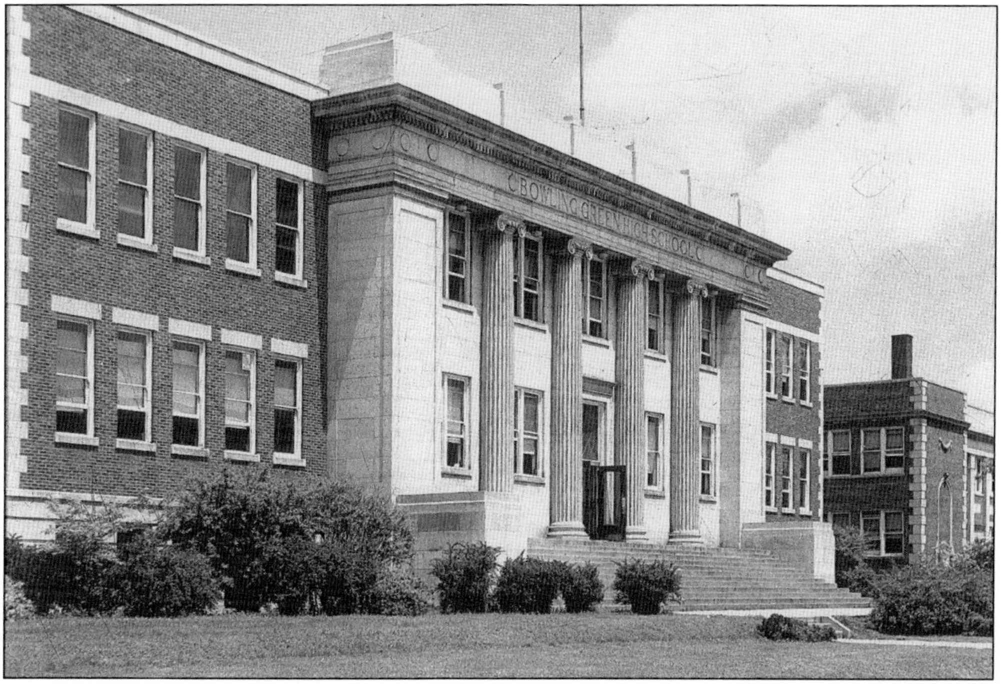

BOWLING GREEN HIGH SCHOOL. This Classical Revival building, designed by Clifford Shopbell and Company of Evansville, was completed in 1923 at a cost of $100,000. Bowling Green Junior High, the building to the right, was constructed in 1929. The high school moved in 1970 and the junior high left in 2001.

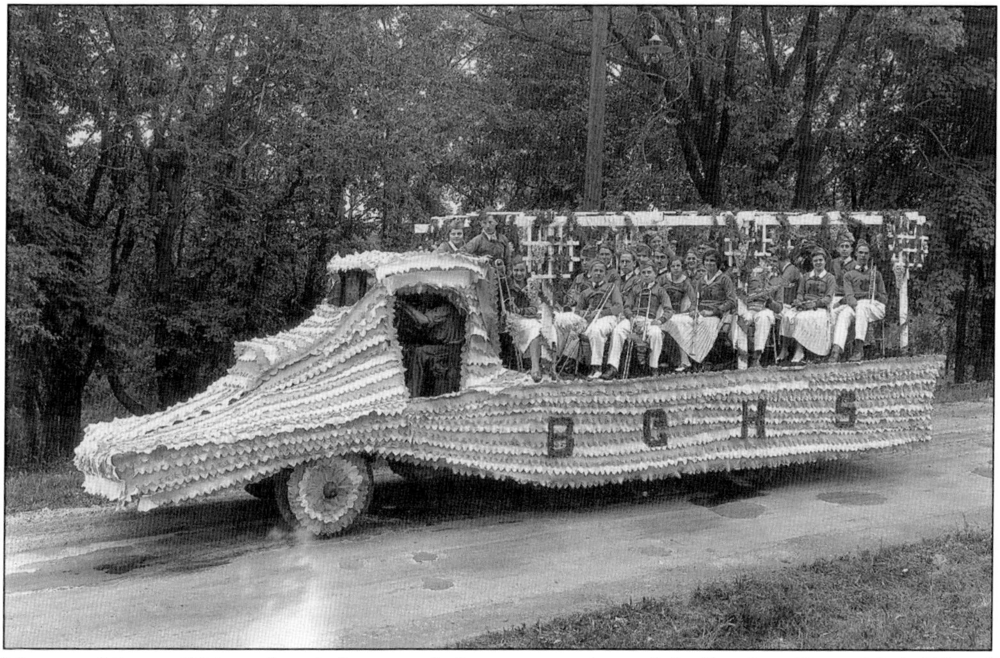

MOVING MUSIC. This undated photograph features members of the Bowling Green High School band preparing for participation in a parade. The float appears to be in the shape of an alligator and somehow the "G" on the side of the float has been turned upside down.

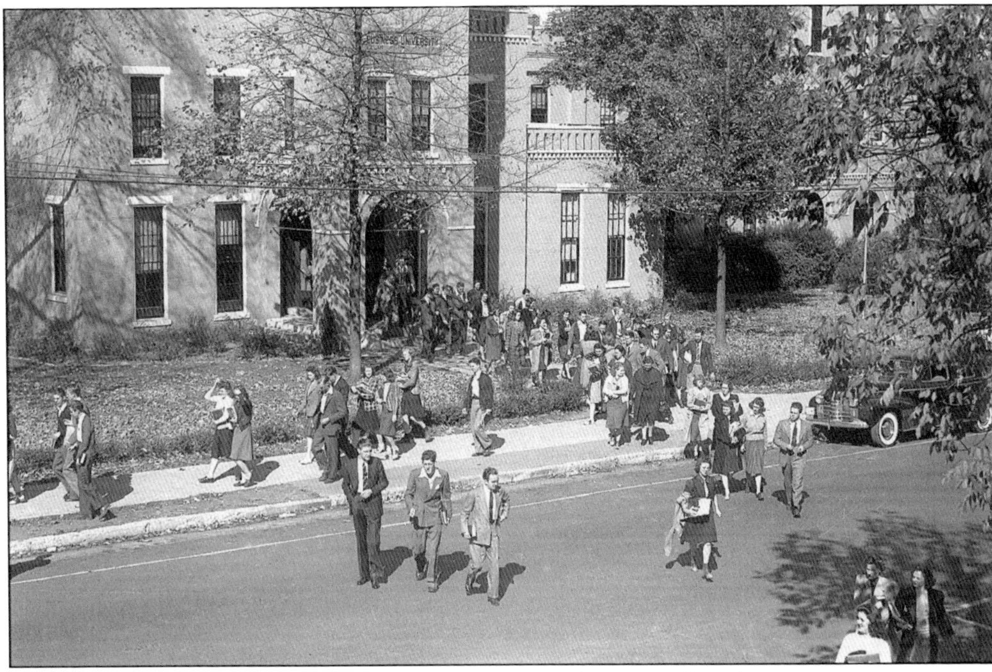

THE OLD BU. Bowling Green Business University, with its castellated parapets, was sometimes called "the castle" and its yearbook was called *The Towers*. This unusual landmark was designed by local architect Creedmore Fleenor. In its heyday, the Business University was one of the largest private commercial schools in the country. It burned in 1964 and soon thereafter merged with Western Kentucky University.

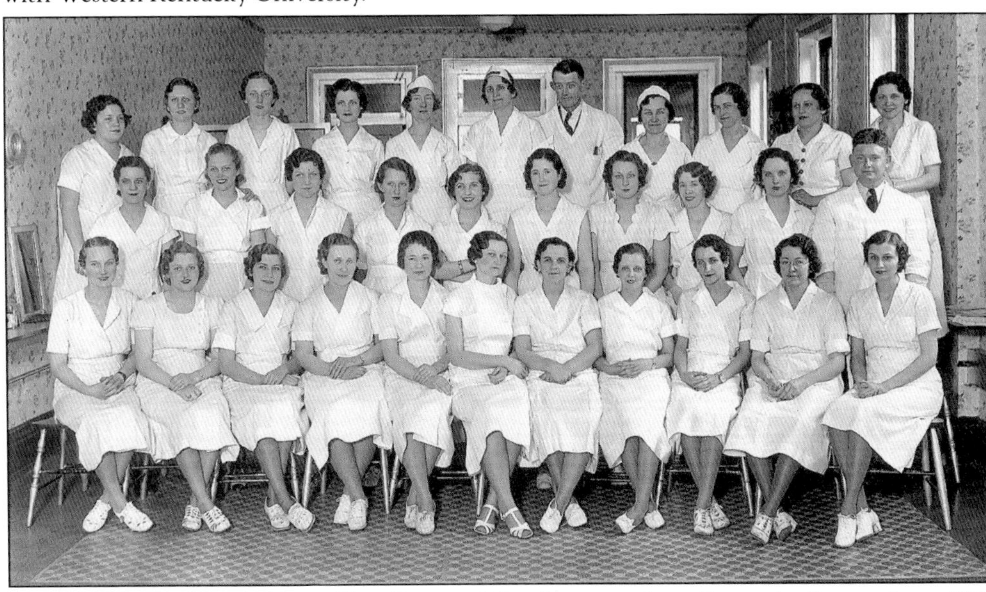

BEAUTY CULTURE. The Lois Glyn Beauty School operated on Fountain Square from 1930 through the 1970s. The school's founder, Glyn Fisher, is the male standing in the back row, although many credit his wife Edna with running the establishment. Mr. Fisher also owned a series of beauty shops in the area. His school trained thousands of beauticians and was considered one of the finest schools of its type in the state.

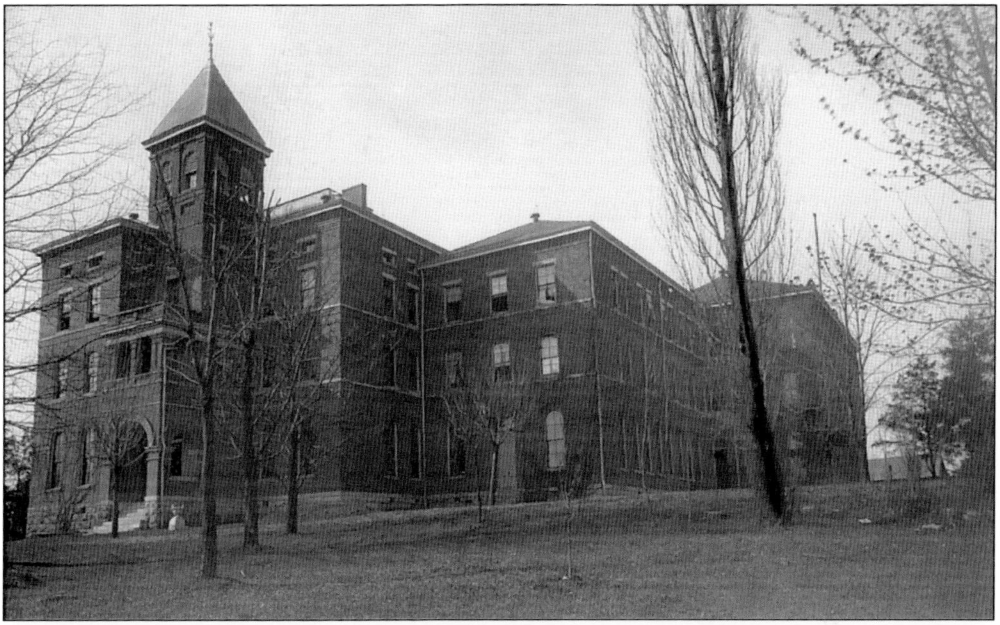

POTTER COLLEGE. Founded in 1889, Potter College's mission was to provide a liberal arts education for young ladies. The campus consisted of this imposing building at the top of Vinegar Hill and the home of B.F. Cabell, the institution's president. After the college went defunct in 1909, Western Kentucky University purchased the building and the school's property.

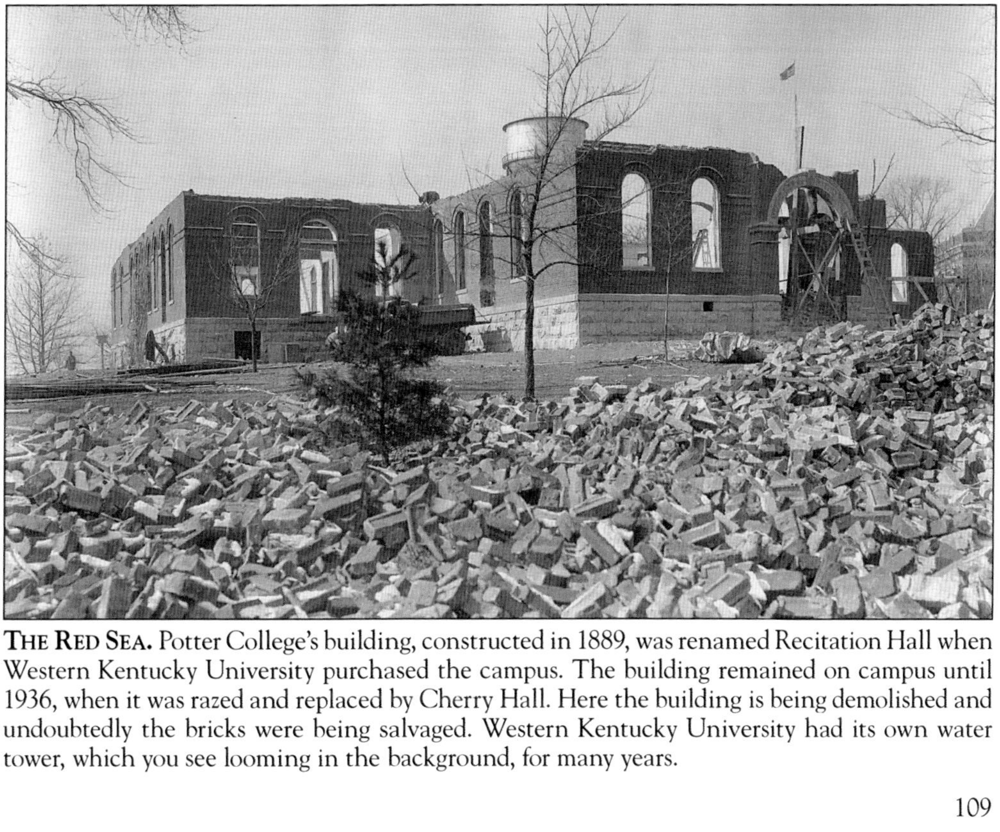

THE RED SEA. Potter College's building, constructed in 1889, was renamed Recitation Hall when Western Kentucky University purchased the campus. The building remained on campus until 1936, when it was razed and replaced by Cherry Hall. Here the building is being demolished and undoubtedly the bricks were being salvaged. Western Kentucky University had its own water tower, which you see looming in the background, for many years.

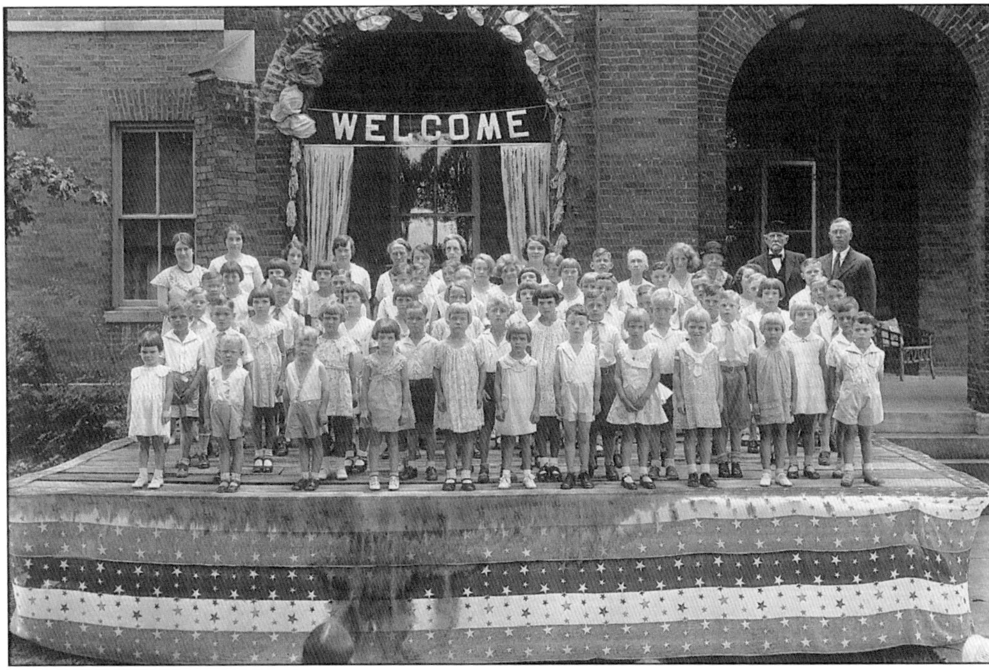

POTTERS ORPHAN HOME. Clinton and Mary Potter established this institution initially as a school for training young ministers in 1901. This school closed in 1912 and an orphanage and elementary school were started. This group has obviously been assembled for a program held in front of the building. This building burned in 1941.

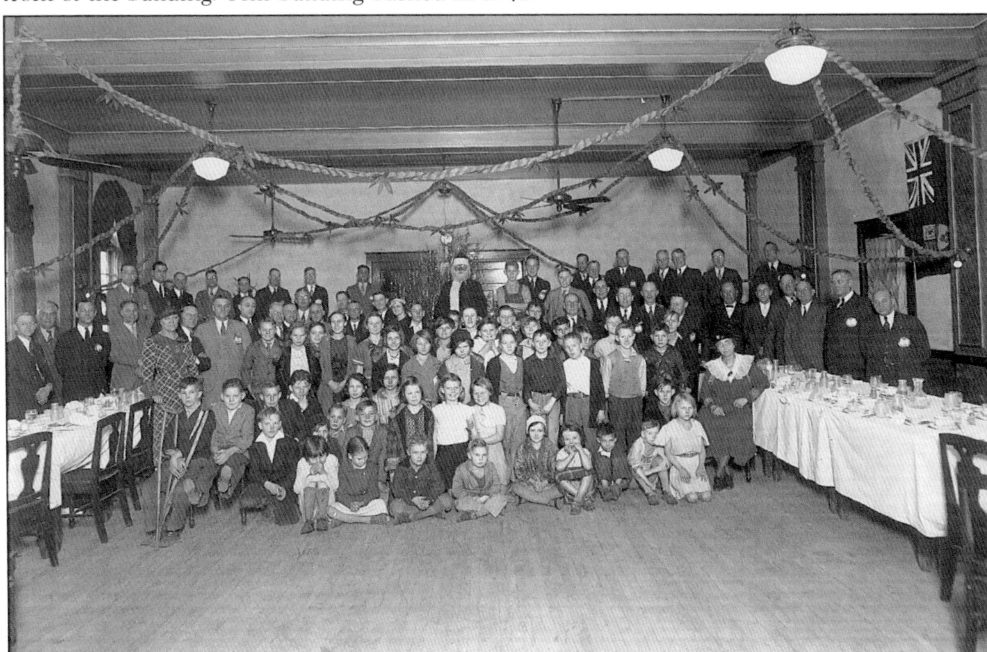

FOR THE KIDDIES. Here the combined efforts of the Bowling Green Kiwanis and Rotary Clubs helped a number of needy children receive a good meal and a small gift at Christmas in the mid-1930s.

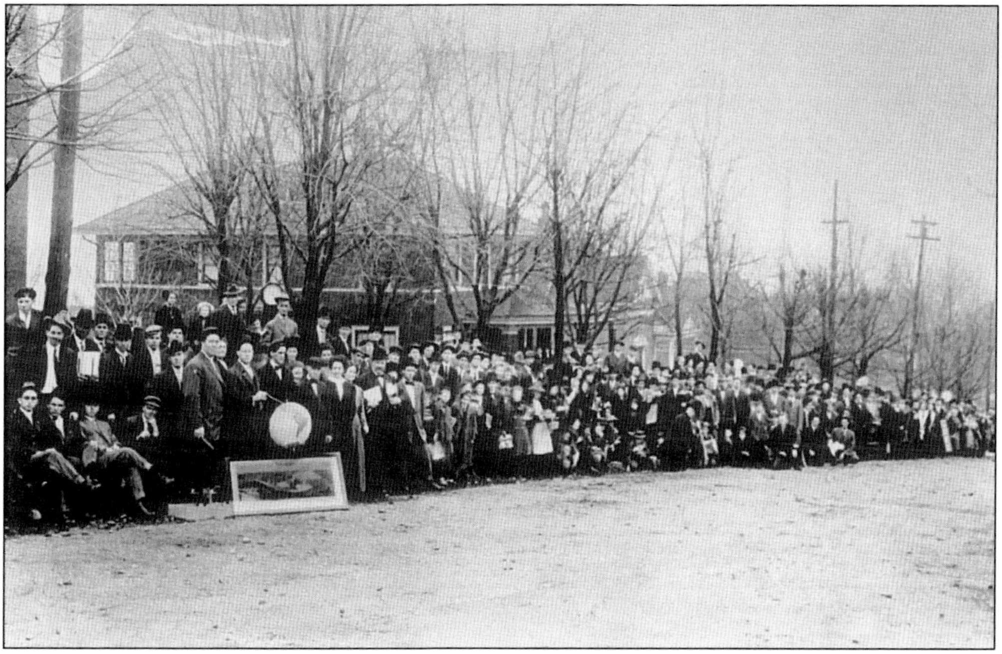

MOVING ON UP. What appears to be a parade is actually the faculty, staff, and students of Western Kentucky State Normal School moving from their facilities downtown to the school's new campus atop College Hill. The old Potter College building, Cabell Hall, and the new Van Meter Auditorium were ready for occupation.

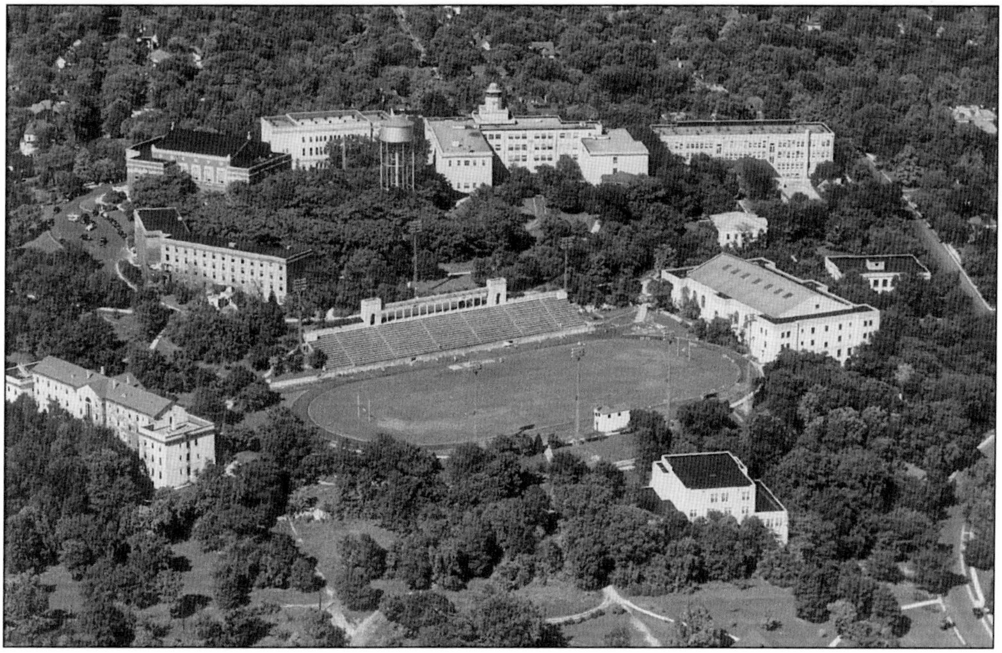

FLYING HIGH. This is an aerial view of Western Kentucky University in the mid-1940s. The football field located in the center of campus occupied an abandoned rock quarry. The playing field was moved in 1972 when L.T. Smith Stadium was constructed, but the bleachers, built into the side of the hill, were retained and made a natural amphitheater.

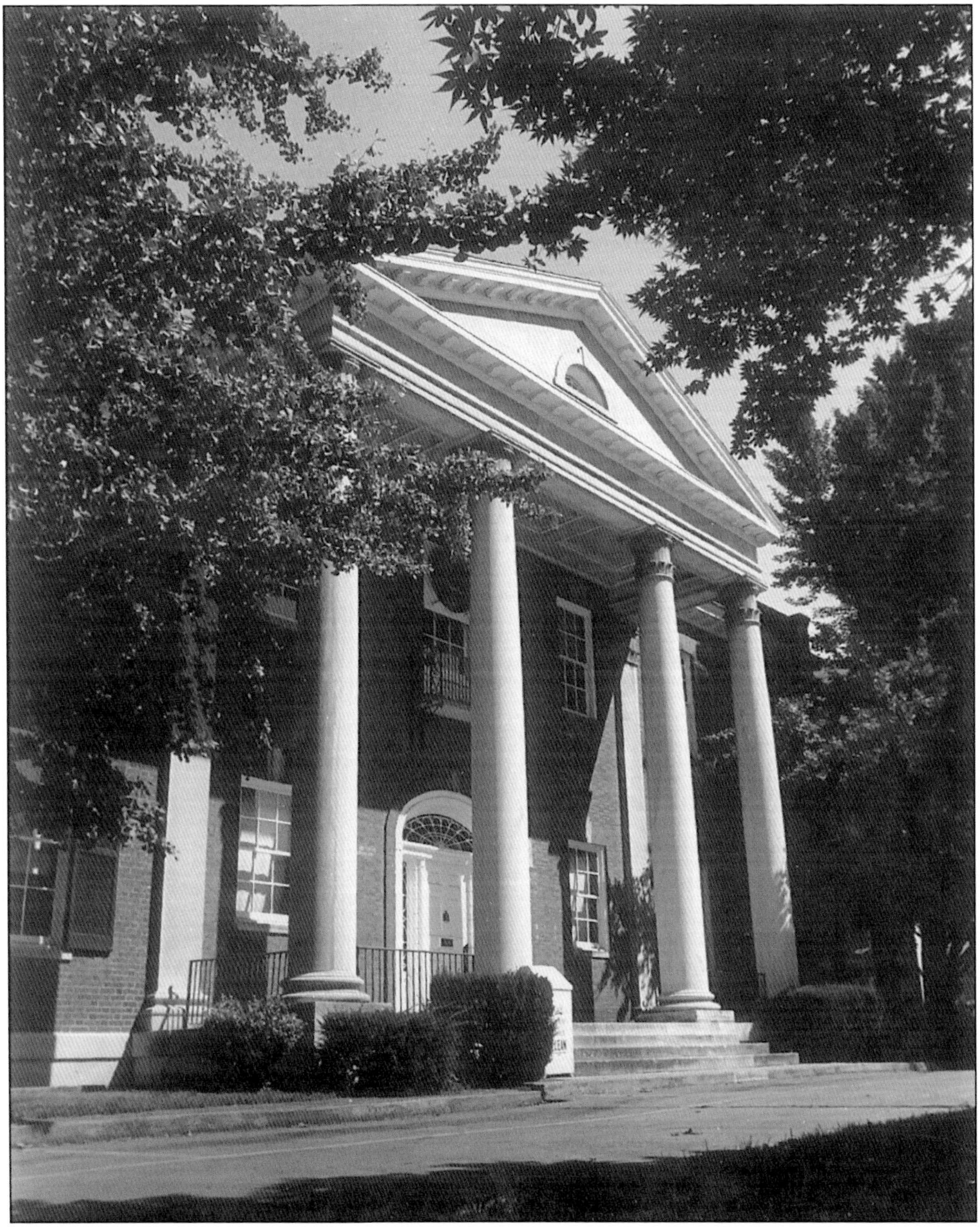

Treasure Chest. The Kentucky Building on Western Kentucky University's lovely campus houses the Kentucky Library & Museum. Located here are books, manuscripts, and artifacts related to the cultural heritage of the state. Collecting Kentuckiana at WKU began with a few concerned history professors who felt the need to preserve the Commonwealth's unique history. WKU's president, Henry Hardin Cherry, championed the idea in the late 1920s and fundraising began. Construction on the building, designed by Louisville architect Brinton B. Davis, began in 1929, but the Great Depression halted construction. With money from the Public Works Administration and with the assistance of local architect, James M. Ingram, the building was completed in 1939. Each portico column is turned from a single shaft of Bowling Green limestone. A substantial addition was built in 1979. (Photo by Robert Stuart.)

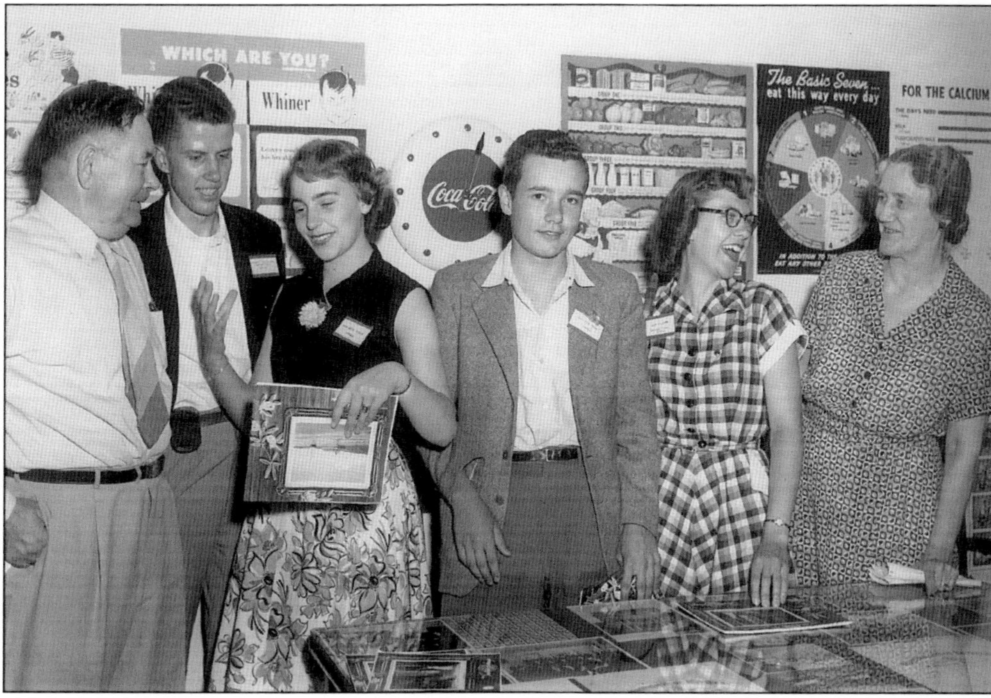

FOREIGN VISITORS. In the summer of 1952 a group of 34 foreign students spent several days in Bowling Green absorbing American culture. The Warren County Tuberculosis Association sponsored their stay. The youth visited local farms, were guests at a swimming party, toured the Kentucky Building, went to a drive-in theater, attended chapel at the Bowling Green Business University, and spent time with local teens at various events.

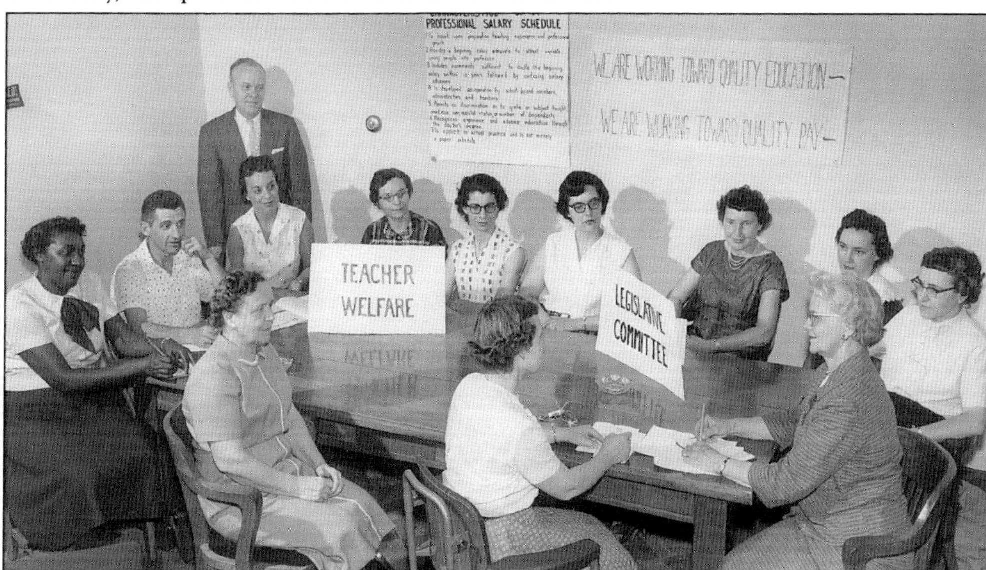

TEACHERS UNITE! This conclave of teachers met in 1959 to advocate a "professional salary schedule" for Bowling Green educators. Their poster notes that such a scale would "Permit no discrimination as to grade or subject taught, creed, race, sex, marital status or number of dependents." (Photo by Love's Studios.)

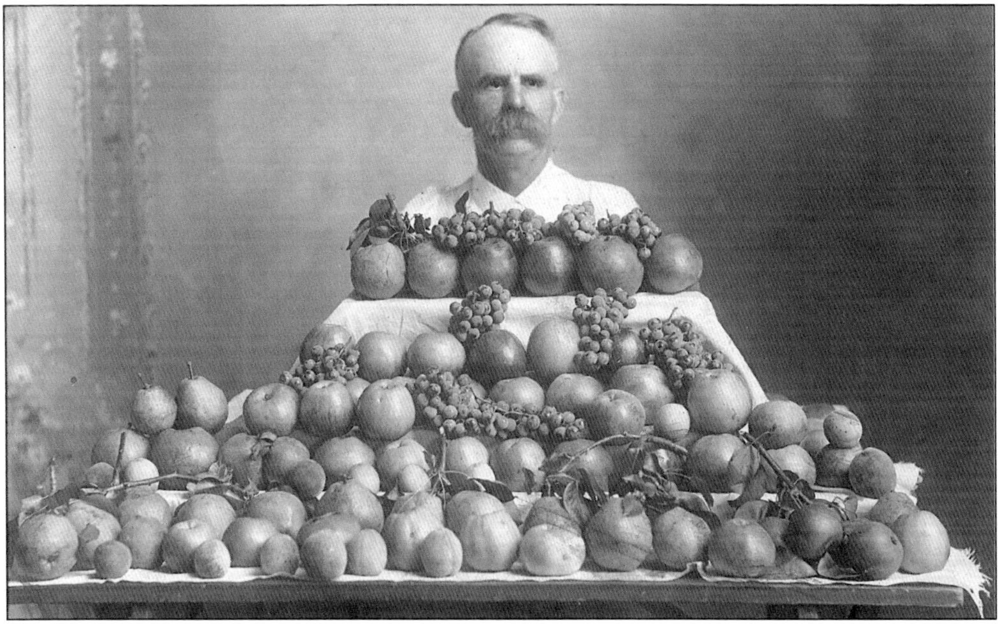

FRUITFUL. E.G. Young of Richardsville poses with his fruit display that was produced for the Farmers Chautauqua held in his area in 1912. These farmers' meetings were created and produced by WKU, and their goals were to promote efficiency in farming, hygiene in the rural home, and school consolidation. These lecture series and accompanying demonstrations were held throughout the county. (Photo by S.G. Rogers.)

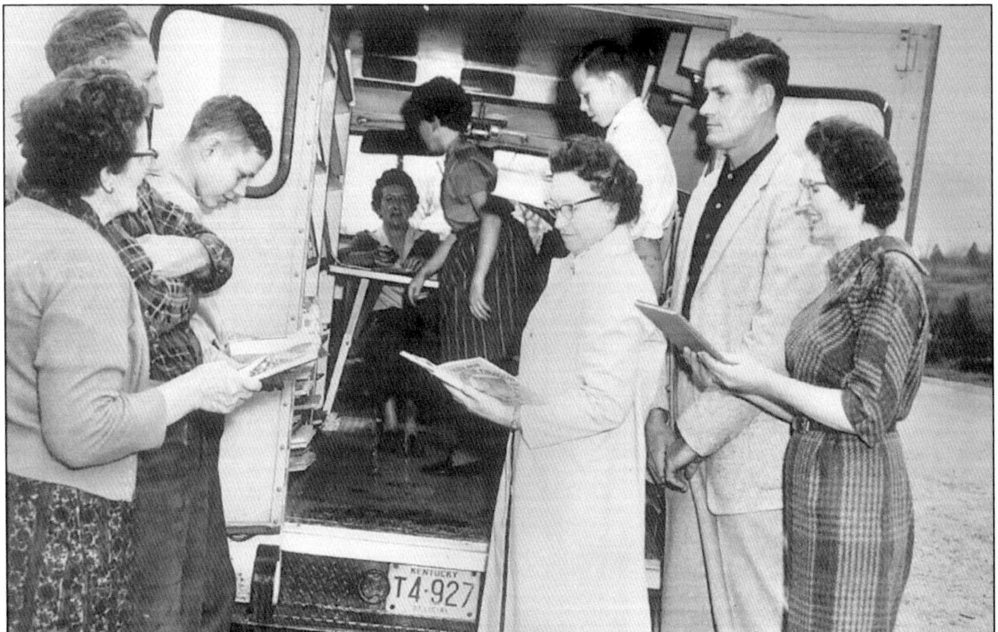

ROADSIDE READING. The Friends of Kentucky Libraries banded together with citizen and corporate support to purchase over 50 bookmobiles for Kentucky counties in 1954. Honey Krust Bakery donated the funds necessary to purchase a bookmobile for Bowling Green and Warren County; it made its first run on January 15, 1955.

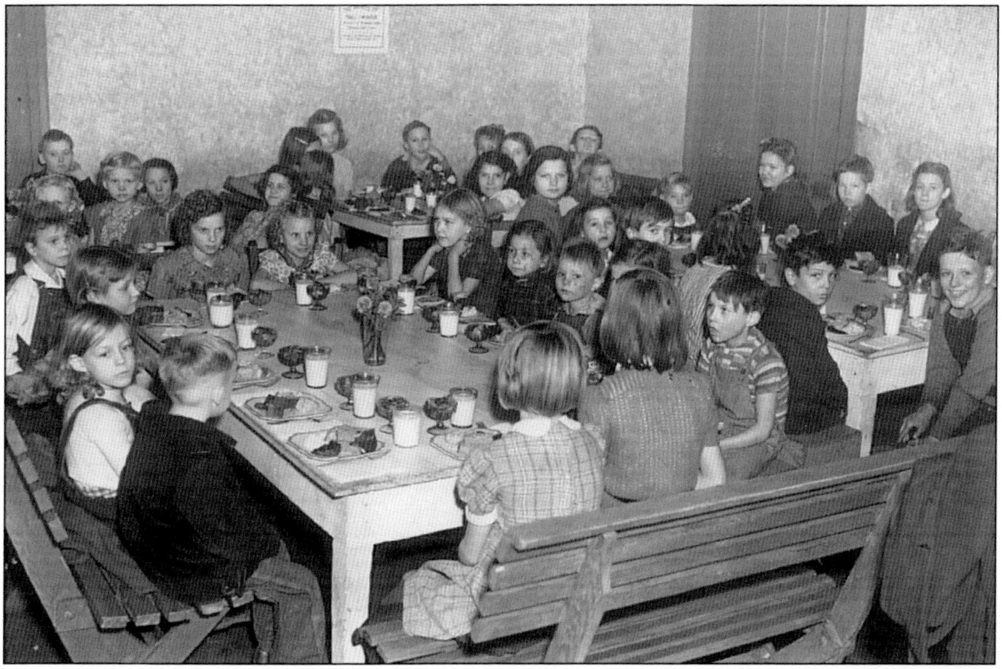

HELPING HANDS. Feeding needy children a hearty and healthy lunch was a project undertaken by the Welfare Center, which was established in the early 1920s in reaction to the deaths of four children due to exposure and malnutrition. In addition to the physical food, the local Business & Professional Women's Club provided mental nourishment with a story hour each week.

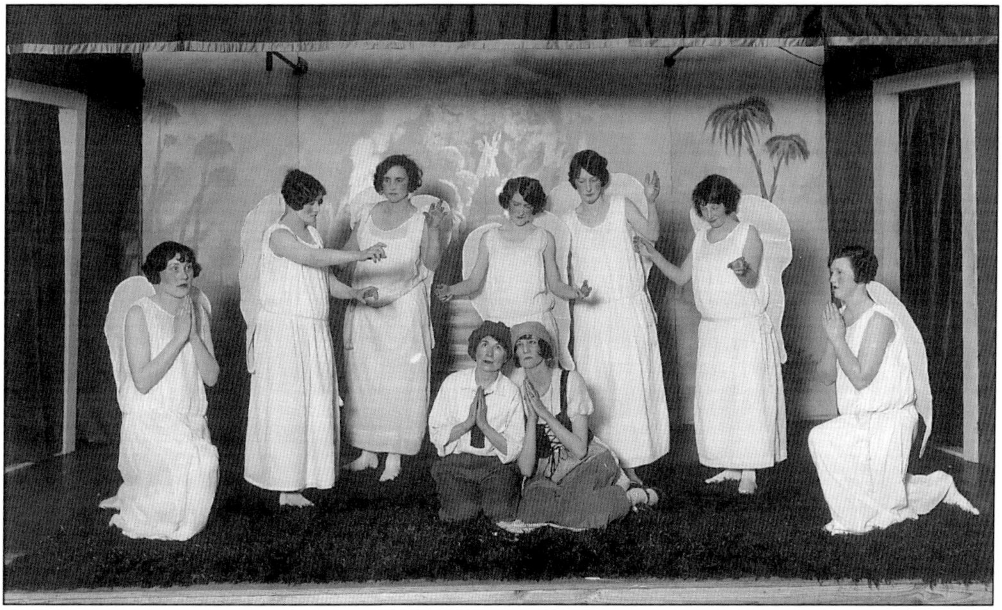

HEAVENLY TABLEAUX. Here the local Rebekahs are participating in some program to raise money for benevolent or educational purposes. The Rebekahs are the female auxiliary of the Independent Order of Oddfellows. They exist to support each other emotionally and financially and to uphold the maxims of the Oddfellows organization: Love, Friendship, and Truth.

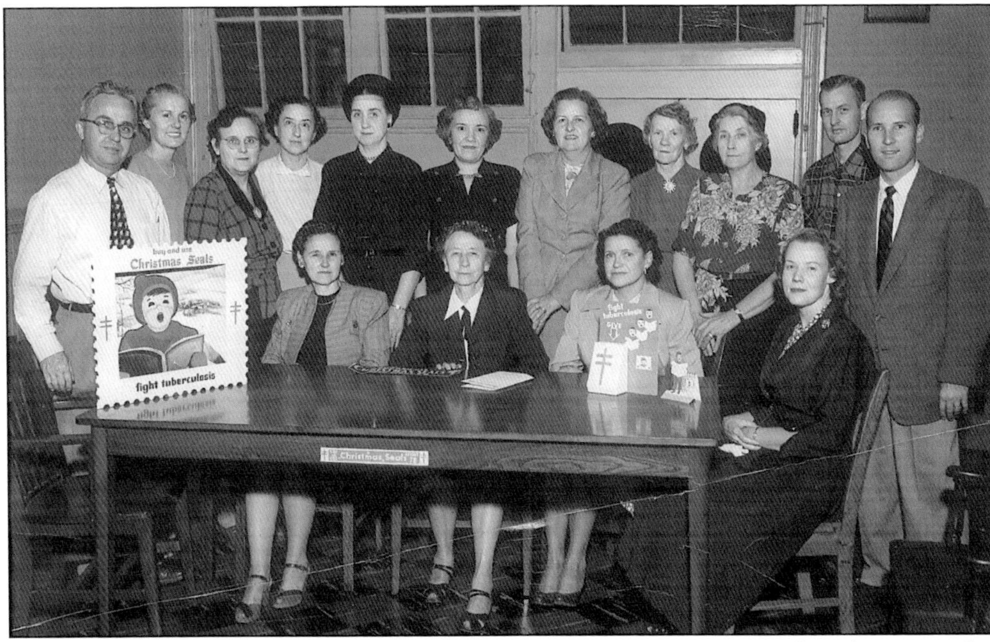

FIGHTING THE WHITE PLAGUE. This eager group of concerned citizens gathered in November 1953 at the American National Bank to kick off the annual Christmas Seals campaign. Throughout the 1950s, tuberculosis was a major cause of death in the United States and was sometimes referred to as the "White Plague."

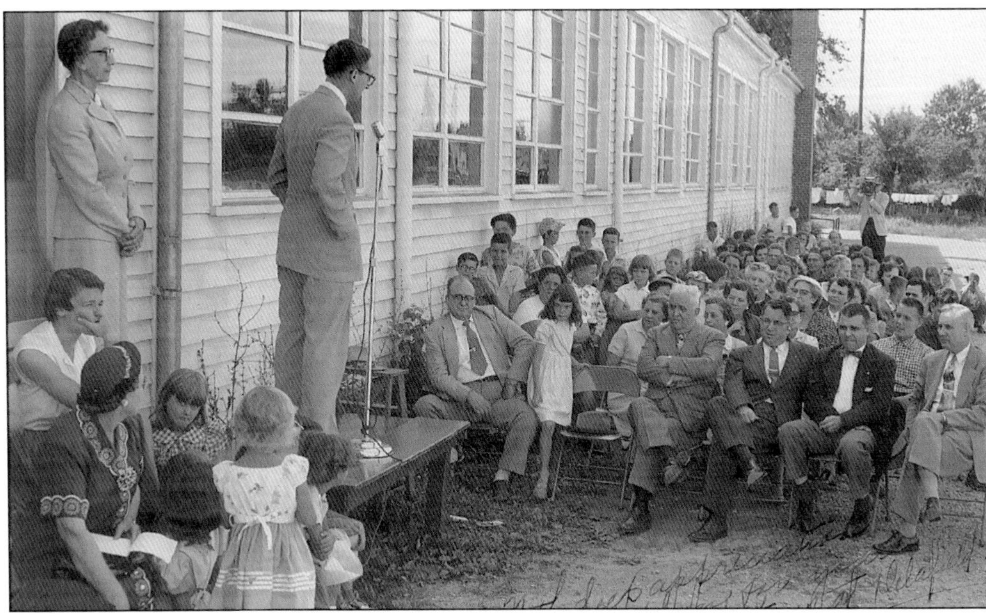

RECREATION HAVEN. The occasion for this August gathering is the launching of the Delafield recreation program in June 1955. The Boys Club eventually took over administration of this program. The duo standing on the stage is Paul Lemmon, assistant regional director of Boys Clubs of America, and Nell Gooch Travelstead, a local music teacher and advocate for the needy. The Delafield Improvement League, headed by Travelstead, was responsible for this initiative.

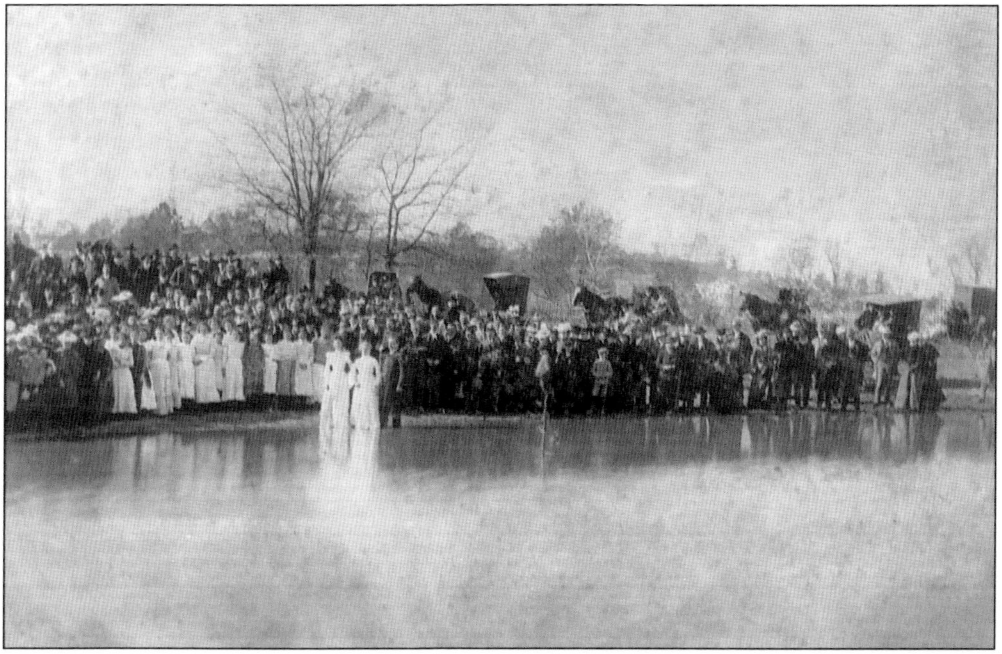

BAPTISM. Warren County is blessed with an abundance of streams, rivers, lakes, and ponds. A baptismal spot was not difficult to locate. Only extreme cold weather prevented the event. Here a congregation and friends gather at a large pond for the ceremony on November 15, 1901. Indoor baptisms were not common, particularly in the county, until after 1960.

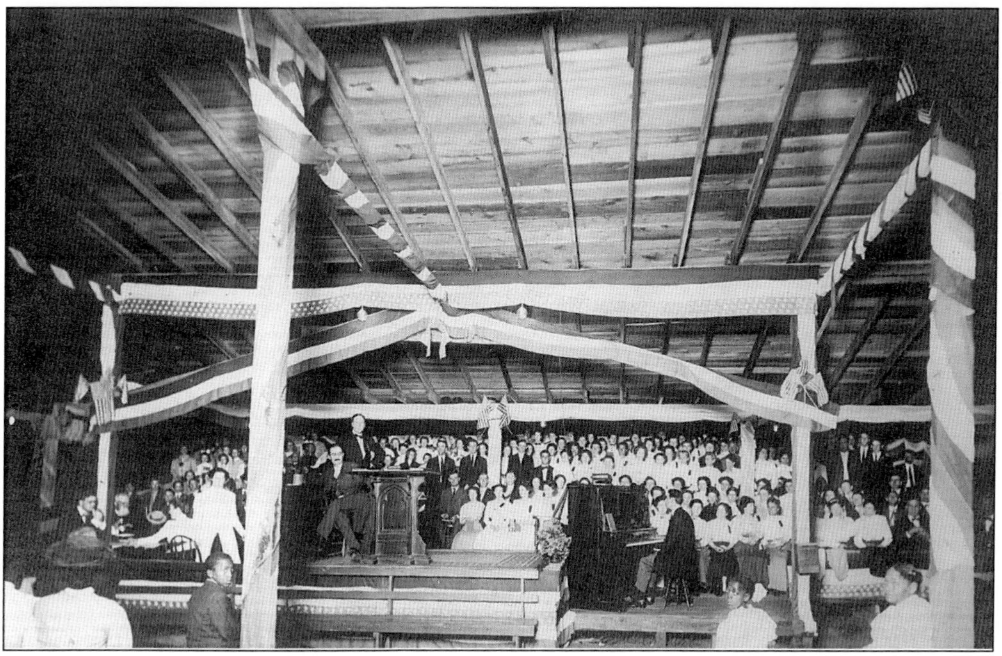

HAM-SCHOFIELD REVIVAL. Mordecai Ham and his singing associate held several revivals in Bowling Green. This one dates from June 1910, when Bowling Green was in the throes of a local option election. Ham is sometimes credited with helping to defeat the organized saloon owners and liquor stores in that election. Mr. Ham is seated next to the pulpit.

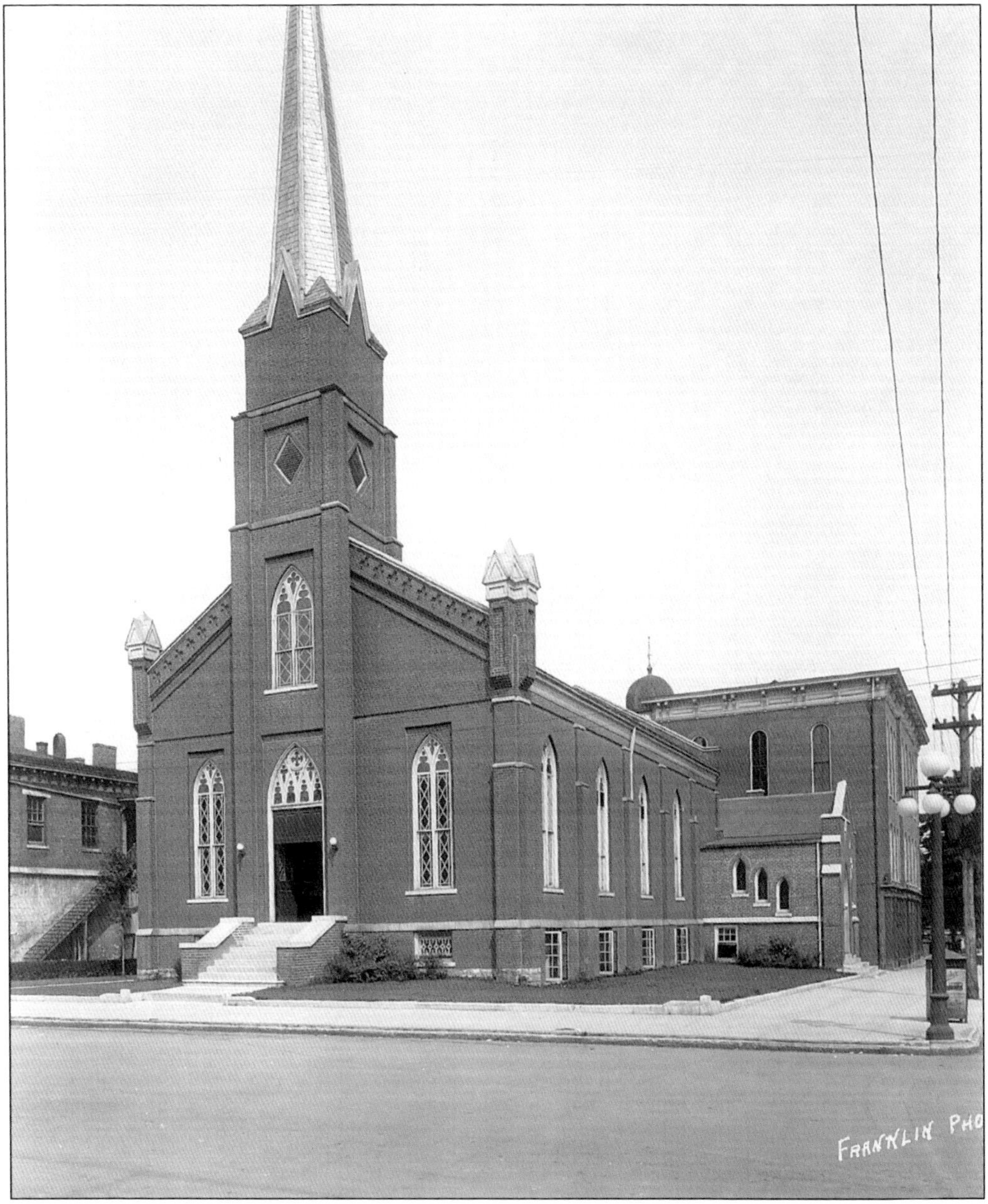

THE PRESBYTERIAN CHURCH. The first Presbyterian congregation in Bowling Green organized in 1819. They erected a building in what is now Pioneer Cemetery, but it burned in the early 1830s. Renowned architect Hugh Roland designed the present masonry building with Gothic detailing and an elegant steeple; construction began in 1833. Besides the church, this photograph also provides hints about others buildings. The building to the left of the church is the old Warren County Jail, built in the mid-19th century and used until the 1930s. The building directly behind the church is the Cooke Building, which contained professional offices, particularly those of attorneys who practiced at the Courthouse. This Italianate building, which boasted round arched windows and bracketed eaves, was purchased by the Presbyterian Church; it was razed when an addition was made to the building in the early 1990s. A portion of the courthouse cupola is visible above the Cooke Building.

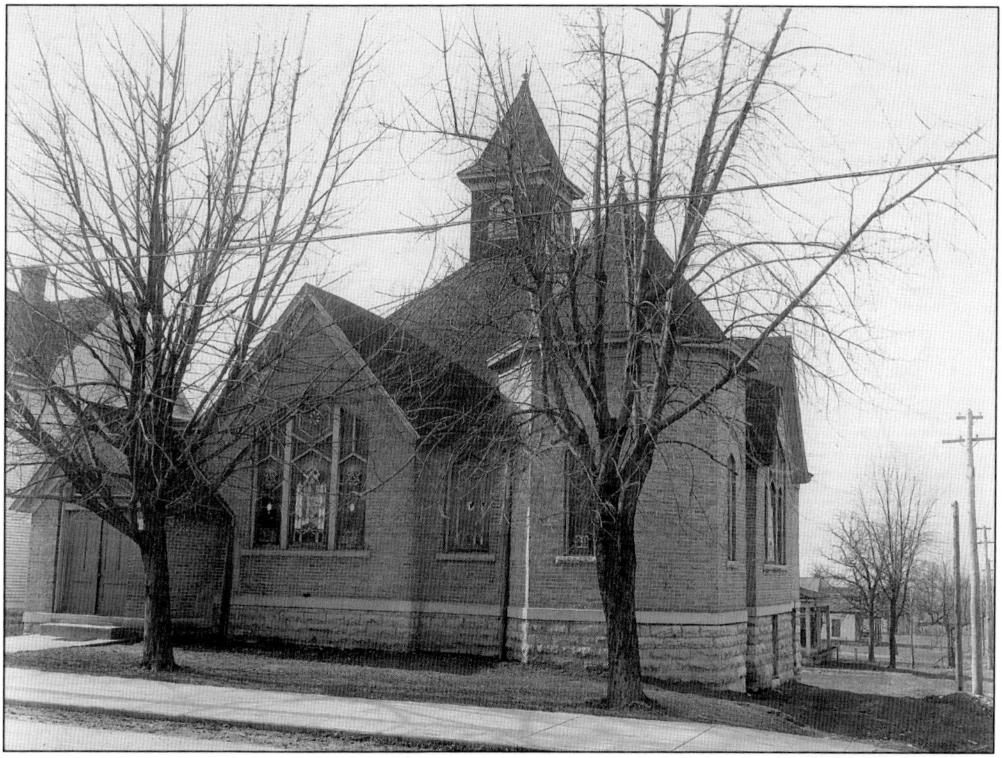

BROADWAY METHODIST CHURCH. This church organized as a mission from State Street Methodist Church in 1906 and initially met in a grocery store. With 45 members, the congregation built this fine house of worship in 1909 at the corner of Broadway Street and Laurel Avenue. The church moved to its present location at the end of Elizabeth Street in 1959.

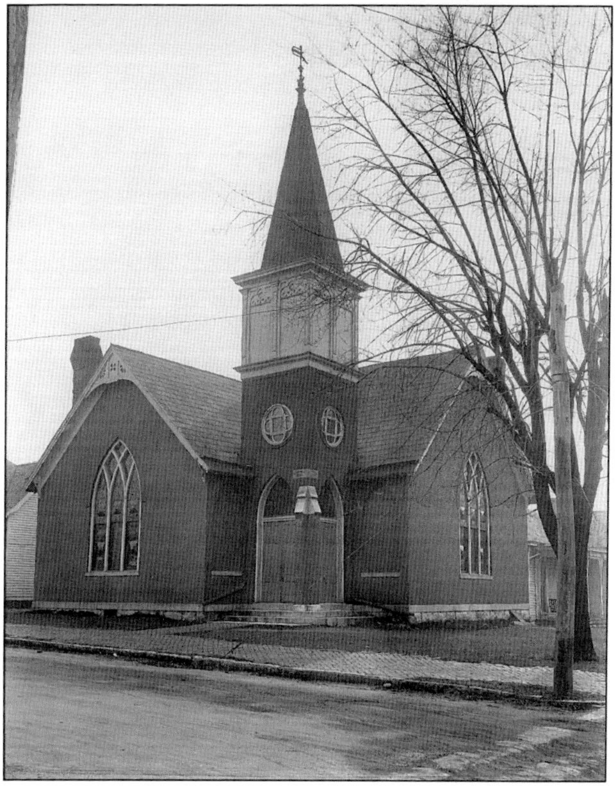

KERR MEMORIAL METHODIST CHURCH. This church, located at the corner of 12th and Adams Streets, was organized in 1890 as the First Methodist Episcopal Church under the benevolent eye of Rev. Daniel Farmer Kerr. This congregation erected this $6,000 structure in 1891. In 1937, the church voted to change its name to Kerr Memorial. This congregation merged with Faith Methodist Church in 1999.

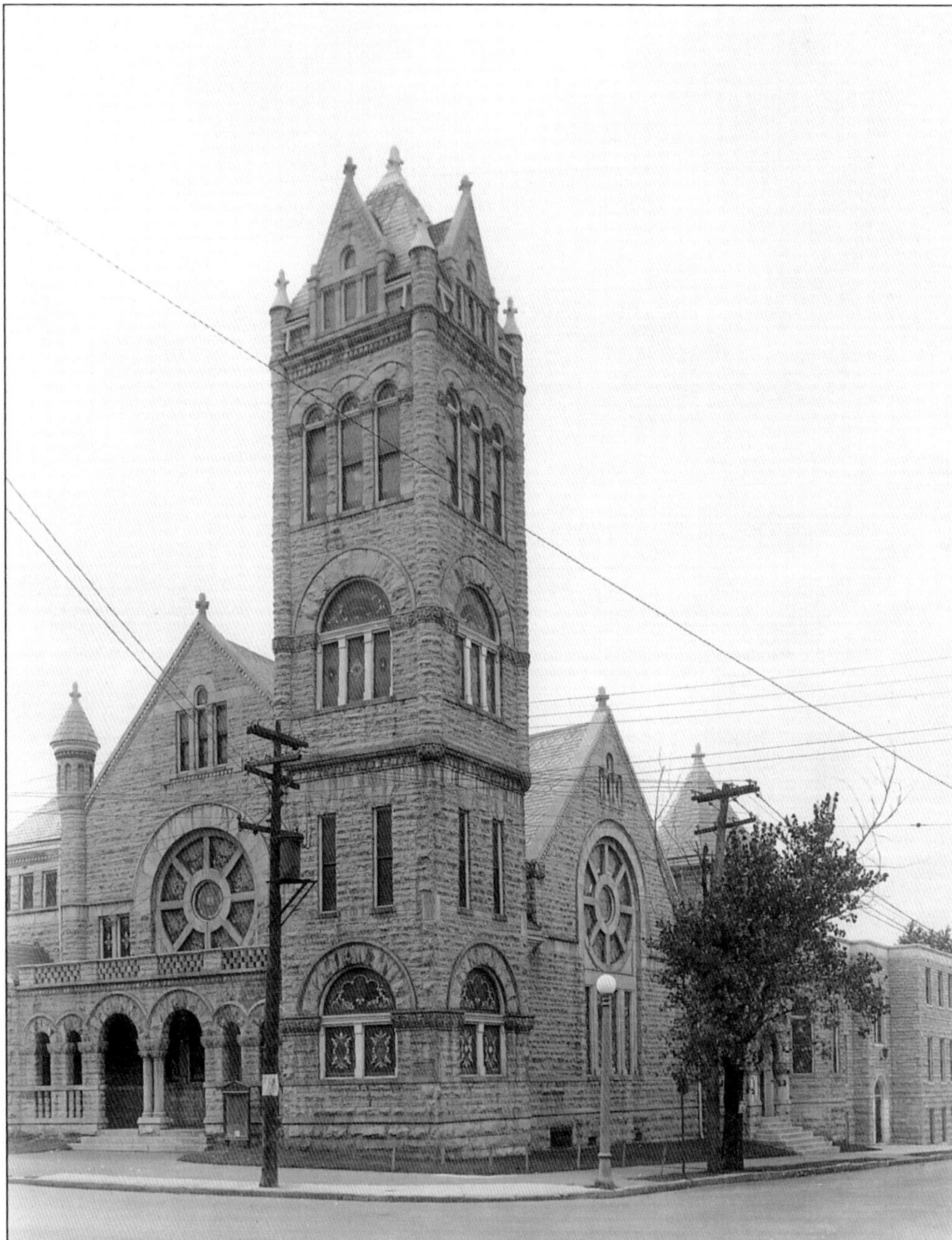

State Street Methodist Church. Methodists first organized in 1819 in Bowling Green. Slavery split the church into a northern and southern faction in 1844, but the groups re-united in 1939. This fabulous Romanesque Revival church was designed by Ruben Hunt and built for $20,400. The architect included a five-staged bell tower, variegated window shapes, and artistic massing to make this an architectural treasure. He chose to clad the building in rough ashlar Bowling Green limestone. Those familiar with the building know that the front entrance was drastically altered in a 1950s renovation. One of the church's 77 stained glass windows features a representation of the congregation's previous buildings at 816 State Street.

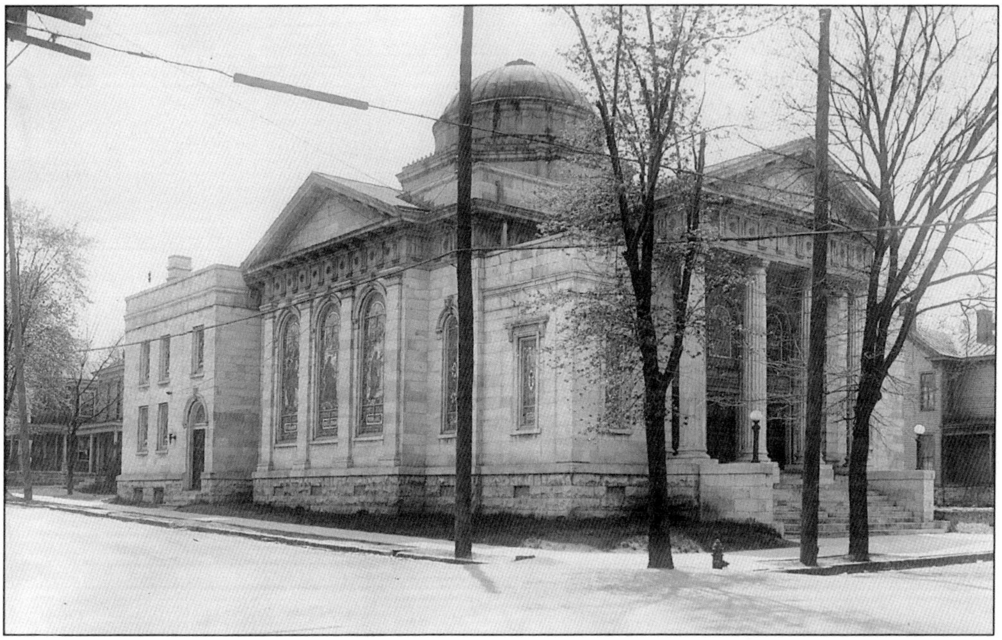

WESTMINSTER PRESBYTERIAN CHURCH. This beautiful worship center was constructed in 1912 for a congregation of the Presbyterian Church USA. The church boasts a beautiful Roman temple front, is crowned with a cast iron dome, and is clad in Bowling Green limestone. The exquisite stained glass windows were memorial gifts from various congregants. The interior picture (below) was taken directly after the April 6, 1946, funeral of Cora Anita Steele. It shows the unusual design of the sanctuary. The area to the left under the arch could be closed off. The massive pipe organ takes up one whole wall. Notice the banner behind the pulpit, which contains stars for the World War II service men from the congregation.

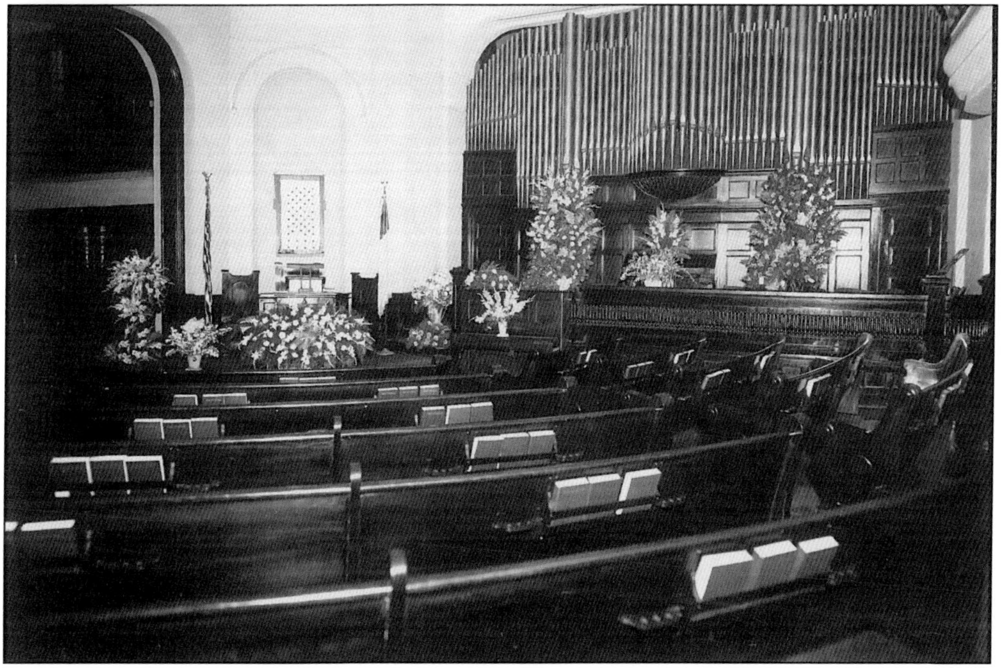

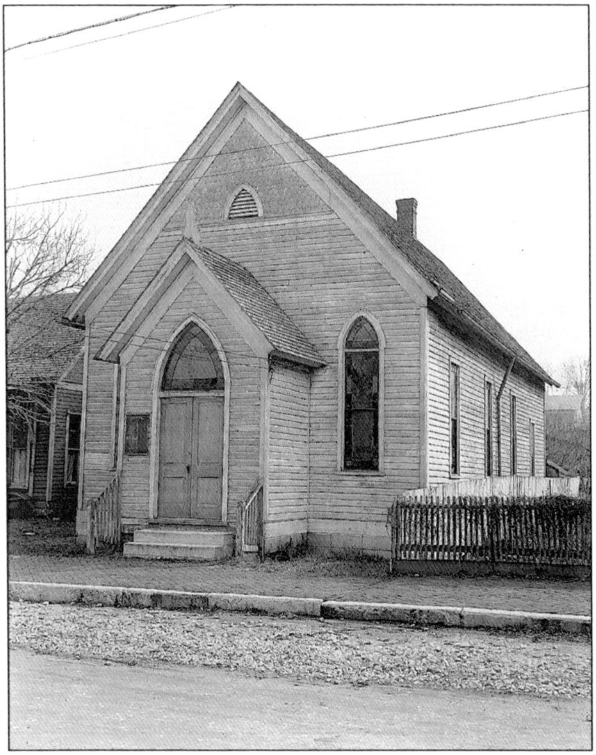

SEVENTH DAY ADVENTIST. This church organized in 1887 with only eight signing the church covenant. In 1900 they constructed this modest frame building at 1122 Park Street. Health education has always been a priority for this denomination. In the mid-1920s the local church sponsored a health clinic and in the 1950s they operated a welfare facility. The congregation built a new church in 1976 on Cave Mill Road.

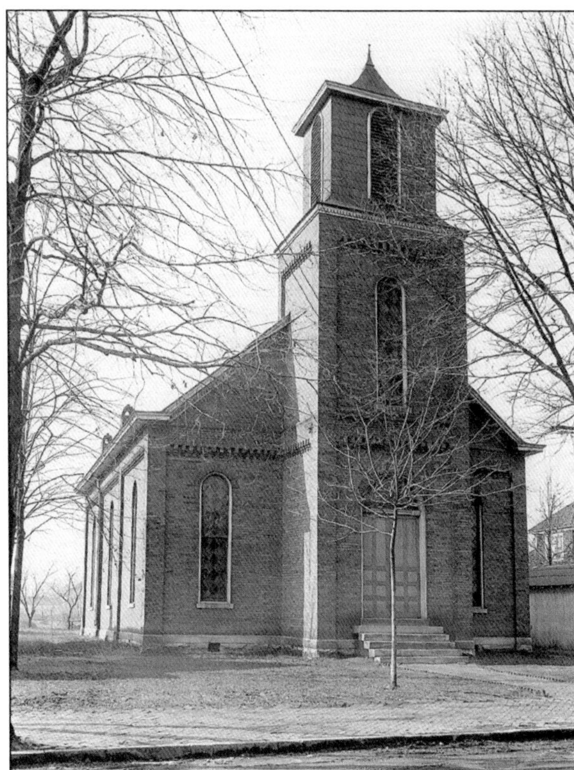

TWELFTH STREET CHURCH OF CHRIST. This building was constructed in 1899 and expanded in 1928. This photo shows the building, with its unusual cupola, prior to additional expansion in 1962. Due to growth, the church moved to a new location on Dishman Lane in April 2002 and changed its name to Lost River Church of Christ.

St. Joseph Catholic Church. Rev. Joseph DeVries organized the Catholic Church in Bowling Green in 1858. The building pictured here was finished in 1887 and designed by Frank Kister to resemble the Cologne Cathedral. The 142-foot steeple tower was heavily damaged in 1923 and was replaced by a shorter, sturdier one. DeVries is buried in the church.

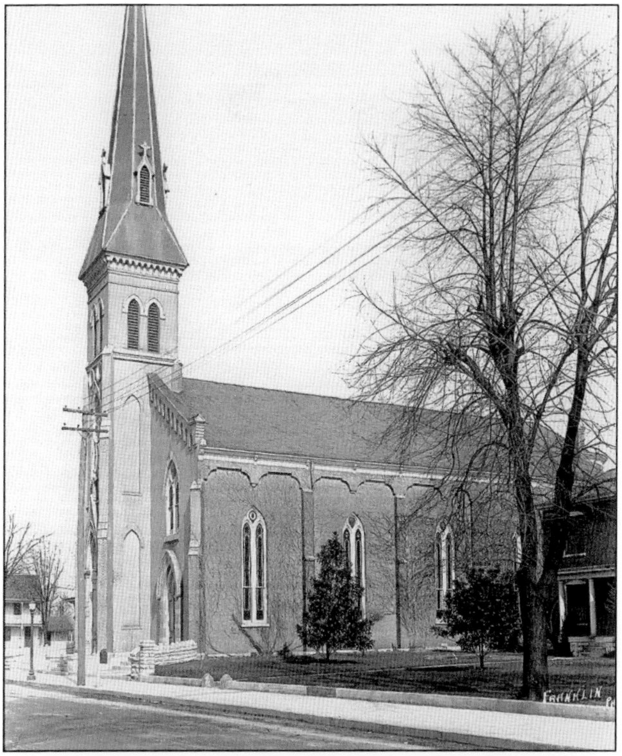

Heavenly Portals. The photograph below, taken in 1937, features the spectacular interior of St. Joseph Catholic Church. The interior has been slightly modified, but it remains a beautiful tribute to the craftspeople who so lovingly created this divine space.

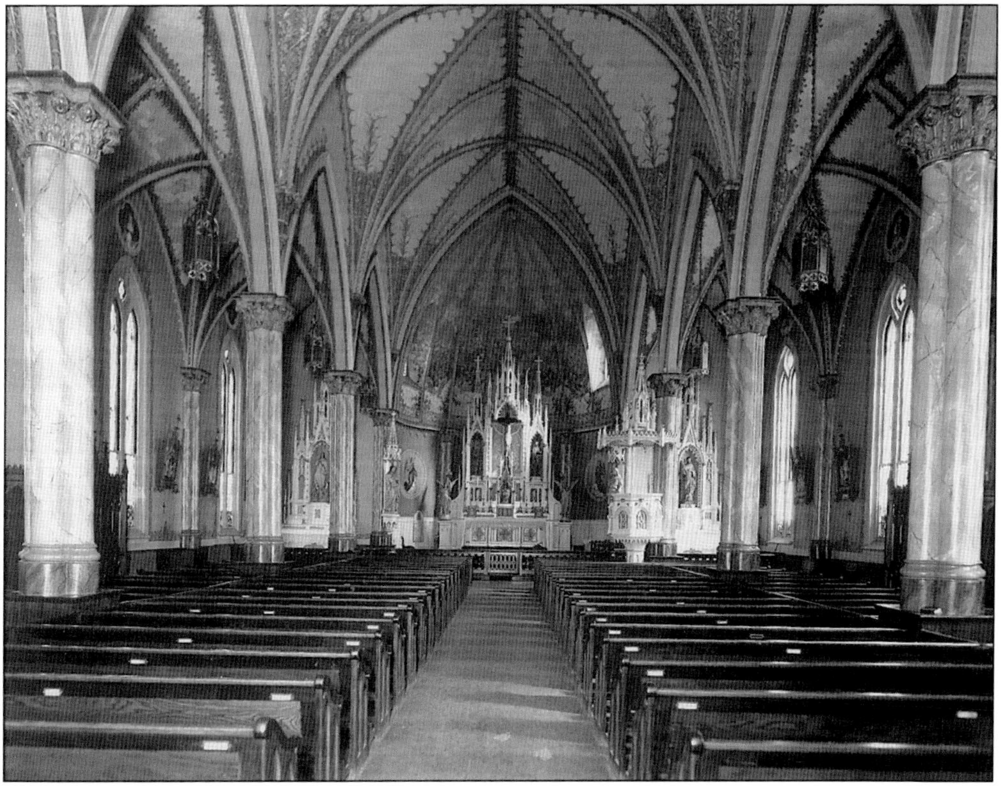

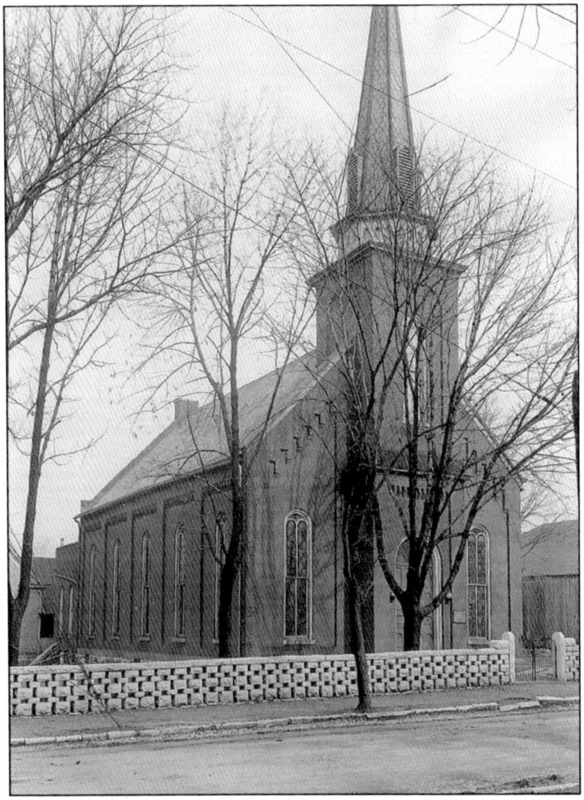

CHRISTIAN SCIENTIST CHURCH. Mary Baker Eddy founded the Church of Christ Scientists in 1879 in Boston. The Bowling Green congregation formed in 1907 and they purchased this building in 1911. The Cumberland Presbyterian congregation built this church in 1869 and worshipped here until 1906. The building was razed in 1967 to make way for a Goodyear Tire Store.

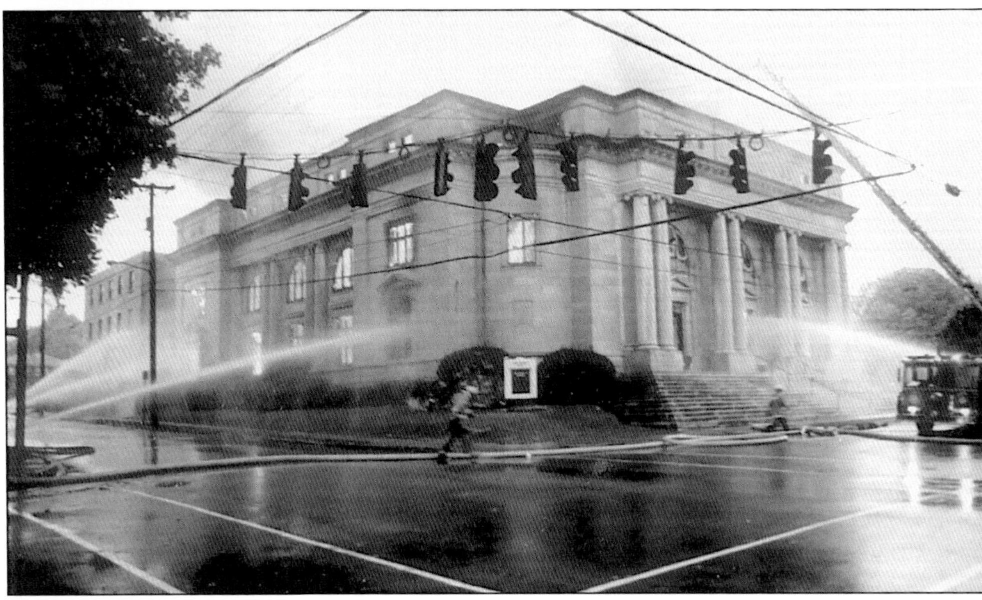

FIRST BAPTIST CHURCH. In 1818, Baptists built a log structure to house its fledgling congregation. In 1854, they erected a commodious brick church in the 300 block of Main Street. Local architect Creedmore Fleenor designed this third structure for the congregation in 1913 and it was built for $135,000. Constructed of local limestone, it was referred to as the "White Temple." It was destroyed in the pictured 1993 fire.

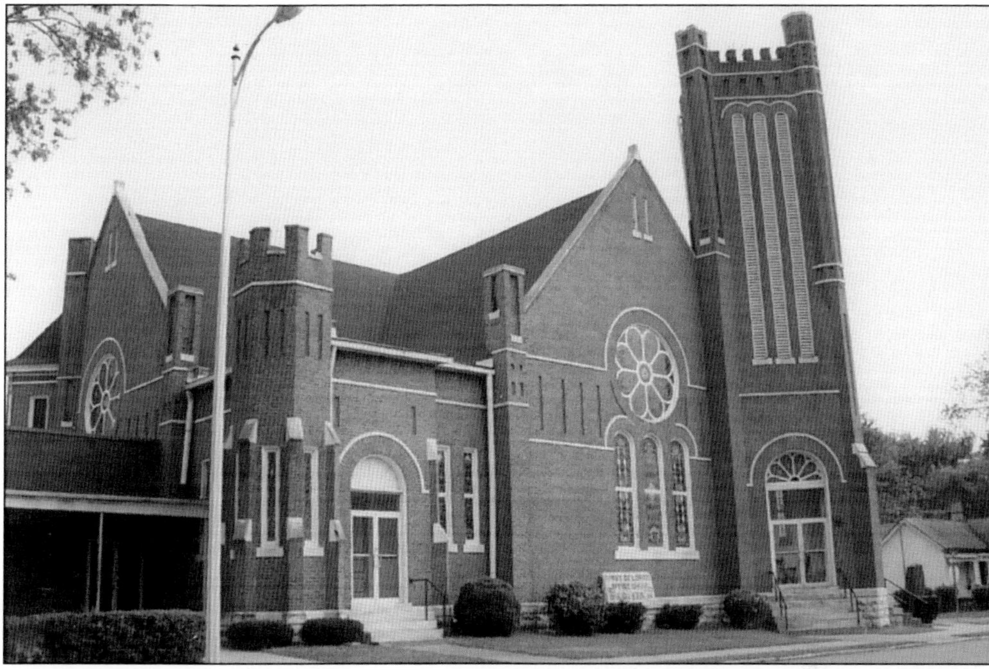

STATE STREET BAPTIST CHURCH. African Americans organized this church from the slave membership of First Baptist Church in 1838. This building was constructed in 1898 after their former house of worship burned. The building is a good example of Gothic-Romanesque Revival architecture and is attributed to local architect Creedmore Fleenor. A devastating fire destroyed the sanctuary in May 2000, but the congregation chose to rebuild using the structure's original walls.

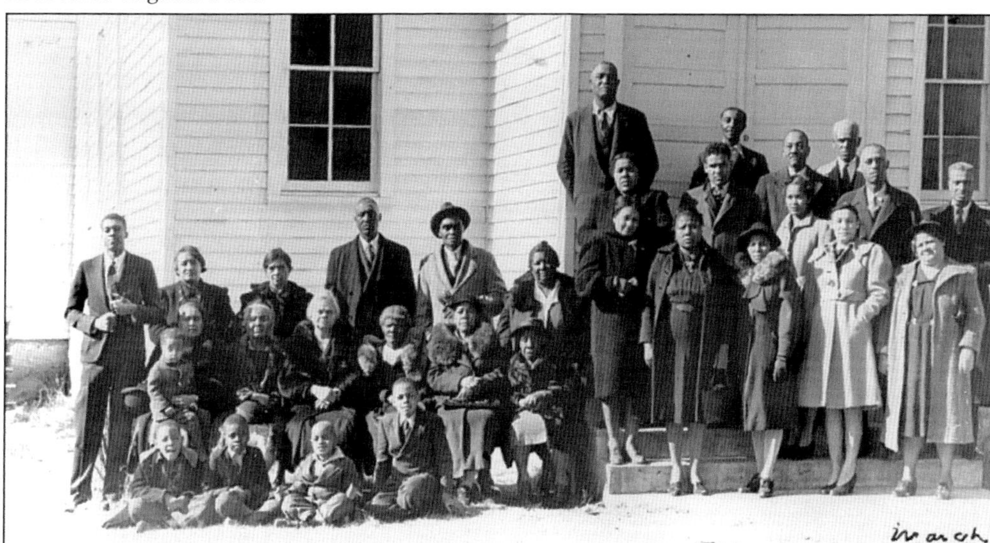

MT. ZION BAPTIST CHURCH. The church has always been a tremendous force in the African-American community for leadership development and spiritual growth. Mt. Zion was located in a segregated African American community known as Jonesville. This March 1943 photo shows the stalwart congregation standing proudly in front of their church building, which fell victim to urban renewal in the 1960s. The congregation continues to meet in another facility.

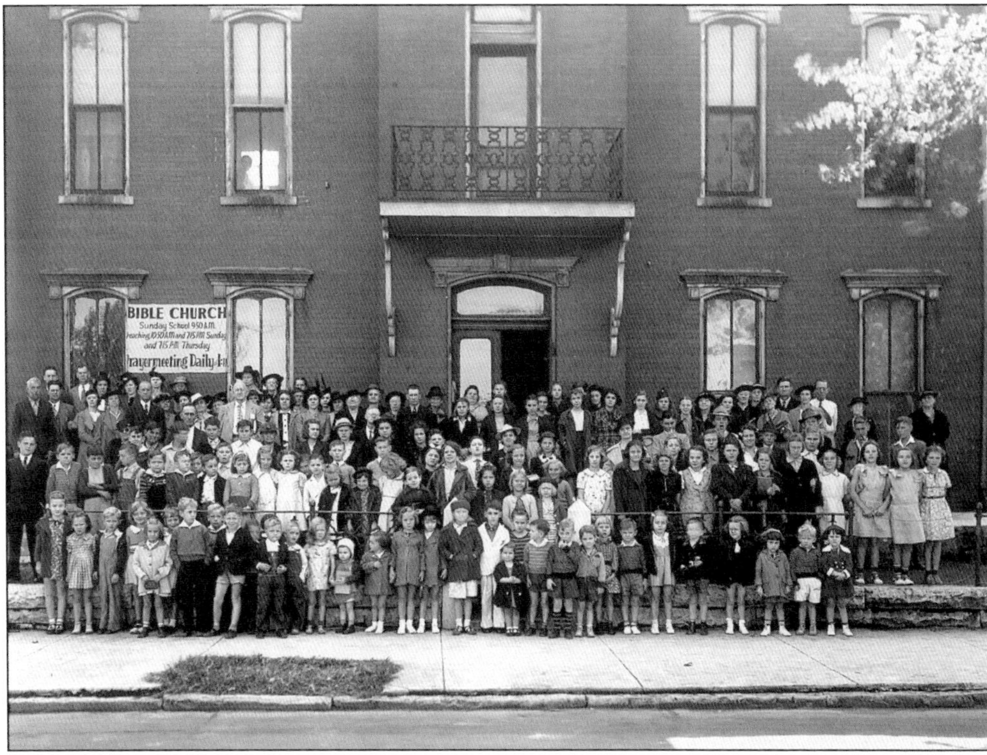

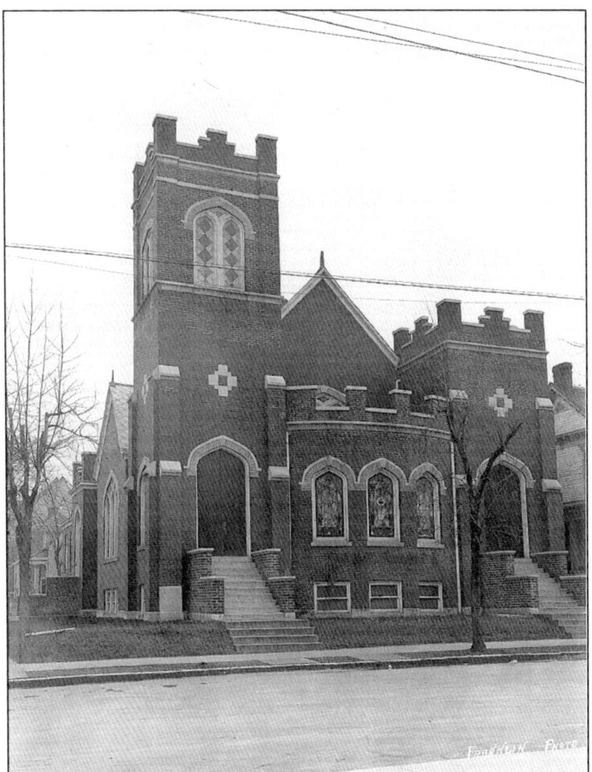

BIBLE CHURCH. The Bible Church, later the Bible Presbyterian Church, was founded on January 31, 1937, by Rev. Eugene C. Comfort. They purchased this home at 822 Center Street in June 1939 and added an auditorium on the north side. Around the time of this photo in the mid-1940s, membership stood at 220, with an average Sunday attendance of 191.

THE CUMBERLAND PRESBYTERIAN CHURCH. Rev. Jesse Grider organized the Cumberland Presbyterian Church in Bowling Green in 1866. The congregation erected the building pictured here at College and Eleventh Streets in 1909 for $20,000. This building was used until the congregation moved to their new church on Campbell Lane in 1971.

CHRIST EPISCOPAL CHURCH. This church organized in 1844. Its first building on East Main Street was dismantled by soldiers during the Civil War. Its current English Gothic building was constructed in 1912 of Warren County limestone on State Street. Designed by George Herbert Gray of Louisville, the church was the congregation's third building.

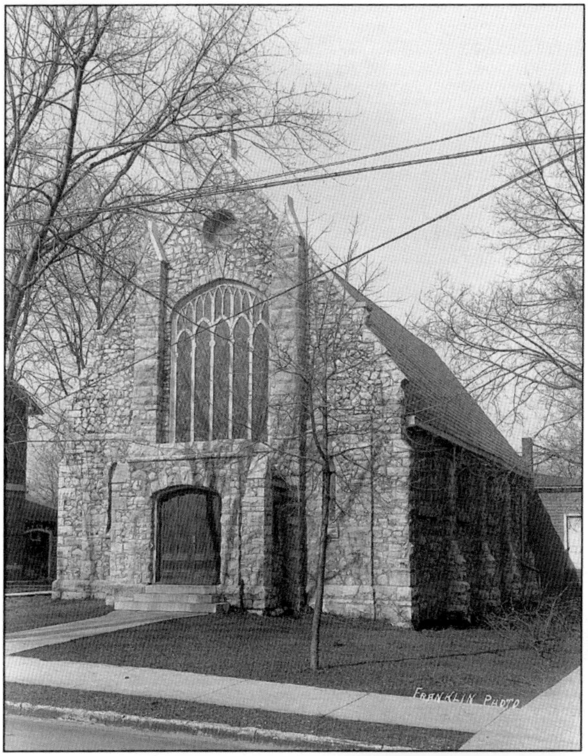

BAZAAR. These ladies are examining some of the handmade materials donated for Christ Episcopal's Bazaar in the mid-1950s.

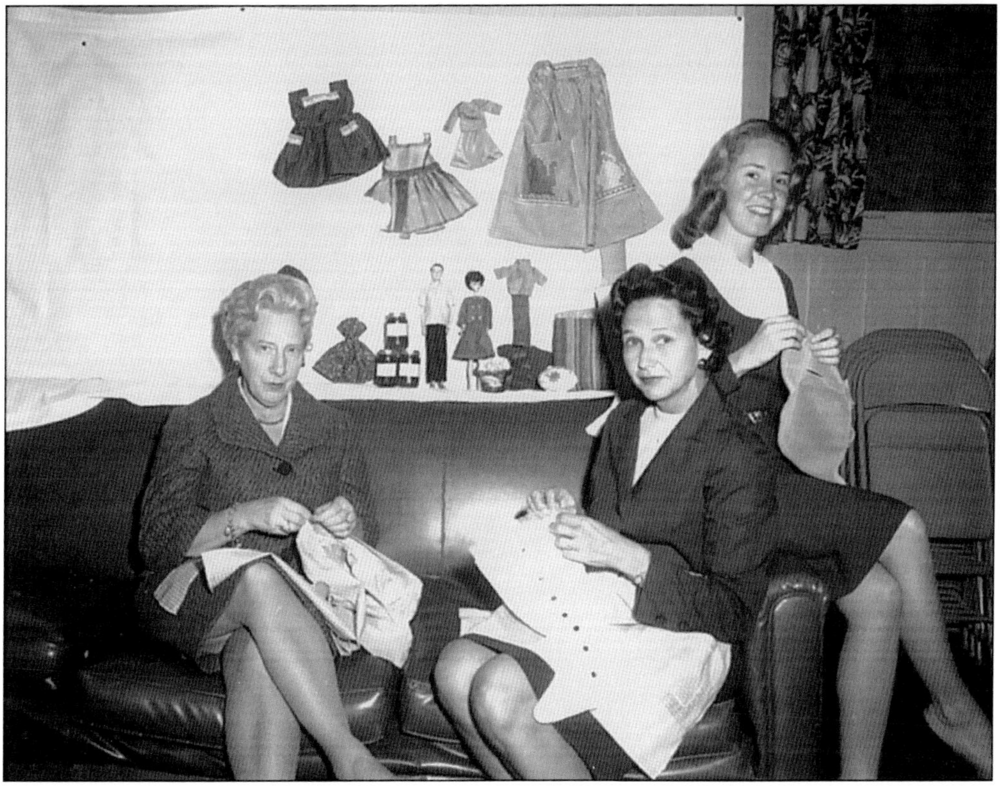

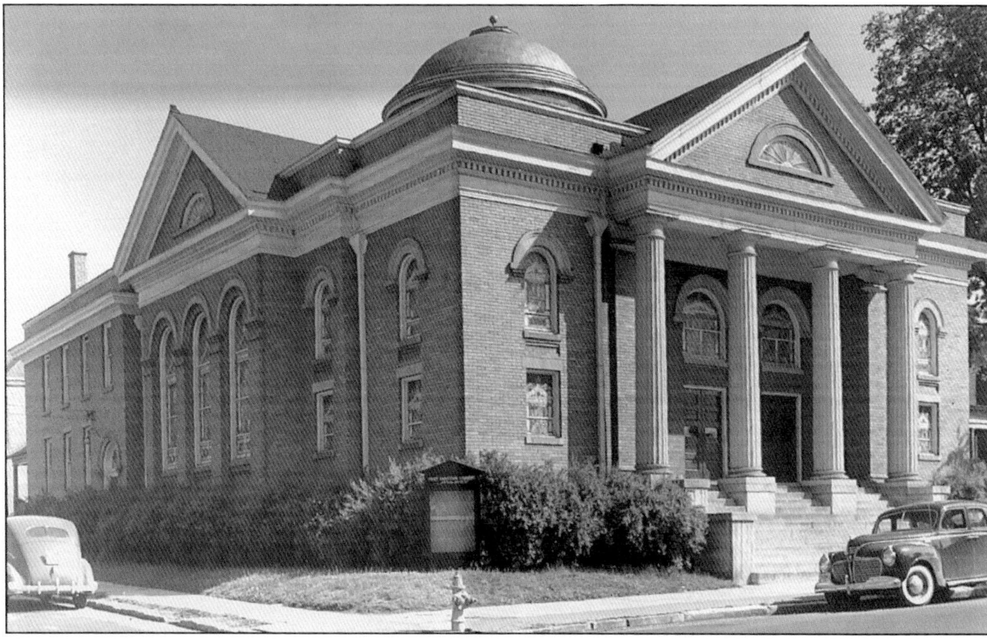

FIRST CHRISTIAN CHURCH. The Christian Church organized here in 1845. The church constructed this house of worship in 1919, making it their third building in the city. The dome began slipping in the 1950s and the building was razed. The congregation met in various locations while a new building was constructed on the same site. That building was completed in 1959; it went through a major renovation in 2001.

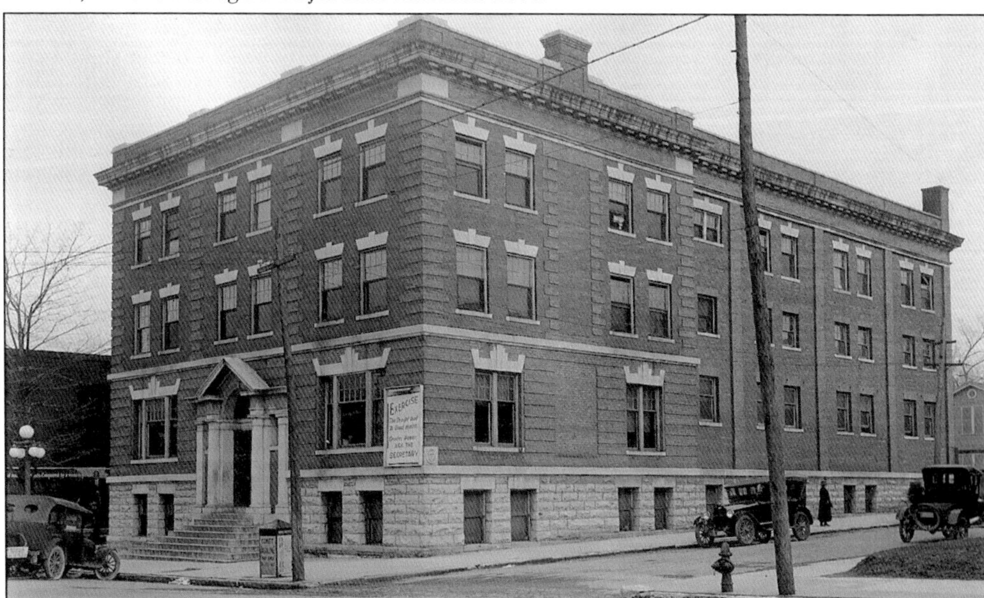

YMCA. The Bowling Green YMCA was opened in 1909 and by 1917 had 380 members. The four-story building, located at the corner of State and 13th Streets, was designed by H.H. Hussey of Lansing, Michigan, at a cost of $29,000. It included a swimming pool, offices, library, reading room, gymnasium, and 22 bedrooms. The building was sold in 1931 and, after extensive remodeling, became the Park City Hotel. It burned in 1985.